RABBITS, WARRENS & ARCHAEOLOGY

RABBITS, WARRENS & ARCHAEOLOGY

TOM WILLIAMSON

Front cover image: Dog kennels, almost like miniature megalithic tombs, built into the earth wall of the dog yard associated with Ditsworthy warren house, Dartmoor. *Inset:* The rabbit, *Oryctolagus cuniculus*. Photograph courtesy of Tracey Rich/ARWP

Rear cover image: Sopwell House, near St Albans in Hertfordshire, and its associated rabbit warren, as depicted on a seventeenth-century estate map. *Courtesy of Hertfordshire Archives and Local Studies*

First published 2007
Reprinted 2020

The History Press
97 St George's Place, Cheltenham,
Gloucestershire, GL50 3QB
www.thehistorypress.co.uk
Tempus Publishing is an imprint of NPI Media Group

© Tom Williamson, 2007

The right of Tom Williamson to be identified as the Author of this work has been asserted in accordance with the Copyrights, Designs and Patents Act 1988.

All rights reserved. No part of this book may be reprinted or reproduced or utilised in any form or by any electronic, mechanical or other means, now known or hereafter invented, including photocopying and recording, or in any information storage or retrieval system, without the permission in writing from the Publishers.

British Library Cataloguing in Publication Data.
A catalogue record for this book is available from the British Library.

ISBN 978-0-7524-4103-0

Typesetting and origination by NPI Media Group
Printed in Great Britain by TJ International Ltd, Padstow, Cornwall.

CONTENTS

	Acknowledgements	7
	A note on sources	8
	Introduction	9
1	The rabbit in Britain	11
2	Pillow mounds	31
3	Other features of the warren	59
4	The landscapes of warrening	89
5	Warrens and archaeologists	127
6	The symbolism of the warren	155
	Conclusion	177
	Bibliography	179
	Index	187

ACKNOWLEDGEMENTS

I have been fortunate, over the years, in the many people who have encouraged or at least tolerated my obsession with the archaeology of rabbit warrens. Many have provided help, inspiration or information: I would like to thank, in particular, David Austin, Mark Bailey, John Barnatt, Joe Bettey, Ed Dennison, Paul Everson, Graeme Guilbert, Sarah Harrison, Catherine Hills, Rosemary Hoppitt, Robert Liddiard, Roy Loveday, Anne Mason, Anne Rowe, John Sheail, Robert Silvester, Christopher Taylor, Joan Thirsk, Angus Wainwright, Nicola Whyte, Andy Wood, and the staff of county archaeology units and record offices too numerous to mention. Thanks also to Tracey Rich/ARWP Ltd, for figure 1 and cover picture; to the Cambridge Committee for Aerial Photography, for permission to reproduce figures 10, 16, 17, 18, 45, 57, 61, 62, 63, and 74; to English Heritage, for figures 56, 75 and 76; to Norfolk Record Office, for permission to reproduce figure 6; to the British Library, for permission to reproduce figure 2; to the Ancient House Museum, Thetford, for permission to reproduce figure 5; to Nicola Whyte, who supplied figure 40; to W.A. Baker for figure 72; to John Collis for figure 26; to IBM, for figure 3; to John Barnett for figure 79 and to Barry Cunliffe for figures 14 and 27. Phillip Judge provided the maps and line drawings, and Rik Hoggett plotted figure 9, from information kindly supplied by the National Monuments Record, the Cambridge Committee of Aerial Photography, the Ordnance Survey archaeological records, and the various county Historic Environment Records. Above all, thanks to my family – Liz Bellamy and Matt and Jess Williamson – who continue to put up with my various obscure obsessions with the history and archaeology of the rural landscape.

A NOTE ON SOURCES

Most of the evidence used in this volume is referenced in the usual way. Where particular sites are discussed but no reference is provided, the information is derived from personal observation, from the various county and regional HERs ('Historic Environment Records'), or from the Ordnance Survey Archaeological Records Cards (duplicate set, formerly maintained by English Heritage at Fortress House in London).

The following abbreviations are employed when documentary sources are cited:

BRO – Buckinghamshire Record Office
Cal. Pat. Rolls – Calendar of Patent Rolls
Cal. IPM – Calendar of Inquisitions Post Mortem
ESRO – East Suffolk Record Office
HALS – Hertfordshire Archives and Local Studies
NLW – National Library of Wales
NRO – Norfolk Records Office
TNA: PRO – The National Archives: Public Record Office
WSRO – West Suffolk Records Office

INTRODUCTION

The archaeology of rabbit farming might at first sight appear to be a strange subject for a book. Yet, as I hope to demonstrate, this is not only a neglected but also a surprisingly important topic, well worthy of serious academic attention. Rabbit farming had, before the nineteenth century, an economic and social significance that it is difficult to imagine today: warrens were common features of the countryside and, in some areas and in some periods, occupied more land than any other activity. Indeed, it is striking just how far, and how fast, knowledge of such a significant industry has passed so completely from popular consciousness.

But this is not, it must be emphasised, the first book to examine the story of rabbit farming in England and Wales, for a number of documentary historians have turned their attention to the subject. In particular, John Sheail's survey of 1971 provided an authoritative and comprehensive overview; the eminent medievalist Mark Bailey has written extensively on medieval rabbit warrens, especially in an East Anglian context; while various social and economic historians, most notably Elizabeth Veale, have discussed in some detail the importance of the industry in the medieval and post-medieval periods. This volume differs from such earlier studies, however, in one important respect. It deals primarily, although not exclusively, with material evidence – with the physical remains left by rabbit farming in the form of boundaries, buildings and the specialised structures used for trapping and breeding. It is a work of archaeology, not history.

Of course, I am not the first archaeologist to become interested in rabbits. Many excavators and field workers have been obliged to engage with the past exploitation of these animals, albeit often in a piecemeal or even accidental way. Buried away in local and regional journals, as well as in the various archaeological archives, there is thus a vast amount of information resulting from excavations and survey work. There have also been a number of broader, synoptic accounts of the archaeology of rabbit farming in particular regions, most notably Dartmoor,

Glamorgan and the Tabular Hills of North Yorkshire. But this volume is (with the exception of a much shorter work that I published in 2005) the first overall account of the archaeology of rabbit farming, and rabbit warrens, in England and Wales as a whole.

While an historical approach, dealing primarily with documentary sources, can provide a great deal of information about the ways in which rabbits were exploited in the past, an archaeological perspective can make its own distinctive contribution. It can, for example, add to our understanding of the economic importance of rabbit farming in the medieval and the post-medieval periods simply by demonstrating the incredible scale and sophistication of the industry, both of which are sometimes difficult to appreciate from maps and documents alone. Archaeology can also inform us about the actual practice of rabbit farming for, somewhat surprisingly, many aspects of the way in which this was carried out, even in the eighteenth and nineteenth centuries, appear to be completely unrecorded in documentary sources. Above all, a concentration on the physical remains can throw a shaft of new light on the social and iconographic significance of warrens by examining, in particular, the ways in which they were spatially related to other features of the contemporary cultural landscape, such as great houses and gardens.

Yet there is a further reason why rabbit farming should be a subject of some concern to archaeologists, a reason which has less to do with rabbits and rabbit farming *per se* than with the practice of archaeology itself: for many of the characteristic structures and features associated with warrens have been repeatedly misdated and misinterpreted by archaeologists in the past, and some of these mistakes have become embedded in the archaeological literature. Indeed, it is probable that no other range of field monuments has been so systematically misunderstood by fieldworkers and excavators. In short, far from being some obscure antiquarian backwater, rabbit farming is a topic which should have a major place in the study of British field archaeology and landscape history, and I hope that this volume will help position the warren more firmly on the map of archaeological knowledge.

1
THE RABBIT IN BRITAIN

THE RABBIT

The rabbit (*Oryctolagus cuniculus*) is not indigenous to Britain – or at least, it has not formed part of our native fauna since before the last Ice Age (*1*). It was re-introduced to this country some time in the historic period from mainland Europe, being derived ultimately from the western Mediterranean regions. Until very recently historians were confident that this did not happen until the late eleventh or twelfth century and – like the appearance here of the fallow deer – was the work of the new Norman elite (Sheail 1971, 9-10; Sheail 1978; Sheail 1984; Orgill 1936). Certainly, there is no Old English word for the rabbit; and Caesar, while he refers to hares in his description of Britain in *De Bello Gallico*, makes no mention of the animal. However, rabbit bones were discovered in secure Roman contexts at Lynford in Norfolk in 2001, and at a Roman villa at Beddingham in east Sussex (*British Archaeology* 2006). There have been similar discoveries in the past but these have generally been dismissed as the result of rabbits burrowing into the relevant archaeological layers at a much later date, and dying there. But the rabbit bones at Lynford unquestionably came from a butchered specimen, so this explanation can hardly apply here. The Romans certainly valued the rabbit, both for its fur and its meat, and in their homelands kept them alongside hares in *leporaria*, or hare warrens. The Roman chef Apicius included among his many recipes one for rabbit rissoles (Henderson 1997, 101).

Nevertheless, if the Romans did introduce the rabbit into Britain it was probably on a small scale, and there is no evidence that the species became part of the wild fauna of the country in this period. It presumably died out in late Roman or early post-Roman times, to be re-introduced once more seven centuries later, after the Norman Conquest. What is probably the earliest unambiguous documentary record dates from 1135, when Drake's Island in Plymouth Sound was granted to Plympton Priory *cum cuniculi* ('with the rabbits') (Haynes 1970, 147). By the middle decades of the thirteenth century rabbit colonies had been established as far north as Cramond and Crail in Scotland (Gilbert 1979) and even in parts of Ireland (Henderson 1997, 101). Rabbits were already a familiar enough feature in lowland England by the middle of the twelfth century to be depicted on one of the carved corbels in Kilpeck Church in Herefordshire. Nevertheless, the coney (the word rabbit was, until the eighteenth century, reserved for the young) was initially a domesticated or semi-domesticated animal, kept in special areas. It was poorly adapted to the British climate and vulnerable to a range of predators, and only gradually came to be established on a large scale in the wild.

The natural history of the rabbit has been described by a number of authorities (Thompson and King 1994; Thompson and Worden 1956; Lockley 1964). Although often confused in the popular mind with the hare, the rabbit is a more compact creature, generally around 40-45cm from tail to the tip of the head. Adult males ('bucks') normally weigh 1-1.5kg but can reach as much as 2.7kg (*1*). Rabbits characteristically live in large, hierarchical groups in underground burrow systems which can extend downwards for several metres, and laterally over a wide area. In sandy districts especially the ground can become so riddled with burrows that it is difficult to walk over it or, in particular, ride across it on horseback. Rabbits, contrary to what is sometimes suggested, can tolerate a wide range of conditions, and can at a pinch make their burrows in the heaviest clays. But they have strong preferences which help explain some of the characteristic features of the archaeology of rabbit farming. Firstly, they dislike damp conditions: they drink little and prefer well-drained soil, the young in particular being very vulnerable to drowning, and the animals in general prone to foot-rot. Secondly, they prefer relatively light soil, in preference to clays or stony ground. In Harting's words, 'What suits them best is a light sandy soil, and peaty grounds, as on moorlands, will do well enough, provided it does not lie so low as to become flooded after heavy rain ...' (Harting 1898, 60). Lastly, rabbits cannot easily make their burrows on flat ground, because the excavated soil cannot be moved from the mouth of the burrow. They much prefer sloping terrain, where the excavated material falls away naturally.

Throughout medieval and post-medieval times rabbits were kept in part for their meat, which when the animal was rare was considered a delicacy, and in part for their fur, used in medieval times for trimming clothes, and as late as the twentieth century for making hats (Sheail 1971, 74-8). They are almost entirely covered in fur, which changes in character markedly over the year, becoming thicker in the winter months. Although by the eighteenth century agricultural improvers castigated rabbit warrens as an archaic and wasteful form of land use, not least because of the problems which escapees caused to surrounding farmland, rabbits made rather good use of agriculturally marginal areas because of

1 The rabbit, Oryctolagus cuniculus, is today a common sight in the countryside but it was originally a semi-domesticated animal – an introduced alien which was poorly suited to the British environment

their ability to survive on thin, coarse or rank vegetation, and in the absence of good supplies of running water. They also breed, it need hardly be said, with some rapidity. Does can give birth five or even six times in the breeding season, which runs from February through to September, if abundant food is available (if it is not, or if the doe is under some other form of stress, the embryos are reabsorbed by the body). They give birth, usually to between six and eight offspring at a time, in short tunnels called *stops*, the mouths of which are closed (with vegetation) during absences, to hide the young not only from predators but also from the buck rabbits, which tend to kill the young. The young rabbits grow up quickly, and are independent of their mothers within six weeks. They usually take up residence on the fringes of the colony, and will only have a chance to become one of the dominant males during subsequent years.

Some of the earliest rabbit warrens to be established in Britain were on offshore islands where the rabbits could be kept relatively safe from predators: early examples are thus recorded on the Scilly Isles, on Lundy, and on Hayling Island in Hampshire (Sheail 1971, 17; East 1981). Others were in areas of coastal sand, where the rabbits could burrow easily and where at least one side of the warren was bounded, by the

2 Women catching rabbits with ferret and purse net, from the fourteenth-century *Queen Mary's Psalter*. The low earth mound in which the rabbits are living is probably an artificial warren or 'pillow mound'

sea: examples include the two royal warrens referred to in the Patent Rolls for 1306 at Esington and Kilnese on the coast of Holderness in Yorkshire (Henderson 1997, 105). But warrens were also soon established in areas of inland sand, especially in the East Anglian Breckland, and on the Suffolk coastal heaths (Bailey 1988 and 1989). Moreover, by the thirteenth century rabbits were also widely bred in enclosures located beside elite residences – castles, palaces, monasteries – and, in particular, within deer parks (*2*). Medieval accounts suggest that such enclosures might be surrounded by paling and also on occasion by hedges, and entered through gates which could be locked. In 1457, for example, the Bursar's accounts for Fountains Abbey (North Yorkshire) record payments for the 'making of the hedges around the garden of the rabbits' (*in factura sepium circa ortum cuniculorum*), while at Petworth in Sussex in 1349 locks were bought for 'the two larger gates of *la Conyghere*', which was itself listed as one of the 'enclosure of the parks'(Faull and Moorhouse 1981, 755). This suggests that the barriers around medieval domestic warrens were, in some cases, more for protecting the rabbits from poachers and predators, than for preventing the animals themselves from straying (Faull and Moorhouse 1981, 755). Some warrens may have been bounded by water-filled ditches: an artificial island, flanked by a complex of fish ponds and containing mounds of spoil, at Northill in Bedfordshire is one suggested example.

References to rabbit enclosures within parks are particularly numerous. A royal order of 1235 thus refers to the ten rabbits which were to be taken from the park at Guildford in Surrey (Henderson 1997, 105). At Petworth in Sussex William, 8th Baron de Percy (1193-1245), had a 'new small park in which is his *cunegaria*'. On the estates of the Bishop of Winchester the earliest reference

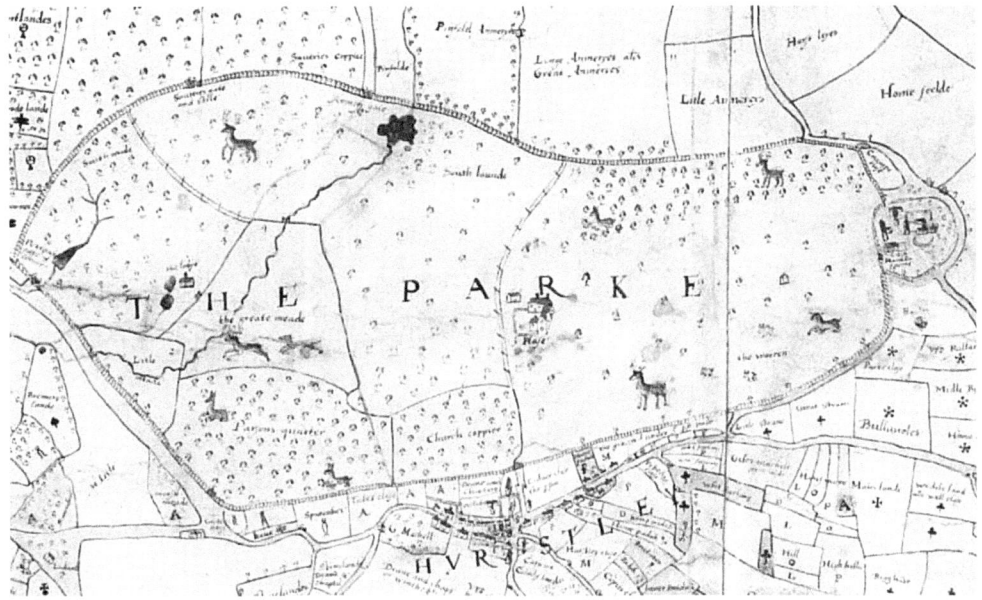

3 The medieval deer park at Hursley, Hampshire, as shown on an early sixteenth-century map. The rabbit warren is clearly labelled in the south-eastern section of the park

to rabbits concerns an attempt to stock Bishopstoke Park in Hampshire with rabbits brought from Bittern Park in 1236-7. By 1243 there were also warrens in the bishop's parks at Merdon near Hursley in Hampshire, and on the Isle of Wight (Roberts 1988, 77). The majority of early medieval warrens, in fact, were probably located within parks (*3*).

As most readers will be aware, parks were securely fenced, usually well-wooded enclosures in which deer were farmed and hunted. They usually lay at a distance from their owner's residence, having been carved out of some dwindling remnant of woodland on the fringes of cultivated territories. Some care must be taken, in that references to warrens and parks at the same location need not necessarily indicate that the one lay within the other. As at Knebworth in Hertfordshire, they might have occupied neighbouring but separate sites. Nevertheless, a large number of parks did contain warrens, just as they often contained fish ponds, and for similar reasons: they were relatively secure areas, clearly fenced off from the outside world, and were thus a good place to protect desirable foodstuffs from poachers.

Parks were not impregnable, however, and we often hear of the warrens within them in connection with legal cases concerning, not so much the poaching activities of local peasants, but episodes of deliberate park-breaking by neighbouring landowners. To enter another man's park, and to hunt in it openly, was the supreme affront. In 1360 various 'evildoers' thus broke into the

4 Catching rabbits with nets, from the fourteenth-century Livre de Chasse

parks at East Dereham and Shipdham in Norfolk 'and entered the warrens there, hunted in these, felled trees, trod down and depastured with cattle the grass there and carried away the said trees and deer from the park and hares, conies, pheasants and partridges from the warrens' (Cal. Pat. Rolls 1358-61, 403). There are innumerable similar examples, from throughout the country. Some legal cases describe how park breakers actually hunted the rabbits: and this in turn raises the question of the extent to which rabbits were likewise hunted, on a recreational basis, by their owners in the Middle Ages. Gaston Febus' *Livre de Chasse* contains several sections on rabbits, describing how they can be flushed from their holes by ferrets or smoke, and caught in nets or by dogs. Rabbits were not highly esteemed as quarry, but they were evidently hunted on occasions (Almond 2003, 108-110) (*4*).

The word 'warren' was originally used in the term 'free warren' which meant, not an area of ground occupied by rabbits, but a tract of land over which an individual was granted the right to take game – which otherwise, under the terms of feudal law, was reserved to the monarch. The lawyer Manwood, writing in 1598, defined the 'beasts of warren' as the coney, hare, pheasant and partridge, 'and none other' (Harting 1898, 53): but roe and fallow deer were also generally included, as at various times were other species such as the woodcock. The special areas in which rabbits were bred and kept in the early Middle Ages were generally referred to as *coneygarths* (latin *cunicularium*, from the Middle English *coning-erth*, 'rabbit warren' (Faull and Moorhouse 1981, 753). The term 'warren' was first used in this sense only from the mid-fourteenth century, and then usually (although not exclusively) for the relatively small number of extensive, more commercial warrens on islands or in areas of sand. In the course of the sixteenth and seventeenth centuries, however, the term became the usual one for all rabbit reserves, and by the seventeenth century was also being applied to the burrow systems within which any rabbits, wild or otherwise, made their homes.

So far as the evidence goes the number of rabbit warrens increased steadily in the later fourteenth and fifteenth centuries, spreading down the social scale from great magnates to the local gentry. They became a more common feature of parks, and also proliferated on areas of marginal land, especially commons. In the period immediately following the Black Death they represented one of the ways in which major landowners could diversify their agricultural incomes, and they were a good way of making money from areas of poor-quality land, especially unenclosed wastes and commons, the law holding that a grant of free warren permitted manorial lords to establish colonies of rabbits in such locations regardless of the impact that this might have on the grazing available to the beasts of the commoners. To quote Harting again, 'no action will lie against a lord of the manor for keeping coneys on land over which he has a right of warren' (Harting 1898, 57). In the sixteenth and seventeenth centuries large commercial warrens thus began to proliferate in lowland forests like Ashdown and Rockingham; on Dartmoor; in the Mendip Hills and on the Cotswolds; and widely across the chalklands of Wessex (Aston and Bettey 1998, 133-5; Haynes 1970; Bettey 2004). Some extensive warrens had probably existed in most of these areas in medieval times, but the extent of post-medieval growth is what is really noticeable. The later seventeenth and the first half of the eighteenth centuries, another period of agricultural depression, saw not only the further expansion of rabbit farming in all the areas in which it was already well-established, but also the spread of commercial warrens into new districts – the Tabular Hills, the Yorkshire Wolds, the Lincolnshire Wolds, and probably the Welsh Moors, although once again a few large warrens may already have existed in some of these districts (Harris and Spratt 1991; Harris 1970; Doughty 1965).

As warrens proliferated, however, the status of rabbits gradually changed. In the Middle Ages they were a luxury item: a single rabbit in the thirteenth century was worth more than a workman's daily wage (Rackham 1986, 48). Their meat was esteemed as a delicacy, suitable for a feast, and their fur was used for trimming the robes of the great. They were a source of prestige and profit, as well as food: even the smaller warrens usually produced rabbits for sale and exchange, as well as private consumption, and carcases might be sent many miles to supply peripatetic noble households. In 1347 it was reported in an *Inquisition Post Mortem* that there had been no recent profits from the warren at Beavoir in Leicestershire because the rabbits had been used 'for the enthronement of the archbishop of York, and for the lord's maintenance, and sent to Stoke Daubeny from the feast of St Michael to the day of his death' (Cal. IPM Vol 8 Ed.III, 336*)*. Even in the seventeenth century rabbits were a greatly esteemed foodstuff, exchanged between landowners and sent many miles as gifts. But by the end of the eighteenth century they were becoming a food for the poor and, while some fur was still being sent abroad, to be used in the traditional way, increasing quantities were used as 'wool' – separated from the skins and used as felt for hat-making. Moreover, as a range of agricultural innovations, and the spread of enclosure, allowed the cultivation of much formerly marginal land, warrens were increasingly rendered uneconomic, and considered a backward and anti-social form of land use which undermined the more progressive policies of neighbours.

Already, by the early eighteenth century, warrens were beginning to be abandoned on the Wessex chalklands (Bettey 2004, 390-1), and by 1800 the tide was turning against them on the Wolds of Lincolnshire and Yorkshire (Beastall 1978,144-5). In the later eighteenth and early nineteenth centuries enclosure, reclamation and improvement saw the demise of warrens in other areas – the Mendips, the Cotswolds, most lowland forest districts – in which the new techniques and the single-minded improving zeal of the 'agricultural revolution' were able to convert rough grazing into productive arable land or improved pasture. By the middle decades of the nineteenth century commercial rabbit farms had become largely restricted to the East Anglian Breckland, and to certain areas of high moorland where – on Dartmoor and in the Welsh uplands especially – entirely new enterprises continued to be established. It was normally only in such particularly marginal areas, and especially on the Tabular Hills, on Dartmoor, and in Breckland, that the industry continued on a significant scale into the late nineteenth and early twentieth centuries (Harris and Spratt 1991, 202-5; Haynes 1970; Clarke 1937, 108-117; Crossing 1903). Nevertheless, a scatter

5 Warreners at North Farm, Barnham, Suffolk in 1921, with dogs, long-handled staves, and ferrets (in the boxes). The East Anglian Breckland was one of the few districts in which commercial warrens continued to flourish well into the twentieth century

of commercial rabbits farms in less inhospitable areas continued to operate into the twentieth century, as at Wood Hall, Carperby, in Wensleydale (Dennison 2004, 140). In some cases warrens survived because they provided raw materials for particular industries, such as hat-making in the Ribble Valley in Lancashire. In the East Anglian Breckland, as late as the 1920s, nearly half the area of the Elveden estate near Thetford was given over to warrens. Thirty warreners were employed and 120,000 rabbits were taken per annum (Parry 2003, 77). Some of the warrens around Brandon continued to function into the 1950s, the rabbits being sold both for meat and for fur, the latter going to the hat factory at Brandon (5). Only the advent of myxamotosis in 1954 finally brought this ancient Breckland industry to an end.

It will be apparent from this brief account that commercial warrening in the post-medieval period was associated with relatively marginal land, and in particular with areas of moor and heath – Breckland, the Suffolk coastal heaths, Dartmoor, the Welsh moors, the Tabular Hills. Indeed, many of the warrens in 'forest' areas were in fact established, not in well-wooded environments ('forest' was a technical term, for an area subject to forest law, rather than an environmental one), but on sandy commons. To a large extent this was simply a function of the low value of such land, and the fact that rabbit farming made more economic use of it than most other kinds of enterprise. But it also reflects the liking of rabbits for sandy and peaty soils and also, perhaps, the importance of heather and gorse in the vegetation of moors and heaths. Both plants made excellent feed for the rabbits, and gorse was used as winter fodder and also to cap the banks forming the perimeter of the warren. One rabbit keeper told a House of Commons Select Committee in 1875 that 'Gorse is a very despised article, but I appreciate it very highly' (Sheail 1971, 50).

Not all post-medieval exploitation of rabbits, it should be noted, took the form of large commercial warrens. Small domestic warrens continued to exist close to many manor houses well into the eighteenth century, and there were numerous relatively small warrens which lacked a full-time warrener, and remained untended for much of the time. Rabbits were also caught on a regular, systematic but small-scale basis by farmers living in some marginal areas, as a useful way of supplementing the income from more mainstream agricultural enterprises — a form of exploitation which has been described as the 'farm warren' (Harris and Spratt 1991, 180).

The rabbits were mainly born in May and June and the majority were normally killed in November, December and January, when their fur was fully developed, although on some warrens, where supplies of winter feed were low and/or meat rather than fur was the main concern of the warrener, systematic culling might begin in the summer. Most of the rabbits kept in medieval and post-medieval warrens were of the common-grey variety – the normal wild rabbit – but black rabbits were also kept, their skins in great demand as ornamental trimming for clothes until the middle of the eighteenth century. The silver-grey or silver-blue was also greatly valued: it seems to have been bred only from the seventeenth century and was particularly associated with the warrens in the north east of England, although it could be found more widely. It may have derived ultimately from Ireland (Dennison 2004, 140). Large quantities of its fur were exported to Europe and beyond in the eighteenth century, but the market contracted in the nineteenth and by the start of the twentieth century the silver-blue was only really kept for its meat (Sheail 1971, 74-8).

THE WORK OF THE WARRENER

Warrener, like warren, is a word with a range of meanings, sometimes referring to the individuals who managed the enterprise, sometimes to the skilled workmen who looked after the rabbits. They were responsible for protecting the stock of the warren from vermin – especially rats, stoats, weasels, polecats, foxes and cats, but also birds of prey – as well as from poachers; for minimising the numbers of rabbits which escaped from the warren; and for ensuring that they were adequately fed. Rabbits will consume a wide range of vegetation, but warreners were well aware that they were larger and healthier – and reproduced most rapidly – when they fed on grass which was kept in good heart, rather than on the kinds of tough weeds and thistles which generally remained after several years of intensive rabbit grazing. In parts of Lincolnshire in the eighteenth century, and sporadically elsewhere, warrens were sometimes subdivided by banks to exclude the rabbits from particular areas, which could then be ploughed and cultivated with grain crops for a few years, before being returned to grass, in a form of 'convertible husbandry' (Sheail 1971, 49-50). It was claimed that the resulting improvement in the quality of the sward allowed the warren population to be more than doubled. Some writers advocated the planting of dandelions or groundsel for feed. Nevertheless, there was seldom enough grazing in the winter and warreners were obliged to make use of fodder crops, sometimes grown within enclosures on the warren, sometimes brought in from elsewhere. The need for fodder was especially acute when thick snow covered the ground, for rabbits find it hard to dig their way through drifts.

Hay was the main form of fodder used, together with – from the early eighteenth century – turnips, the rabbits in Thetford Warren in Norfolk reportedly eating their way through the produce of 80 acres (32ha) during one particularly severe winter in the eighteenth century. In earlier periods especially, young bracken and other 'rowe', or coarse grass, was employed, and branches were cut from pollards or coppices to provide 'leafy hay' and also – when laid on top of the ground – to give the animals in their burrows extra protection from the elements. A lease for the warren at Knebworth in Hertfordshire, dating from 1722, thus allowed the tenant 'once in every yeare' during the 21-year lease 'to Lopp sixty Pollards for Browse for the Rabbitts' (HALS 46606). Hazel, elder and ash were especially favoured as feed and on the Mount Misery warren in North Yorkshire coppiced stools of ash and hazel still survive, growing from the tops of the stone walls surrounding enclosures and on the warren boundary, presumably to offer some protection from the rabbits (Harris and Spratt 1991, 193).

There are some indications that fodder crops were used on a larger scale in the post-medieval period, and especially from the later seventeenth century, significantly raising the numbers of rabbits which could be kept on the warren. But as stocking levels rose it became harder to keep the rabbits within the area of the warren, for in over-crowded conditions the young rabbits in particular were more prone to stray onto surrounding farmland, where they might be killed or cause damage to crops. This in turn made it more important to secure the warren boundary with some sort of rabbit-proof barrier, such as a wall or bank. This was not an entirely new development. Small medieval coneygarths had usually been enclosed and even the larger warrens had often been surrounded, at least in part,

RABBITS, WARRENS & ARCHAEOLOGY

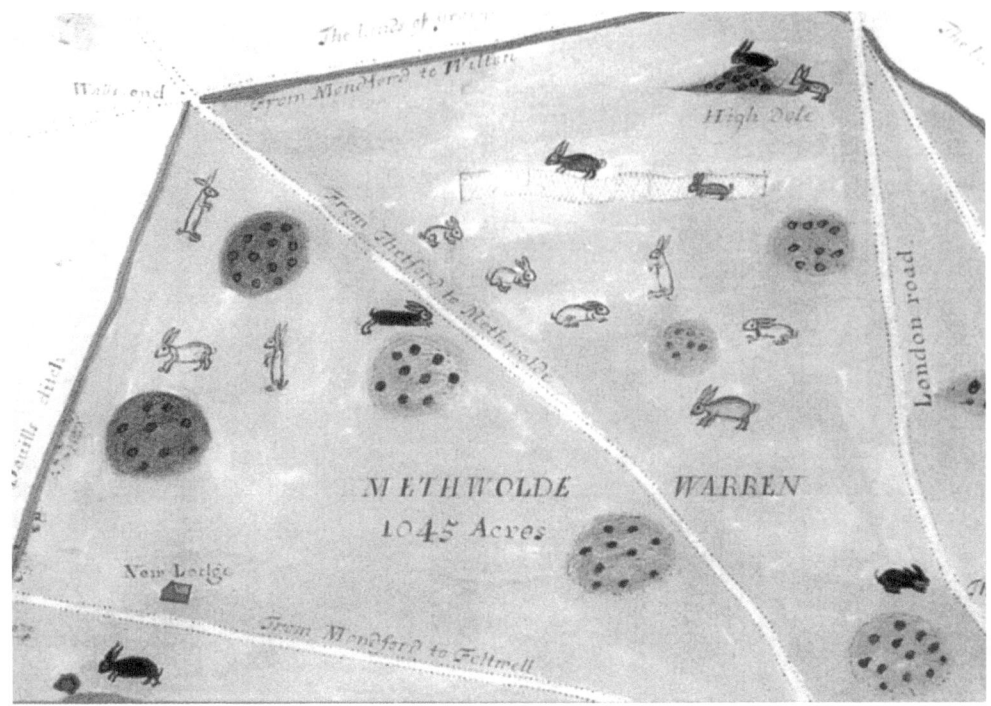

6 Methwold Warren in west Norfolk, as depicted on an estate map of 1699. As well as the rabbits themselves, the map shows the warren boundaries, which to the west formed by the Dark Age earthwork called the Fossditch; the 'new lodge'; and a long net or 'haye', used to catch the rabbits. The circular features may be pillow mounds, but could also be natural sand dunes or prehistoric barrows in which the rabbits have taken up residence

by a bank and ditch. But the scale and extent of enclosure certainly increased during the post-medieval period, and many formerly open warrens were provided with perimeter banks and walls for the first time, as at Kirton in Lincolnshire, where in 1736 the freeholders actually paid the lord of the manor of Redbourne £60 to enclose his warren (Sheail 1971, 44-7). In the later nineteenth century wire netting was increasingly employed, often to firm up particularly vulnerable stretches of boundary, but it was expensive and did not last very long.

Besides ensuring that they were well-fed and protected from predators, warreners looked after their rabbits in a host of other ways. They often, for example, attempted to restore some of the scrub which their stock invariably stripped from the warren, planting thorns, gorse or even juniper to provide shelter, especially in winter. But the warreners were also, of course, responsible for catching and killing their charges, something achieved in a variety of ways. On some warrens special tip traps were used but for the most part, in medieval and post-medieval times alike, the rabbits were caught using some combination of dogs, ferrets and nets. A long net (or 'hay'), as much as 150m in length, might be erected between the rabbits and their burrows, often at night when they were feeding, and the animals either wandered into it as they returned to their burrows or were driven into it by dogs, usually lurchers or tumblers. Alternatively, ferrets might be introduced into the burrows, and the bolting rabbits caught in purse nets placed at the various entrances to the burrow system, or in long nets enclosing its entire area. The ferrets were usually muzzled, for if they killed a rabbit in the deep burrows they might drink its blood and then fall asleep, and would have to be recovered with much laborious digging. In some cases the ferrets were attached to a long line, and might be put into one burrow after another, so that the rabbits either bolted or were forced to huddle together in one section of the system, from which – with digging – they could be extracted. Sometimes dogs and ferrets were used together, as Clarke described in Breckland in the early twentieth century:

> The ferrets were first turned in the burrows unmuzzled, and directly their presence was made known, the rabbits fled pell-mell from their hereditary enemies. Directly the rabbit came out of the "bolt hole" he dashed for dear life to the northward. In most cases he had gone but a few yards when a lurcher caught him up, and brought him to his master … . A few rabbits reached the net, into which they bolted headlong, and were cast back by the slackness, or got their heads or paws entangled in the meshes (Clarke 1925, 138)

In the Middle Ages warrens were generally administered directly by their owners, as part of the manorial demesne. From late medieval times, however, it became common for the larger examples to be rented out to professional warreners, usually for a period of 7-21 years. The lease agreements usually state, in some detail, what was expected of the leasee, especially how many rabbits – i.e., the breeding stock of the warren – were to be left at the end of the tenancy. At Nacton in Suffolk, for example, the tenant was to leave 'five hundred couple of coneys good, well conditioned and alive' when the lease expired in 1646 (ESRO H93/3/48). Such prescriptions could be quite detailed, as at Hertingfordbury in Hertfordshire in 1634, where the tenant was bound to leave 'one hundred and twenty female Conyes and twenty male Conyes wheirof the better halfe to bee black' (HALS D/EP T264). The rent was often paid in part, and occasionally entirely, in rabbits. When the warren at Easton Royal in Wiltshire was leased by the Earl of Hertford for twelve years in 1608 the two warreners agreed to pay an annual rent of £5, together with 500 couples of coneys, 'good, swete and mete to be served', which were to be delivered to the Earl's home (Bettey 2004, 385). The annual rent for the warren at Hertingfordbury in 1634 was set at £16, plus:

Six cupple of fatt good and sweete Conyes att the Feaste of St Michell Tharchangell every yeare duringe the said terme or att any other tyme upon reasonable warninge beinge att such tyme as Conyes are in season (HALS D/EP T264)

Sometimes the owner was allowed to help himself to the rabbits, within stated limits. When Westwood Lodge Warren in Blythburgh was let for £15 per annum in 1690 (ESRO HA 30: 50/22/3.43) the contract, drawn up between Sir Charles Blois and John Atkins, gave the latter all the 'Coneys or rabbits now being or remaining in and upon the lands', although Sir Charles reserved the right, when resident at Westwood Lodge, to 'have kill and take upon the said warren ... five couple of coneys every week from St James to Candlemass in every year'.

More importantly for the archaeologist, leases also often note that the various buildings and facilities on the warren should be maintained in good condition, and describe what equipment should be left at the end of the tenancy. They can thus be an important source of information about the field archaeology, and the material culture, of warrening, although sometimes the terms they employ are vague or formulaic. The tenant of Knebworth Warren in Hertfordshire for example was obliged, by the terms of the lease he signed in 1722, to 'repair preserve maintain and keep ... the hedges Gates Stiles Posts Railes Pales Trapps Mounds and Fences whatsoever as well belonging to the said Warren ...' (HALS 46606). The 1608 lease for Easton Royal in Wiltshire describes how the warren, which covered around 60ha, had been 'newly enclosed' and contained a 'lodge or dwelling house'. The new tenants agreed to keep in good repair 'the boundes fences ... burrowes, banckes, and berryes, flapps, trappes and falls nowe being within or upon the same' (Bettey 2004, 385). Some of these terms and clauses seem to have been standard components of leases: an example drawn up in 1624 between the Earl of Hertford and one Thomas Cary, for a warren at Durley in the same county, similarly refers to the need to maintain the 'burrowes, banckes, berryes, flaps, traps and falls' in good repair (Bettey 2004, 385-7). Leases sometimes allowed the tenant to take materials for repairing the warren, or for feeding the stock over the winter, from adjoining areas of ground. Another Wiltshire lease, for the warren in Burderop Park in Chiseldon, thus gave the tenant the right to take 'convenient browse for the Conies in hard weather' from the surrounding land (Bettey 2004, 387). They also sometimes reserved the right of the owner to graze other stock in the warren, especially sheep, at certain times of the year, although on occasions the warrener himself was allowed to keep other forms of livestock there. A lease for the warren at Micheldever in Hampshire, for example, allowed the tenant to keep 60 sheep around the warren lodge, as well as pigs and cattle (Sheail 1971, 82).

Figures for the stocking densities on warrens are very variable. On Lincolnshire warrens in the eighteenth and nineteenth centuries between five and six rabbits were usually over-wintered per acre (*c*.2-3 per hectare), but on some of the warrens in the Tabular Hills the figure was as low as four or even two (Doughty 1965, 16). Strickland in 1812 suggested that a Yorkshire warren in good heart could produce as many as 20 rabbits per acre (*c*.eight per hectare) per annum, but this seems to have been optimistic: the produce of the nearby Lincolnshire warrens varied from four to ten rabbits per acre per year, while on Low Hunsley Warren on the Lincolnshire Wolds the figure was around twelve (Strickland 1812, 251-2; Doughty 1965, 16; Harris 1970, 440). In reality, variations in the quality of the feed, and in the extent to which imported fodder was used to feed the rabbits, make it virtually impossible to generalise. As Harting put it in 1898, 'The question of how many rabbits should go to the acre can only be answered in general terms, for it is obvious that an acre in one county may contain double the quantity of food found on another where the soil and the nature of the vegetation may vary considerably' (Harting 1898, 65). Moreover, populations fluctuated markedly from one season to the next, and from one year to the next, so that figures for a single point in time are usually a poor guide to the average performance. As Daniel described in 1801, 'The Spring and Summer of 1798 were so favourable to the breeding of the Rabbits, that the Warrens in all parts were supposed to have never been more plentifully stocked, but great numbers of the young ones perished by a disorder, supposed to be produced by the continued wet in the Autumn' (Daniel 1801, 348).

THE FEATURES OF THE WARREN

Rabbit warrens were noticeable features of the landscape. They are often depicted on early maps and frequently gave their name to adjacent roads and fields (*6*). Some, to judge from maps and documents, were wood-pastures, filled quite densely with pollarded trees which had presumably become established before the introduction of rabbits into the area in question – in some cases because the warren had been created within an existing deer park. The 1634 lease for the warren at Hertingfordbury in Hertfordshire thus allowed the tenant to 'take the lopes of the bouldings or pollards within the said Warren or Close called the little Parke for repayringe of the hedges aboute the said Warren and Close … . And also for his necessary Fyerwood' (HALS D/EP T264). At Shrubland Park in Suffolk a map of 1668 (Shrubland Hall archives) shows 'The Warren' as an area planted densely with trees, apparently sweet chestnuts to judge from survivors which still grow there (below, p.173). But most warrens, especially the large commercial enterprises created in marginal areas of heath, moor and downland, were open, treeless environments. In areas of heathland, in particular, intense grazing gave them a distinctive, often desolate appearance. The rabbits stripped the turf, exposing the sand beneath to the force of the wind and leading to the formation of mobile dunes, like those which, blown out of Lakenheath Warren in Breckland, partly engulfed the village of Santon Downham in 1668 and blocked the river Little Ouse (Wright 1668). Under the pressure of intense grazing plants like clover and trefoil declined in abundance; nettles and the tougher grasses tended to flourish (Sheail 1971, 53-4). But as well as being distinctive by virtue of their ecology and appearance, warrens also contained a number of characteristic structures, which are the main subject of this book.

Firstly, as already noted, many warrens were surrounded by banks or walls, to prevent the rabbits from straying. Escaped rabbits not only meant a loss of profit. They might cause damage to neighbouring crops, leading to prosecutions from other landowners. Indeed, as early as 1392 a colony of feral rabbits at Iken on the coastal heaths of Suffolk – descendants of escapees from Dunningworth Warren, some four kilometres to the west – caused serious damage to farmland (Bailey 1988, 5). The extent to which owners bothered to erect walls, fences and banks was in part related to the character of adjoining land, and in part a function of the warren's size: smaller warrens were not only cheaper to enclose than larger, but rabbits were less likely to roam away from a large warren, at least if feed was adequate. Many warrens also contained internal subdivisions and enclosures, similarly defined by walls or banks, sometimes to allow more efficient management of the grazing, sometimes to allow fodder crops to be cultivated, sometimes to allow forms of 'convertible' husbandry to be practiced, sometimes for other purposes.

Secondly, most of the larger warrens contained 'lodges' or warren houses. These mainly served as a home and workplace for the warrener but could also be used as bases for recreational hunting, and more generally for the owner's pleasure, and medieval examples in particular could be well-built, elaborate structures. The warrener needed to be resident in order to protect the warren's occupants from predators and poachers. Hungry peasants must have looked with envy at well-stocked warrens, but in the Middle Ages many convicted poachers came from more affluent sections of the community. In the early fifteenth century Augustinian canons from Blythburgh Priory in Suffolk were regularly convicted of poaching in the warren at Westwood near Dunwich. One, Thomas Sherman, was actually described in a court roll of 1425 as 'a poaching canon' (Bailey 1988, 17)!

Thirdly, warrens were supplied with special traps to catch the various vermin that prayed on the rabbits, and these have sometimes left archaeological traces. So too have the rather larger traps which, on a minority of warrens, were used to catch the rabbits themselves. Lastly, and most importantly, on many warrens the rabbits were provided with purpose-built accommodation. This usually took the form of low, oval or rectangular mounds called 'pillow mounds' by

7 A pillow mound, one in a group of two, on the Dunstable Downs in Bedfordshire. The neat, rectangular ends and flat top are typical of examples found in the south and east of England

archaeologists (*7*). Many examples survive, many have been excavated, and great is the confusion which they have caused to archaeologists over the years, a subject to which I shall return. Round mounds, cross-shaped mounds, and mounds of irregular shape were also used to house the rabbits, and on occasions various kinds of earlier earthwork, sometimes suitably modified. All these features provided soft dry earth, and sloping ground, suitable for the rabbits to burrow in, but some were also specially designed to make it easier to trap the animals.

Not all warrens, it should be emphasised, contained all these features. Small, untended warrens, for example, did not have lodges while the distribution of certain other features is strongly regional in character. But the majority of warrens contained at least some of these elements, although they have not necessarily survived, in archaeologically visible form, to the present.

THE RABBIT IN THE WILD

The decline of commercial warrens from the middle of the eighteenth century was accompanied, perhaps paradoxically, by a continued expansion in the number of rabbits in the wild. Colonies of feral rabbits were already causing widespread damage in some districts even in medieval times, as already noted, and by 1555 the Swiss naturalist Gesner was able to comment that 'There are few countries wherein coneys do not breed, but the most plenty of all is in England' (Topsell 1607, 110). In areas where warrens were large and numerous they aroused great resentment because of the damage the rabbits caused, not only to the herbage on the common lands on which many of the larger warrens were located, but also to the crops growing on the surrounding arable. Warrens came to have a symbolic significance, as statements of class and privilege. They were targets for rioters and rebels — and features to be proudly displayed in parks, and beside great mansions.

By the middle of the eighteenth century rabbits were becoming a significant pest in many districts, and often frustrated the planting plans of country gentlemen. William Windham of Felbrigg in Norfolk noted despairingly in his planting book: 'the hares and rabbits have destroyed the plantations on Harrisons Brake entirely, not withstanding the great cost of fencing' (NRO WKC 7/134). Nevertheless, over large areas of Britain rabbits were still comparatively uncommon, especially upland districts, such as Cumbria. Indeed, as late as 1813 it was said that rabbits were rare across most of the high, mountainous interior of Wales (Davies 1813, 347). While the growth in the numbers of rabbits in the eighteenth and nineteenth centuries, and their appearance in new areas, was clearly a continuation of an existing trend of expansion and colonisation, there is no doubt that the two centuries after *c*.1700 saw the triumph of the rabbit in the wild. By the end of the nineteenth century rabbits were abundant almost everywhere in England (Sheail 1978).

A number of reasons have been suggested for the rabbit's evident success in the post-medieval period, and especially during the eighteenth and nineteenth centuries. To some extent genetic mutation and natural selection simply worked, over the long centuries, to make the rabbit better adapted to the local climate, and in particular better able to resist the various diseases which unfamiliar levels of damp and cold engendered. But environmental changes may also have been an important factor. Until the middle decades of the eighteenth century a large swathe of country running diagonally across England from Yorkshire to Dorset had been open, 'champion' land, in which extensive arable open fields, devoid of hedges, thickets and pasture, had occupied most of the land surface. In such landscapes, rabbits could find few places to make their homes. The enclosure of the champion lands had been continuing slowly for more than three centuries but in the period after 1750, with the advent of enclosure by parliamentary act, it speeded up considerably (Williamson 2002, 29-51). By the early nineteenth century the open, boundless prospects of the Midlands had been replaced by a network of fields, surrounded by neat hawthorn hedges: a landscape in which, to quote the poet John Clare,

> Fence now meets fence in owners little bounds
> Of field and meadow large as garden grounds
> In little parcels little minds to please
> With men and flocks imprisoned ill at ease
> (Robinson and Powell 1984, 168)

– and one in which rabbits could far more easily make their burrows. More importantly, over large areas of the Midlands the enclosure of the open fields was associated with the conversion of arable land to pasture, again providing the rabbit with a larger number of places, undisturbed by the regular passage of the plough, in which burrows could be safely made.

The parliamentary enclosures were one facet of that complex collection of change in the landscape and economy of rural England which historians often refer to as the 'agricultural revolution'. This involved, among other things, the development of new systems of farming involving the cultivation of fodder crops, especially turnips, and this may also have been a factor in the expansion in rabbit numbers. In traditional farming systems there had been little to sustain wild rabbit populations over the winter months. Wheat and rye were the principal autumn-sown crops and these provided only meagre grazing by December or January, while the rest of the land was either fallow or awaiting spring cultivation. Turnips, however, came into widespread cultivation during the eighteenth century and these, sown around midsummer and eaten off in the fields over the winter, provided ample sustenance (Sheail 1978).

Perhaps the most important factor in the increase in rabbit numbers, however, was the rise of organised game keeping in the later eighteenth and nineteenth centuries. As landowners vied with each other to maximise the 'bag' of game birds, particularly pheasants, gamekeepers were obliged to wage war on their various predators, especially foxes, stoats, weasels and pole cats, animals which had also served to keep rabbit numbers in check (Munsche 1981). As the preservation of pheasants and partridges increased and became more organised wild rabbits were themselves initially given no special protection and in some cases local villagers were allowed to take them, in order to control their numbers: not least because they competed with game for food, and attracted vermin. But during the nineteenth century there was a growing interest in shooting rabbits themselves, and by 1861 no less than 3333 were shot in a single day at Bradgate

Park in Leicestershire (Sheail 1971, 113). Efforts were now made in many districts to protect rabbits from both their animal and human predators. This caused severe problems to farmers, whose crops were frequently decimated by them. Leases often placed restrictions on the extent to which their numbers could be controlled by tenant farmers, terms which were bitterly resented – as was the fact that the rabbit, although a common pest, was given similar protection to true game (hares, pheasants, and partridges) by successive Game Laws, resulting in the punishment of numerous poor country-dwellers for casual poaching. Only in 1880, with the passing of the Ground Game Act, were occupiers of land (as much as owners) given the right to kill rabbits, although on tenanted land the landowner also retained the right to hunt them.

Interest in rabbit shooting increased still further with the onset of agricultural depression from the late 1870s. The areas most badly affected by the late nineteenth-century fall in grain prices tended to be those characterised by light, poor arable land, such as the East Anglian Breckland, in which warrens and rabbits were already well-established in the landscape. Indeed, destruction of predators 'so that game birds may survive in abundance' (Williamson and Haggard 1943, 54), coupled with the spread of derelict arable land in the more marginal areas of the country and the increasingly scrubby nature of many heaths and commons, led to an explosion in rabbit numbers, especially in the arable areas of eastern England. By the 1940s rabbits had become a serious problem in most parts of the country. Indeed, by the outbreak of the Second World War it was estimated that there were about 50 million in England alone, four times the number of sheep; a figure which had risen to 'somewhere between 60 and 100 millions' by the 1950s (Sheail 1971, 9-10). Various attempts at limitation, or even eradication, were made under the aegis of Rabbit Clearance Societies. The animals were shot and trapped on a large scale, and in the first half of the twentieth century experiments were made with gassing them underground using chlorine and mustard gas, while in the 1920s cyanide gas began to be employed. But the interests of sporting landowners ensured that small numbers of rabbits were usually allowed to survive each eradication campaign, and they remained a serious pest in most districts until 1953-4, when the virus *Myxomatosis cuniculus*, intentionally introduced into Europe from south America, spread into southern England from France. The rabbit population fell with extraordinary rapidity – around 99 per cent of the population was wiped out and the opportunity was taken to intensify eradication campaigns, in order to remove the small percentage of animals which were immune. Rabbit populations have never returned to the levels seen in the 1940s, but resistance has spread and the animal is now, once again, everywhere fairly common in the wild and, at a local level, once again a serious nuisance.

2
PILLOW MOUNDS

INTRODUCTION

The most common and important of the archaeological remains left by rabbit farming are 'pillow mounds' – low, rectangular or ovoid mounds which provided accommodation for the population of the warren, or for some proportion of it. Well over 2000 individual examples are recorded in England and Wales, in county HERs, other archaeological archives, and in the archaeological literature. In most cases they are quite unassociated with any other obvious signs of warrening activity – most, for example, do not appear to lie within any kind of enclosure. The term 'pillow mound' was coined by the archaeologist O.G.S. Crawford in the 1920s (Crawford 1927, 341) but the mounds had been described, and in some cases excavated, by archaeologists for several decades before this (Greenwell 1877, 201-2). Their function and age was for a time a matter of some debate. As early as 1879 Pitt Rivers suggested that they were artificial rabbit accommodation, for he had seen some examples still being used for this purpose on Dartmoor (Price 1881, 321-22, 331). But early twentieth-century archaeologists, living in a landscape over-populated with rabbits, found it hard to understand why they should need to be provided with specially-built accommodation. This was particularly so given that some mounds were located in areas of dry sandy soil, or close to earlier earthworks, places where (in Crawford's phrase) 'such temptations to burrow seem rather superfluous' (Crawford 1927, 341). Crawford eventually became convinced that the mounds were, indeed, artificial warrens, but well into the second half of the twentieth century many archaeologists continued to believe that while *most* pillow mounds may have been built for this purpose, *some* had rather different origins, and were perhaps considerably earlier in date.

The term 'pillow mound', like many in archaeology, is in some ways unsatisfactory and confusing. The mounds do not resemble pillows in the modern sense so much as old-fashioned bolsters: that is, the majority tend to be relatively long and thin in shape. More importantly, it is clear from post-medieval documents — especially leases for rabbit warrens — that the usual term for these features by the sixteenth century was 'berries', 'buries', or 'burrows'.

Pillow mounds display much variation in both their morphology and their dimensions (*8*). Some are rectangular, with fairly square ends; others are more ovoid in plan. Most have a ditch which runs all the way around the mound (unlike those associated with Neolithic long barrows, which usually only run down the sides): but when, as if often the case, mounds are placed on a slope the ditch can be absent from the downhill side. Although pillow mounds generally have the same width and height throughout their length the more rectangular examples, in particular, tend to have broad level tops, while the more ovoid forms generally have higher and more rounded backs. Either way, few true pillow mounds are more than 1.5m in height and most are lower than this. Low, flat-topped, rectangular examples tend to be characteristic of lowland areas, while the more rounded and ovoid forms are more typical of the uplands of the north and west, but this is only true in very general terms and there are many exceptions. Where stone is freely available — again more in upland than in lowland areas — the sides of the ditch are sometimes retained by dry-stone walling, or by large slabs of stone, while large flat stones are sometimes evident on the upper surface of the mound, and masses of rubble near the base.

Perhaps the most striking aspect of variation is in the size of the mounds. Smaller examples can be less than 9m long but the largest mounds can reach 200m and one at Hartfield in Sussex is no less than 234m in length (Tebbut 1968). While extended mounds of this kind can be found scattered throughout England, they are a particular feature of Sussex and Surrey. Whatever their length, few pillow mounds are more than 10m wide, a very small number more than 15m, and the majority have transverse dimensions of 4-7m. This, perhaps, is the most important defining feature of this class of earthwork (Williamson and Loveday 1988, 300-01).

A minority of mounds display a characteristic which Crawford termed 'segmenting' — that is, their surface is cut by a pattern of shallow grooves (Crawford and Keiller 1928, 162). These are most obvious from the air but are often quite clear on the ground, as at Minchinhampton in Gloucestershire where some of the mounds are dissected by rough trenches around 30cm wide and as much as 40cm deep. Some mounds have a single longitudinal groove; some display varying numbers of transverse grooves; others have both. Their layout often appears irregular, or haphazard, in that individual grooves run at a skewed angle across the width of the mound and frequently do not lie precisely parallel with, or at right angles to, the other grooves.

It is important to note, partly because it has been a fruitful source of archaeological confusion, that two or more mounds can be 'conjoined': that is,

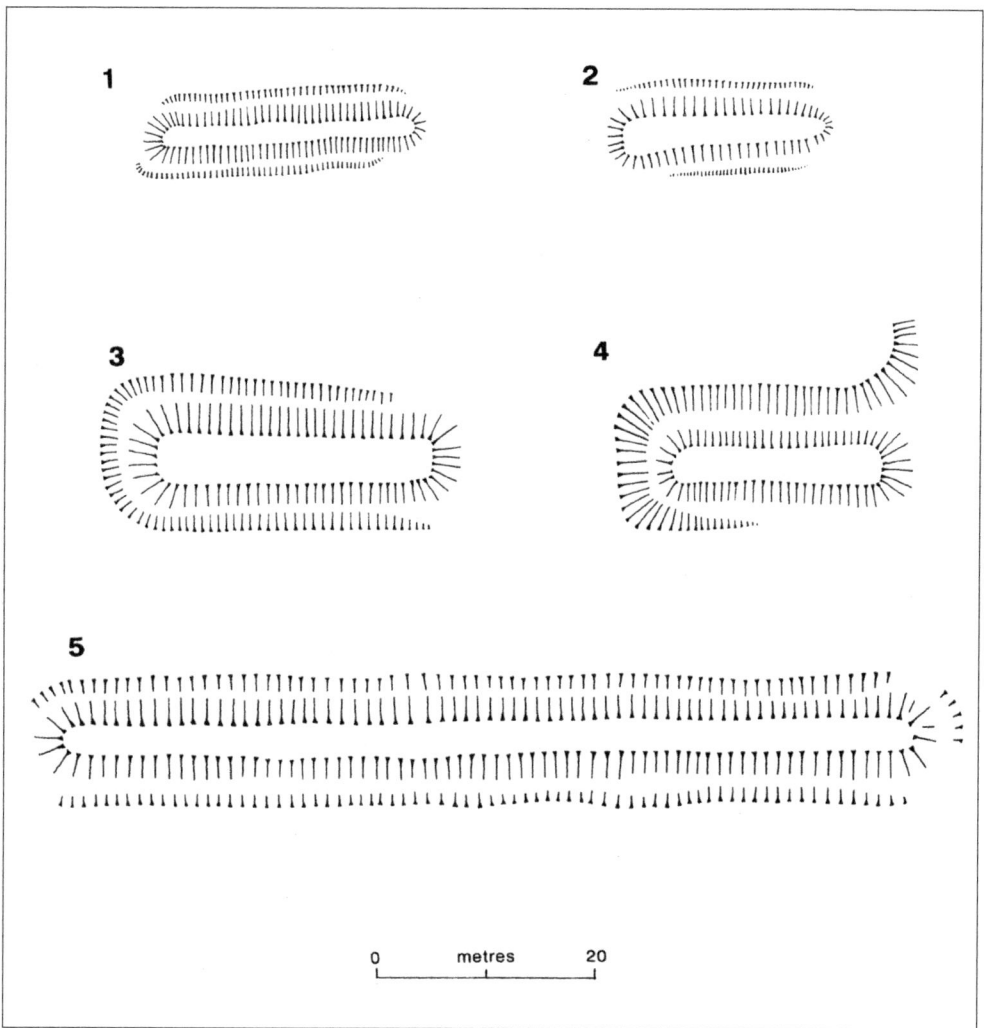

8 Typical pillow mounds: 1 Llanelwedd, Powys (after RCAHM, Wales); 2 Penmaen Burrows, South Glamorgan (after RCAHM, Wales); 3 Cwm Ednant, Darowen, Powys; 4 Stoke Doyle, Northamptonshire (after RCHME); 5 Hartfield, Sussex (after Ordnance Survey archaeological records). Pillow mounds can vary greatly in length, as shown, but seldom have a width much in excess of 15m

joined together at the ends in such a way that they share the same ditches. In this manner they can form long, straight lines, as at Quarrendon near Aylesbury (Buckinghamshire); shallow arcs, as at High Beech in Epping Forest (Essex); open polygons, as at Worth (Sussex) or Hawkesbury (Avon); or even a square, as at Pilsdon Pen (Dorset).

THE LOCATION AND DISTRIBUTION OF PILLOW MOUNDS

Pillow mounds can occur singly; in small clusters; or in large groups containing as many as 90 or even 100 mounds. As figure 9 shows, the largest groups are generally to be found in the west and to some extent the north of the country, and especially in areas of high moorland, in southern and central Wales and on Dartmoor. Here they are often associated with other evidence of rabbit farming – warren houses, tip traps and vermin traps, fodder enclosures and the rest. Moreover, local knowledge of their use as rabbit accommodation survived – and in some cases the actual use of the mounds continued – into the twentieth century (Lineham 1966; Haynes 1970; RCAHM 1982, 316-8). Large groups of mounds also occur in the Mendip Hills; in the Cotswolds; and in the chalklands of Wessex – all areas in which the documentary evidence suggests rabbit farming formed an important element in the local economy in the sixteenth, seventeenth and eighteenth centuries. In central and eastern England, in contrast, small groups of mounds, or single mounds, are more usually encountered, although some larger concentrations, such as that at High Beech (Essex), are known. This north west/south east division is mirrored, to some extent, in the overall distribution of individual mounds and mound groups, the majority of which are found in the former rather than the latter regions.

Of course, to some extent these distributions are the consequence of current, and recent, patterns of land use. Pillow mounds are fairly slight features, easily destroyed by ploughing, and in the course of the later eighteenth and nineteenth centuries arable farming became increasingly concentrated in the east of England, and pasture farming in the centre and west. At the same time, large areas of rough grazing (especially heaths and chalk downland) in the east of the country were converted to arable, potentially destroying any pillow mounds which had existed there (Williamson 2002). In this context it should be noted that a number of documentary records suggest that pillow mounds were, indeed, once a more common feature of the landscape of the east than they are today. In the county of Norfolk, for example, there are now only a handful of examples. But in 1596, during a court case concerning an area of heathland in the parish of Swainsthorpe, the judge enquired whether there were 'any great highe burrowes upon the said pece of ground such as be commonly in warrens', and the witness replied: 'yea my lorde' (Rutledge 1980).

Nevertheless, the fact that the largest *groups* of mounds, as well as the greatest number of individual mounds, are found in the west strongly suggests that the present distribution is only in part the consequence of structured destruction by later land use. Moreover, a number of areas in the east where rabbit farming was unquestionably important during the medieval or post-medieval periods – such as the East Anglian Breckland, the Suffolk coastal heaths or the Tabular Hills of

PILLOW MOUNDS

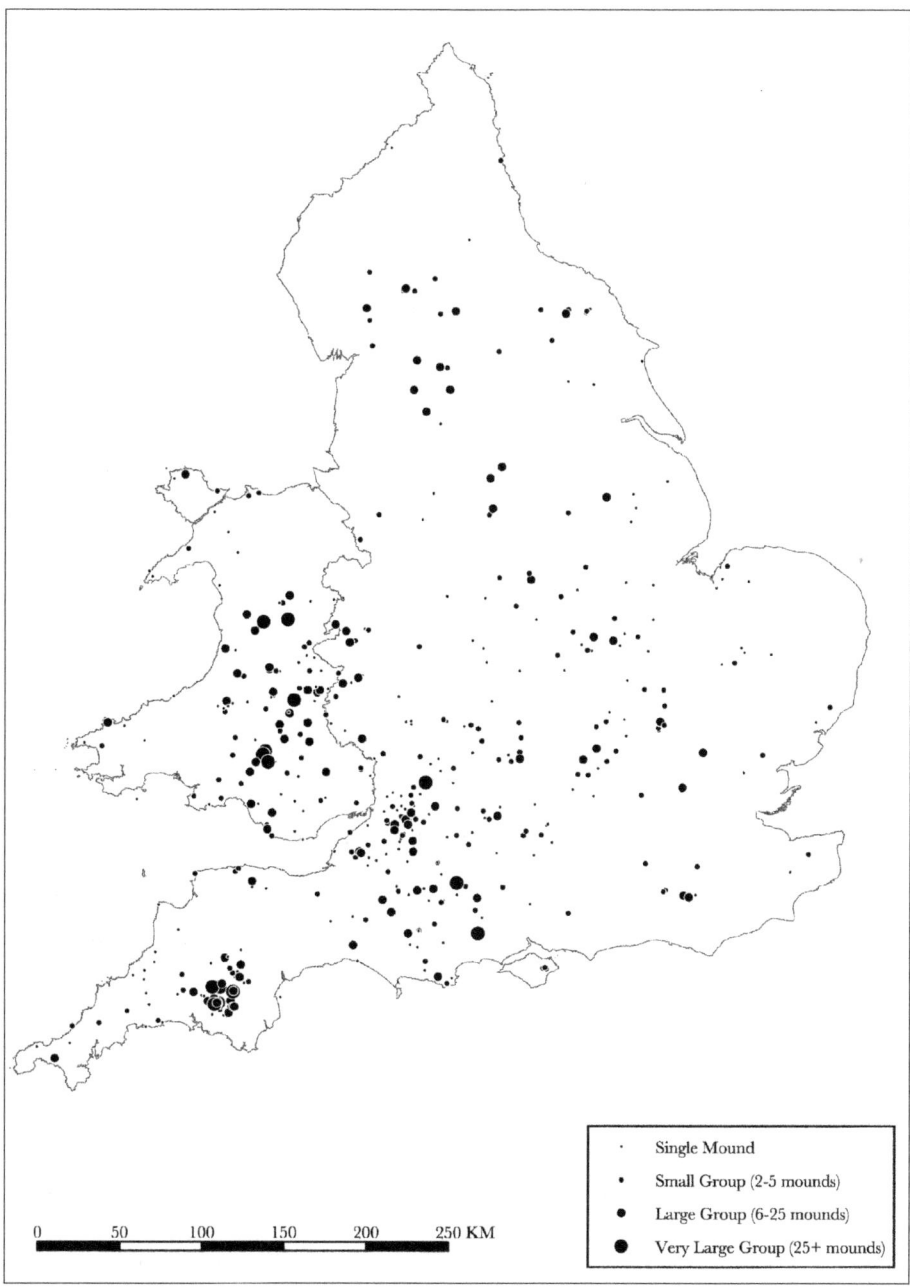

9 The distribution of pillow mounds in England and Wales, still surviving or destroyed since c.1900 (source: RCHME, RCAHM, Ordnance Survey Archaeological Records, Cambridge University Aerial Photography Library, county Sites and Monuments Records/Historic Environment Records). Although unquestionably incomplete, the map does indicate the broad pattern of distribution in the country. The majority of mounds, and most of the larger groups of mounds, are found in western Britain

North Yorkshire – have very few recorded pillow mounds, in spite of the fact that extensive areas of unploughed ground still survive there, or survived until recently. There was thus clearly a greater need to house rabbits in mounds in the west of the country than in the east.

A high proportion of pillow mounds, around two thirds, are found in areas which are still, or were until the parliamentary enclosures of the eighteenth and nineteenth centuries, common land. Given what has already been said about the use of commons and manorial 'wastes' for rabbit farming this is exactly what we would expect. It is *partly* for this reason that a substantial number of pillow mounds are located in close proximity to earlier, usually prehistoric, earthworks; features which are likewise concentrated in areas of relatively marginal, unploughed ground (*10*). The large number of pillow mounds found within Iron Age hillforts and related enclosures is especially noteworthy: examples include Dolebury (Somerset); Bury Hill near Bristol; Wapley Camp (Herefordshire); Croft Ambrey (Herefordshire); Danebury (Hampshire); Wains Hill, Clevedon, (Somerset); Dunraven Castle, St Brides Major (South Glamorgan); Pilsdon Pen (Dorset); Marcross (South Glamorgan); Glascwm (Powys); Hollybush (Herefordshire); Portbury (Avon); Largin Castle, Broadoak (Cornwall); Warbstow (Cornwall); Carn Brea (Cornwall); Bur Hill, Buckland (Gloucestershire); and Castell Odo (Gwynedd). Other examples lie close to, but outside, the ramparts, as at Carregwiber Bank, Llandrindod Wells (Powys); Castle Ditches, Tisbury (Wiltshire); Herefordshire Beacon (Herefordshire); Bathampton Down (Avon); Liddington (Wiltshire); Badbury Rings (Dorset); North Stoke (Avon); Twyn Y Gaer, Llanspyddid (Powys); Brean Down (Somerset); Little Sodbury (Avon); and Graigfawr, Nant, near Llandegley (Powys). A number of examples are also closely associated with Bronze Age barrow cemeteries, as at Swanage (Dorset), Alton Barnes (Wiltshire) or Ashley (Isle of Wight).

In some cases mounds are located only in the general vicinity of earlier monuments – at such a distance that the relationship appears casual, rather than causal. Dunstable Downs in Bedfordshire is a steep escarpment, unploughed in historic times, with arable fields above and below it. On the crest are two fine pillow mounds, and a barrow cemetery, the Five Knolls: but the two are separated by more than 100m. In many cases, however, including most of those listed above, the relationship appears purposeful – that is, the mounds were intentionally located within or beside older earthworks. Indeed, in some cases pillow mounds were actually placed on top of the earlier features, as at Twyn Y Gaer, Penpont, near Llanspyddid in Powys, where they have been built into the ramparts of the hillfort; or Hatfield Forest in Essex, where a chain of mounds was created – probably in the 1640s – by adapting an earlier, perhaps prehistoric, earthwork (Rackham 1989, 163-5).

10 A group of pillow mounds at Llanspyddid, Powys. Typically, these are situated on open moorland (since afforested), and are closely associated with the earthworks of a prehistoric enclosure, Twyn Y Gaer

But pillow mounds are not only closely associated with prehistoric features. They also frequently occur within or beside earthworks of medieval date. Numerous examples are thus found within or beside deserted settlements, as at Croydon-cum-Clopton (Cambridgeshire), Stoke Doyle (Northamptonshire), Doddington (Somerset), or Ham Hill (Somerset); within the earthwork remains of monastic complexes, as at Sawtry (Cambridgeshire); and within or beside medieval castles, as at Castle Neroche (Somerset) (within the outer bailey) and Castle Combe

(Wiltshire) (two examples within the outer bailey, two just outside). The difficulty here is that while in some cases the mounds are probably contemporary with the structures with which they are associated, in others they are unquestionably later, as at Croydon, where the mounds overlie the ridge and furrow of the village's fields. Whatever the explanation for the close relationship of pillow mounds and earlier earthworks, it is a subject to which we shall return, for it has important implications for field archaeologist and, in particular, excavators.

THE EXCAVATION OF PILLOW MOUNDS

A large number of pillow mounds have been excavated in the past, often under the impression that they were barrows. Disappointing or negative results have ensured that many of these interventions have remained unpublished, although in some cases reports were archived (such as that for the excavations on Rockford Common, Ellingham (Hampshire) carried out in the 1950s by Colin Bowen for the RCHME). The results of several excavations, moreover, are known only from passing references in early antiquarian works. One of the mounds at Hutton-le-Hole (Yorkshire) was thus excavated some time before 1824, but the only record of the investigation is that 'There were no remains nor was the colour of the earth changed by fire' (Eastmead 1824, 447). Similar brief descriptions have been published for excavations on mounds at Wye (Kent) (Morris 1842, 13-14); Grimston Moor, Gilling (Yorkshire) (Greenwell 1877, 343); and Church Stretton (Shropshire) (Hyslop and Cobbold 1904). Other brief descriptions of excavations by early antiquaries have been preserved, in the Ordnance Survey archaeological records, for mounds at Hinton Charterhouse (Somerset); Bathampton Down (Avon); Heytesbury (Wiltshire); Bucklebury (Oxfordshire); Newark Camp, Gloucester; and Charlecombe (Somerset). In a number of cases, however, no records of the results of excavations survive, if any were indeed ever made: examples include Croydon-cum-Clopton (Cambridgeshire) by T.C. Lethbridge in c.1933 and Stapleford (Wiltshire) by W.F. Grimes in the 1950s. Many other mounds appear to have been dug into at some time in the past, presumably by treasure hunters.

Nevertheless, although archaeologists often found results perplexing, a large number of excavations have been published, in local or national journals, and these provide a wealth of useful information. The earliest fully published example was that carried out in 1879 on mounds at Hollybush Camp and Herefordshire Beacon (Herefordshire) (Price 1880). This was followed a few decades later by excavations of mounds at Sutton-in-Craven (Lancashire) and at Friarhead, Flashby (Yorkshire) (Villy 1912). But it was not until the 1920s, when there was a significant upsurge of interest in these enigmatic features, that large numbers of excavation reports began to appear: 1926 was a bumper year, with the publication of the excavations at Rylstone (Lancashire) (Villy 1926); Bury Hill, Bristol (Davies and Phillips 1926); High Beech (Essex) (Warren 1926); and of the further interventions at Hollybush Hill (Hughes 1926). This was followed by a lull in interest during the 1930s, and through the War years, but the 1950s saw a number of further excavations: at Everage Clough, Burnley (Lancashire) (Willett and Seddon 1953); Shelve Shute, Axbridge (Somerset) (Sylverton 1956); and at Castell Odo (Gwynedd) (Alcock 1960).

Further excavations took place through the second half of the century, including some of the most informative. A number of these were rescue excavations, examining mounds in advance of destruction: as at Farteg Hill (South Glamorgan) in 1953 (RCAHM 1982, 327-8); Llanelwedd (Powys) (Spurgeon 1969); Cold Aston (Oxfordshire) (O'Neil 1966); Cefn Hirgoed (South Glamorgan) (Vyner 1982); and Y Foel (Powys) (Silvester 1995). A few, as at Bodwen, Lanlivery (Cornwall) (Harris *et al.* 1974) and Llanfair Clydogau (Dyfed) (Austin 1988), were carried out as part of research projects. Others were excavated unintentionally, under the impression that they were some other kind of monument, as at Sharpenhoe Clapper (Bedfordshire) (Dix 1983); Pilsdon Pen (Dorset) (Gelling 1977); and, arguably, Croft Ambrey (Herefordshire) (Stanford 1974); or as the side effect of excavating some associated monument, as at Danebury (Hampshire) (Cunliffe 1984).

PILLOW MOUNDS: CONSTRUCTION AND INTERNAL FEATURES

As a result of these excavations, we now know a great deal about the construction, and internal features, of pillow mounds: and it is clear that in these aspects, as in their external morphology, these monuments display much variation. Some appear to have been of simple dump construction, without internal features: they were formed of material dug out from the encircling ditch and piled in the centre (*11*). The mounds at Sutton-in-Craven and Hollybush Hill, however, also contained earth and stones brought to the site from a distance, presumably because sufficient quantities of suitable material could not be obtained in the immediate vicinity (Price 1880, 315; Villy 1912, 330). At Rockford Common the material, including topsoil, turfs, and brown earth was mixed in an amorphous fashion; while at Cilybebyll, similarly, the mound was simply composed of 'topsoil and small stones heaped quite loosely'. But in a number of cases – at Sutton-in-Craven, Rylstone, Everage Clough and Cold Aston – the excavators drew attention to the way that the material within the mound formed distinct layers, which had not been mixed together by the burrowing activities of rabbits, a superficially curious feature to which we shall return (Villy 1912, 331; Villy 1929; O'Neil 1966; Willett and Seddon 1953). Many of the mounds (Hollybush,

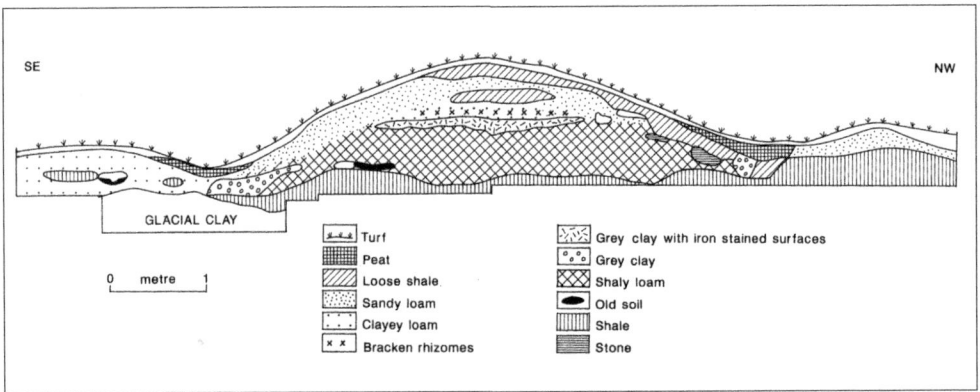

11 Cross-section of a pillow mound at Everage Clough, Burnley in Lancashire, excavated by T. Seddon and F. Willett in the early 1950s (Seddon and Willett 1953). The mound appears to be of simple dump construction, without internal features. It was built in a number of distinct layers which do not seem to have been burrowed into by rabbits

High Beech, Everage Clough, Llanelwedd, and Llanfair Clydogau) overlay areas of burning, perhaps resulting from the clearance of vegetation on the site before construction. In a few cases the excavators noted the fine, loamy and stone-free character of the soil within the mound. At Hollybush, for example, it was described as being 'for the most part fine, as would be found in a garden' (Price 1880). A similar observation was made by Ordnance Survey archaeologists inspecting a trench which had been cut through a mound at Cellan (Dyfed), probably by recent treasure hunters: this revealed only earth and small stones but it was noted that 'The surrounding area is very stony so one can deduce that the stones were removed when the mound was constructed'.

While some mounds thus appear to have been rather simple structures, others were clearly more complex in character. Upland examples have often been found to contain large or medium-sized stones, sometimes arranged in an amorphous fashion at the base of the mound, as at Lanlivery (Cornwall) (Harris *et al.* 1974), but often forming distinct and structured patterns. An example excavated at Llanelwedd (Powys) in the 1960s thus overlay three lines of stones, resting on the old ground surface, which ran the length of the mound, with short transverse lines branching off them and fan-like arrangements at the ends. A second mound covered a similar but more vestigial pattern (Spurgeon 1966, 1967, 1968, 1969, 1970; RCAHM 1982, 319). The mounds at Cefn Hirgoed (Glamorgan) overlay slightly different arrangements, in that the stones formed fairly regular 'grids' of rectangular compartments, arranged in pairs along the length of the mounds, each measuring around 1m x 1.5m (*12*) (Vyner 1982, 852; RCAHM 1982, 319). The mounds at Llanfair Clydogau (Dyfed) covered a mixture of long

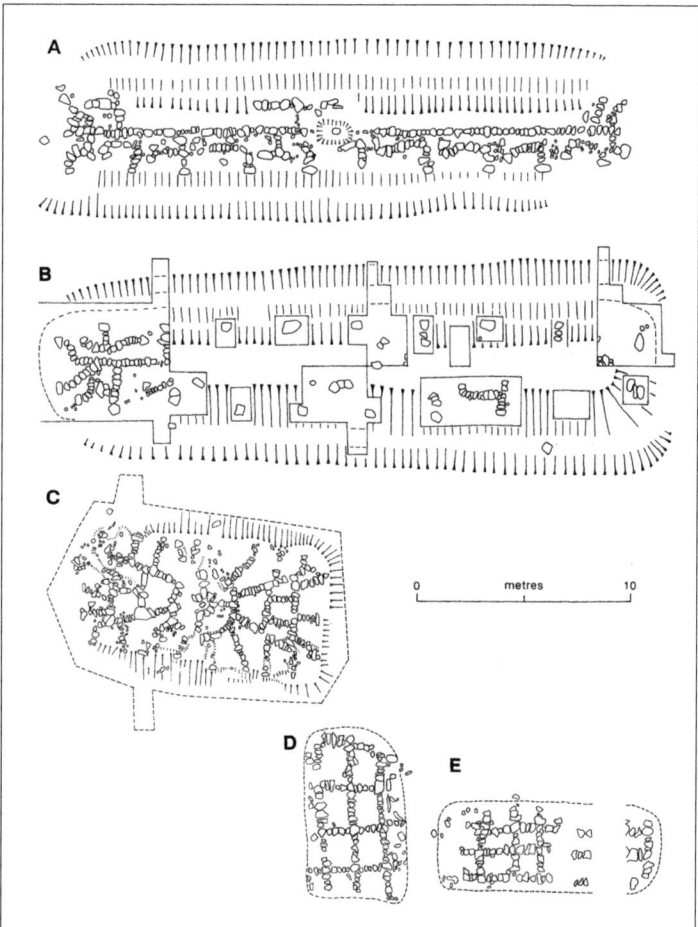

12 Lines of stones capping artificial burrows, dug into the old ground surface, have been discovered beneath a number of pillow mounds, especially in Wales. A and B) Llanelwedd, near Builth Wells, Powys (after RCAHM); C) Llanfair Clydogau, Dyfed (after David Austin); D and E) Cefn Hirgoed, South Glamorgan (after RCAHM)

lines, running the length of the mound, and with short transverse branches; and more complex or irregular patterns (Austin 1982, 146-9). At Castell Odo in Gwynedd, in contrast, the mound covered a single line of stones laid out along its axis (Alcock 1960, 120-1). In all these cases the stones were placed on the old ground surface, with the mound heaped over them. Similar arrangements have sometimes been revealed where other mounds in Wales have been damaged or partially destroyed, as at Mynydd Gelliwion near Pontypridd (RCAHM 1982, 343-4).

Stone lines are not restricted to Welsh mounds. The excavations carried out in 1926 on a mound in Bury Hill Camp near Bristol seem to have uncovered examples, although the report is slightly confused by the excavator's belief that he was dealing with a Roman military building with a 'very crude system of tile drainage' (Davies and Phillips 1926, 10). The latter was represented by lines of 'slanting rows of undressed Pennant flags' running across the width of the mound. The mound here was also retained by a drystone wall, comprising four or five courses of Pennant stone, about 0.3m high. Similar retaining walls and kerbs were recorded at Castell Odo and at Shute Shelve and, as already noted, are a surface feature of many mounds. At the latter two sites there were also signs of a stone 'capping' covering much of the mound, comprising a distinct layer of large stones (Alcock 1960, 120-21; Sylverton 1956, 5).

The lines of stones beneath pillow mounds remained a mystery until David Austin's meticulous excavation at Llanfair Clydoggau in Dyfed (Austin 1988, 146-7). This demonstrated that the stones were not simply laid on the old ground surface, but in fact covered shallow gullies cut into it. Evidently, the builders of the mounds had first cut artificial rabbit runs into the ground to a depth of *c*.20cm, covered them with stones and then heaped the mound over them, thus providing the rabbits with instant shelter from predators and the elements. Most if not all the stone lines discovered elsewhere probably have a similar explanation, although in particularly waterlogged contexts it is possible that some functioned as sub-surface drains. The more amorphous arrangements of stones recorded at other sites probably served a similar range of purposes.

Where mounds were constructed in places where large stones were less readily available, artificial burrows were evidently capped with some inorganic material, and have thus left rather different traces – networks of simple slots cut into the subsoil beneath the mound. A number of examples were excavated by Barry Cunliffe within the hillfort at Danebury (Hampshire), although the overlying mounds had themselves been removed in the eighteenth century, when the interior of the fort was ploughed (*13*) (Cunliffe 1984, 13-14; 1991, 10-12). Very similar features were revealed during the excavation of four mounds, arranged to form a square, within another hillfort – Pilsdon Pen (Dorset) – although their age and purpose were misinterpreted by their excavator (Gelling 1977: see below, pp.139-41). Striations formed by animal claws were observed in the base of some of the Danebury slots and the excavator, Barry Cunliffe, concluded that 'The simplest suggestion is that the structures were created as artificial burrows to encourage rabbits and may indeed have formed the substructure to pillow mounds' (Cunliffe 1984, 14). At both sites the slots were regular in profile, straight-sided and dug into the subsoil (chalk at Danebury, clay at Pilsdon Pen) to a depth of 20-30cm. Some of the complexes comprised a long, single slot, with short projections running off at right angles; others consisted of two or three parallel slots, linked at intervals by transverse slots and again with side branches (*14*). Two broadly similar slots were discovered cut into the chalk beneath the large mound – perhaps too large to be considered a true 'pillow mound' but clearly a related monument – at Sharpenhoe Clapper in the Bedfordshire Chilterns, although

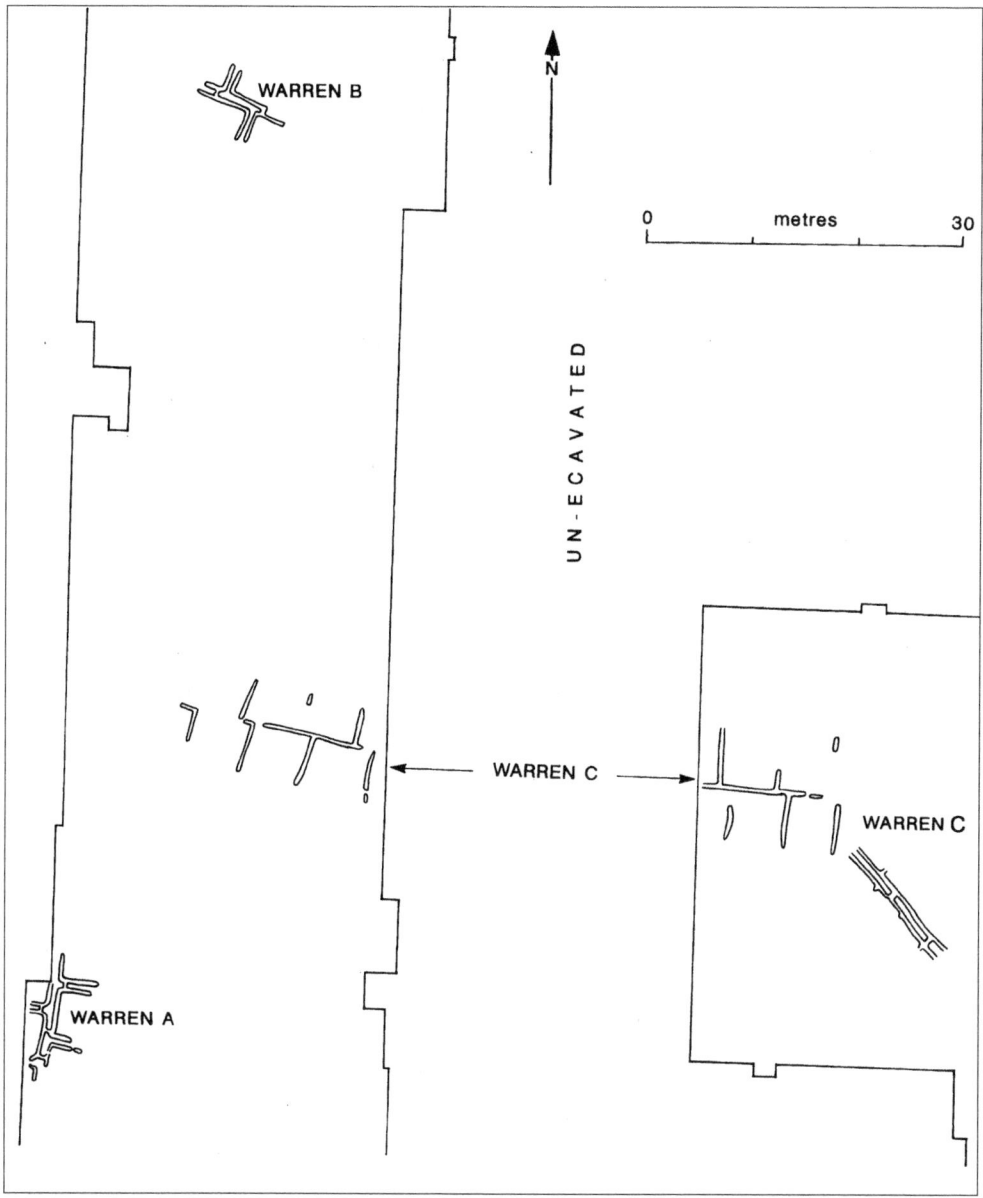

13 In areas in which stone was not freely available, artificial burrows were covered with inorganic materials which have left no obvious archaeological traces. The burrows themselves, however, have sometimes been preserved in the form of linear slots, as here within the area of Danebury hillfort (after B. Cunliffe)

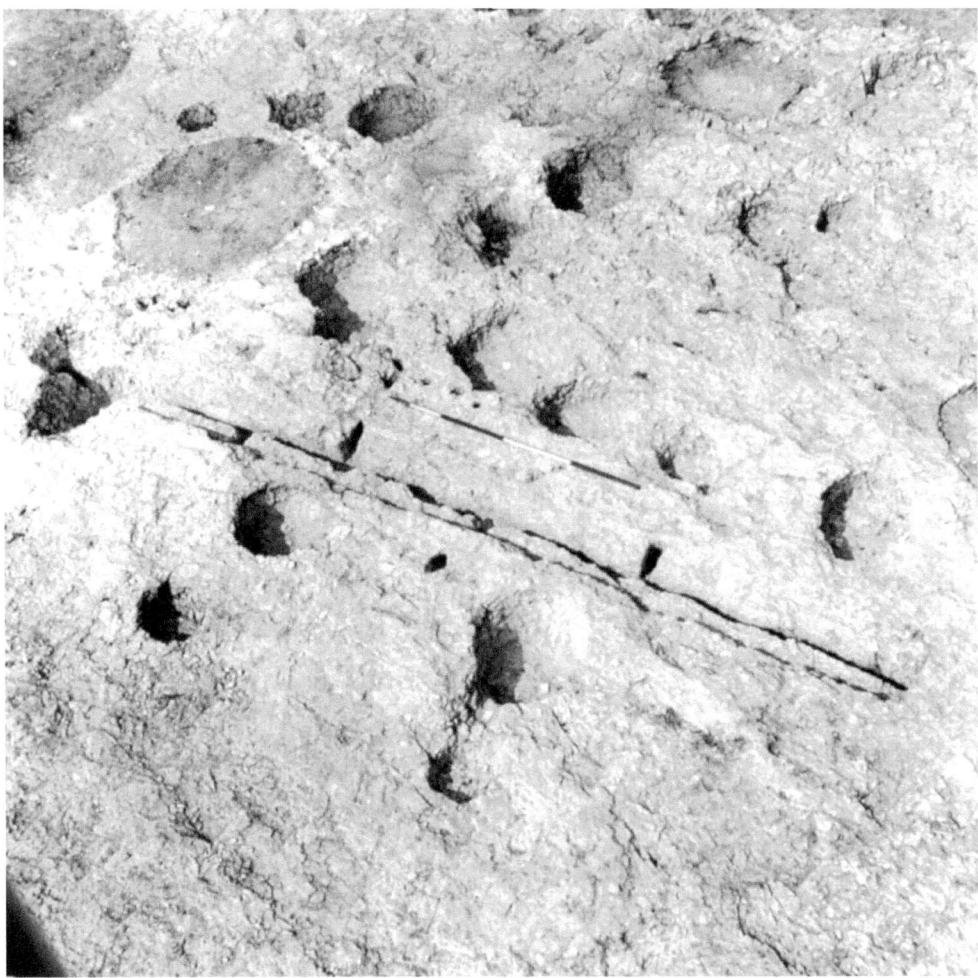

14 The warren slots cut into the chalk within Danebury hillfort in Hampshire were originally probably covered by pillow mounds, which were levelled when the interior of the fort was ploughed in the seventeenth century. The other features shown are of Iron Age date

one was rather larger than the other and it is possible (as the excavator suggested) that this performed some kind of drainage function (Dix 1983, 67-9).

Perhaps the most informative excavation in this context is that carried out on the mounds at Y Foel, Llanllugan (Powys) by Robert Silvester in 1990 (*15*). The mounds were constructed of an orange loam, derived from the subsoil, but they were 'riddled with burrows filled with slightly sticky, loose humic soil' (Silvester 1990, 78). Beneath some of the mounds straight, evidently artificial burrows were discovered, cut into the old ground surface. These had subsequently been augmented, in a less ordered way, by the rabbits themselves. Not all the mounds

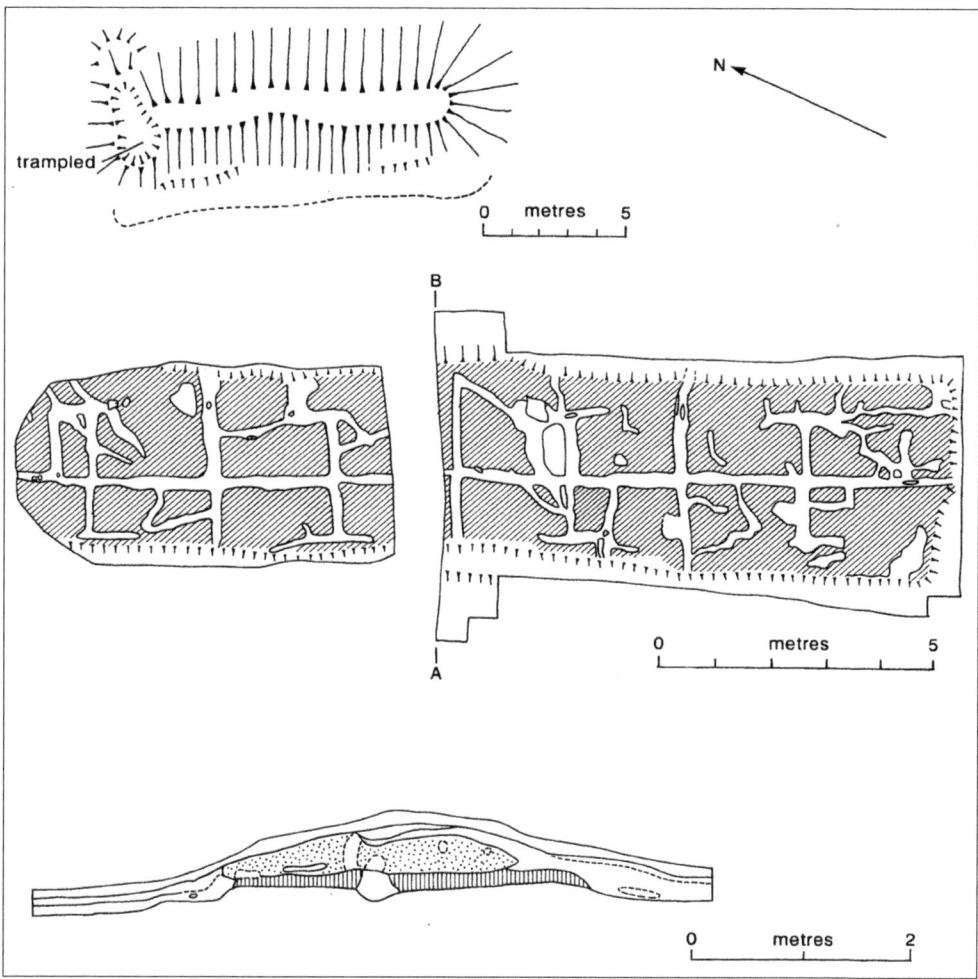

15 Rabbit burrows within a pillow mound at Y Foel, Llanllugan, Powys. Careful excavation by Robert Silvester in 1990 revealed both the original, rectilinear artificial burrows, cut into the subsoil beneath the mound, and the more irregular pattern added by the rabbits themselves (after R. Silvester)

on the warren contained artificial burrows, and Silvester suggested that those that did were the first to be constructed on Y Foel, the original 'colonists' thus being provided with 'fully furnished residences', while their descendants had to make do with less sophisticated accommodation (Silvester 1990, 84).

The burrow slots at such sites must have been capped, in Silvester's words, with 'turves, rushes, or some other organic material' which would 'now be difficult to detect archaeologically' (Silvester 1990, 84). Turfs were certainly employed on Dartmoor, to judge from Crossing's description of 1903 – the only written account of the construction of pillow mounds which seems to exist:

The burrows, or burys, as the warrener calls them, are formed by first digging a narrow trench, with small ones branching from it on each side, but not opposite to each other. Large slabs of turf are then cut, and with these the little trenches are covered. Over this is heaped a mound of earth, and the burrow is finished. A few holes are made for the rabbits to enter, and they quickly take possession of their new abode (Crossing 1903, 62)

It is in fact possible that burrow slots, cut into the old ground surface, were created beneath most pillow mounds, although only noted by a minority of excavators. Where they were capped with inorganic materials they might only be recognised where excavations were particularly meticulous, or where there was a strong visual contrast between the subsoil and the burrow 'fill'. But not all artificial burrows were necessarily cut into the ground surface *beneath* the mound. In some cases they were evidently constructed within it, perhaps because the sub-soil was prone to waterlogging or was too hard and stony for them to be excavated easily. No clear evidence for burrows of this type has been recorded by excavation, but their traces have been noted at a number of places in the form of the shallow surface grooves and trenches which Crawford termed 'segmenting' (Crawford and Keiller 1928, 162). Such grooves, it should be noted, are generally laid out in similar ways to the stone lines and slots found beneath excavated mounds: often, for example, a mound will have a single median groove, with a number of short branches running off at right angles (*16*). The single stone line found beneath Castell Odo is paralleled by the single longitudinal trench observed in mounds at Meifod (Powys) or Lasborough (Gloucestershire). In at least one case a mound originally provided with sub-surface slots seems to have had runs constructed *within* it at a later date. At Bury Hill near Bristol, as already noted, the mound covered stone lines, but the excavator also described how 'at regular intervals shallow transverse grooves had been cut across it', which bore 'no relation to any of the structural features discovered' (Davies and Phillips 1926, 9). There is some documentary evidence that burrows were added to pillow mounds after they had been constructed, although normally by boring holes rather than, as presumably here, digging narrow trenches and covering them over with organic or inorganic materials. During Henry VIII's reign the household accounts for Hampton Court thus refer to the purchase of 'a great long nagre [auger] of irne, to make and bore cony holes within the kynges beries new made for blake conyes in the warren' (Sheail 1971, 43).

16 Pillow mound at Houghton Conquest, Bedfordshire, with a single lengthways groove — traces of a collapsed burrow created within (rather than beneath) the mound

THE AGE OF PILLOW MOUNDS

Excavation has thus contributed greatly to our understanding of the construction of pillow mounds. It has been rather less helpful in establishing the date range of this class of earthwork. Warrens were often established in remote locations, on heaths or downs or moors, far from settlement sites. Many mounds therefore contain little if any debris contemporary with their construction. Proximity to earlier earthworks, moreover, has sometimes meant that they contain residual material of prehistoric or Roman date which has supplied archaeologists with misleadingly early dating evidence. The interpretation of the mound at Bury Hill as a Roman building, for example, was only in part based on its retaining walls and the lines of stones beneath it. It was also due to the Roman and Iron Age pottery recovered in some quantities from within it (Davies and Phillips 1926, 11). At High Beech in Essex, similarly, Warren's interpretation in 1926 of the mounds as Iron Age ritual features was largely based on the presence within them of fragments of Iron Age pottery (Warren 1926, 220, 223). On the other hand, on some occasions material much *later* than the date of a mound's construction has evidently been incorporated by the burrowing activities of the rabbits themselves. The mounds at High Beech were still occupied by rabbits when Warren excavated them and he noted that they contained 'a large amount of the debris of the present-day tripper', including 'high heels from shoes' (Warren 1926, 216). Yet even with these caveats in mind it is clear that the artefacts found within mounds, and in most cases presumably incorporated within them at the time of construction, indicate that a significant proportion are relatively recent features. At Charlecombe (Somerset) the finds made during the excavations in 1911 included the bowl of a clay tobacco pipe; at Lanlivery in Cornwall sherds of late medieval pottery and pieces of coal were recovered (Harris *et al.* 1977); while the mounds excavated by Francis Villy in 1912 at Sutton-in-Craven, Yorkshire, produced forty sherds of medieval pottery, an eighteenth-century trade token, and a George II halfpenny (Villy 1912, 337-8). At Everage Clough, Burnley, Lancashire the excavators commented that the 'superficiality of the ditches ... is suggestive of a fairly recent origin': the quantities of Scots pine pollen recovered from one of the mounds also suggest a post-medieval date, for this species of tree died out in the locality in Roman times and was probably not reintroduced until the seventeenth century. Against this, only one excavation has produced evidence for a medieval date. Fragments of charcoal recovered from the old ground surface beneath one of the mounds at Llanfair Clydogau in Dyfed by David Austin produced radiocarbon dates centring on the late fourteenth century, although it is theoretically possible that these were related to fires made in the area long before the mound's construction (Austin 1988, 151).

Rather more abundant dating evidence comes, not from material recovered from within mounds by excavation, but rather from the relationship of mounds with other archaeological features in the landscape. An example excavated by Bowen on Rockford Common near Ellingham (Hampshire) in the 1950s was thus found to overlie the bank of an enclosure which was itself of post-medieval date, the excavator concluding that the mound was associated with a seventeenth- or eighteenth-century warren. Field observation shows that many mounds overlie 'ridge and furrow', the wave-like corrugations representing the plough ridges of former open fields, fossilised by conversion to pasture in the fifteenth century or later. Examples include the mounds at Aston Sandford (Buckinghamshire), Babcary (Somerset), Benefield (Northamptonshire), Collyweston (Northamptonshire), Croydon-cum-Clopton (Cambridgeshire), Edenham (Lincolnshire), Fotheringay (Northamptonshire), Heytesbury (Wiltshire), Little Sodbury (Gloucestershire), Markenfield (Yorkshire), and Wing (Buckinghamshire) (*17*). Other examples, including those on Dolebury Warren (Somerset), Y Foel and Cwm Ednant (Powys), and Skaigh Moor on Dartmoor (*18*), overlie 'narrow rig', the diminutive form of ridge and furrow which normally dates from the later eighteenth or early nineteenth century, but which in some cases may be slightly earlier. Some mounds are superimposed on the earthworks of late medieval settlement desertion, or lie within the immediate area of deserted settlements with which they can hardly be contemporary, as at Stoke Doyle (Northamptonshire), Hemington (Somerset), Doddington (Somerset), Whetham, Calne Without (Wiltshire), Kegworth (Leicestershire), or Ham Hill (Somerset). At Black Knoll, Plowden, Shropshire, two mounds overlie post-medieval hollow ways. Moreover, as several archaeologists have observed, the general appearance of most mounds – the still well-defined ditches, the sharp profiles – suggests that they are relatively recent additions to the landscape. As the archaeologist Cyril Fox commented in the 1930s, of those in Glamorgan:

> A marked and consistent feature is their perfect condition. The ditches are always complete, frequently lacking that smoothness of profile which great age gives to earthwork. On the other hand, they are old enough to have accumulated a sufficient depth of humus to present the same flora as that of the adjacent undisturbed ground, and therefore have no obvious indications of modernity (Fox 1935, 222)

These features suggested to Fox that the Glamorgan examples were 'not earlier than late medieval'.

Much documentary evidence likewise associates pillow mounds with warrens of late medieval or post-medieval date. The reference to constructing 'buries' at Hampton Court in the early sixteenth century has already been noted. At Rockingham (Northamptonshire) a group of mounds lies within a warren created in 1616; at Weekley (Northamptonshire) a single mound lies within an area called 'The Warren' on seventeenth-century maps (Brown and Taylor 1984); at Edensor (Derbyshire) several lie within an area described as 'Conygarth' on Senior's 1617 survey of the Chatsworth estate (Senior 1617; Barnatt and Williamson 2005, 32-3); while at Hartfield (Sussex) two separate groups of mounds occur in areas referred to as 'The Warren' and 'Warren Lodge' in a parliamentary survey of 1646. The warren slots excavated by Cunliffe at Danebury lay within an area described in 1678 as 'anciently and till since the memory of man a warren', but this had probably only been established in the sixteenth century, when the area in question ceased to be used as the site for a fair (Cunliffe recovered a single sherd of post-medieval pottery from one of the slots) (Cunliffe 1985, 184). The mounds in Hatfield Forest in Essex are almost certainly the 'Coney Burroughs' which Lord Morley constructed in the 1640s, and for which he was repeatedly fined in his own manorial court (Rackham 1989, 164). While some of the groups of pillow

17 A large group of pillow mounds at Little Sodbury, Gloucestershire partly overlies an area of medieval or later 'ridge and furrow'

mounds on Dartmoor, such as those at Trowlesworthy and Ditsworthy, may be associated with medieval warrens most lie within ones with sixteenth century or later origins (Haynes 1970). Of course, warrens could be long-lived enterprises, and some of these examples, and their mounds, may have existed in medieval times: but the recurrent association with sixteenth- and seventeenth-century warrens is noteworthy. 'Burroughes' were certainly a common feature of the sixteenth- and seventeenth-century countryside. When Thomas Tusser wrote his *Five Hundred Pointes of Good Husbandrie* in 1580, his advice for January included the injunction to 'Spare labour nor monie/store borough with conie' (Tusser 1580).

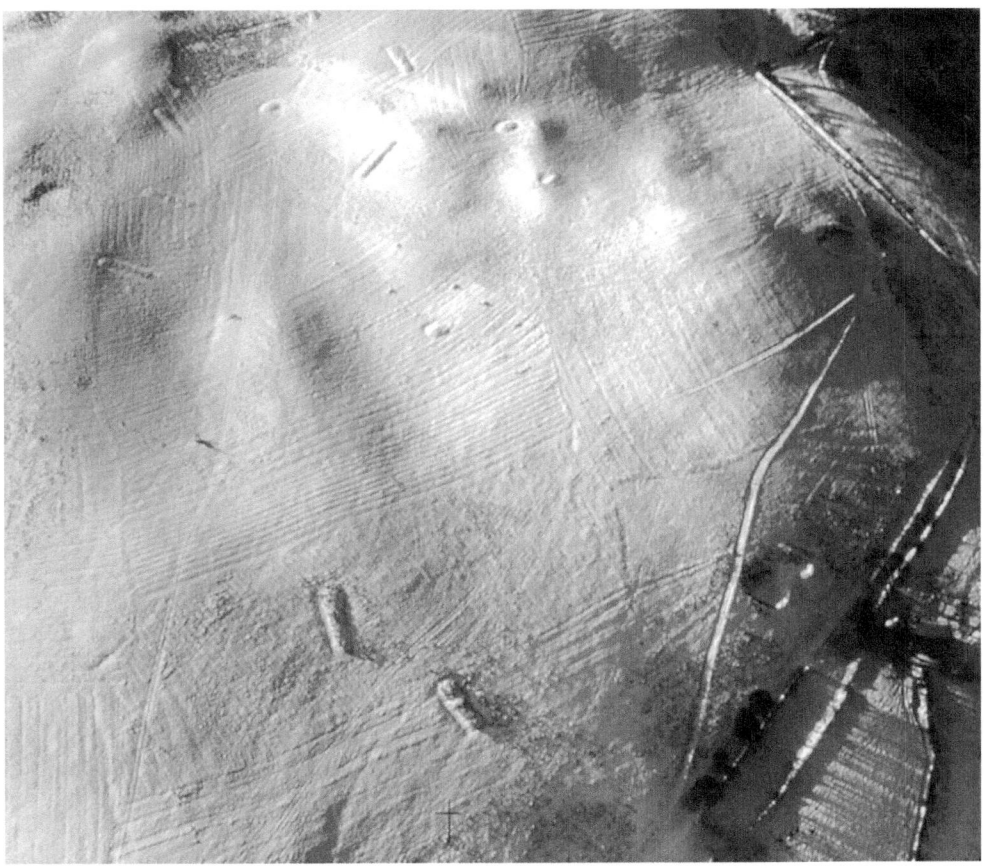

18 A group of mounds, including both circular and rectangular examples, partly overlying 'narrow rig' of eighteenth- or nineteenth-century date at Llandegeley, Powys

A significant proportion of pillow mounds, however, are later – of eighteenth- or nineteenth-century date. Thus the mounds at Trelleck in Gwent, according to the local estate records, were erected some time before 1719 by the landowner, Colonel Henry Probert. Many of the mounds on the moorlands of southern and central Wales have been plausibly dated to the later eighteenth or early nineteenth centuries (not least because agricultural writers and others make it clear that the rabbit was virtually unknown in the interior of that country before this time) (e.g. Davies 1813, 347). Some are quite closely dated. The large groups of mounds at Ystradfellte and Cray in Powys lie within part of the Great Forest of Brecknock which was not sold off by the Crown until 1820 (RCAHM 1982, 314-5; Spurgeon 1967, 1969). Several of the groups on Dartmoor (such as Beardown or Huntingdon) are similarly located within warrens first established in the early or even mid-nineteenth century. Here, and perhaps in a few other areas, the construction of new mounds, as well as the utilisation of existing ones, continued to the very end of the nineteenth century and possibly into the twentieth (Crossing 1903, 62). Hazeldine Warren interpreted the mounds at High Beech (Essex) in 1926 as prehistoric ritual structures but a number of local people informed him that they had been constructed in their own lifetime as warrens (Warren 1926, 221). At Walford in Herefordshire Ordnance Survey archaeologists were assured in 1958 by local people that a group of four mounds had been constructed a mere 70 years earlier.

The documentary and archaeological evidence thus suggests that the majority of surviving mounds are of post-medieval date, and this would fit in well with the more general historical evidence already outlined, for an expansion of warrening in areas of waste and common land from the fifteenth century. But there is no doubt that pillow mounds were constructed in the Middle Ages. Probable examples are depicted in a number of medieval illustrations, such as that in the fourteenth-century *Queen Mary's Psalter* (see 2). Moreover, the archaeological evidence is to some extent biased by the simple fact that, given the slight dimensions of pillow mounds and their vulnerability to destruction, they are unlikely to be found *underlying* such features as ridge and furrow (although the RCHME have suggested one possible example, at Sulby in Northamptonshire). It is also important to note that mounds occur in a number of places where medieval warrens are documented – that on Barry Island, Glamorgan, for example, lies within the area of a warren mentioned in 1491, while examples in the park at Castle Combe, Wiltshire, can probably be associated with the warren which was leased in 1416. This is one of several cases where mounds are associated with parks with probable medieval origins, including Acton Court (Avon); Broughton Park (Oxfordshire); Clarendon Park (Wiltshire); Cornbury (Oxfordshire); Hardington Park (Somerset); Lasborough Park (Gloucestershire); Levens Park (Cumbria); Miserden (Gloucestershire); Prinknash (Gloucestershire); Shobden Park (Somerset); and Tortworth Park (Avon). The pillow mounds scattered across the former parkland around Markenfield Hall, near Ripon in North Yorkshire, are almost certainly of fourteenth- or fifteenth-century date. They overlie ridge and furrow and are associated with a residence which was constructed in 1310 on a grand scale, but which had declined to the status of a farm house by the early sixteenth century. Other pillow mounds are associated with the earthworks of medieval monastic precincts with which they appear to be contemporary (as at Isleham and Sawtry in Cambridgeshire, and Bruton in Somerset). We should also perhaps pay some attention to the evidence of minor place names. Where mounds lie in an area bearing a name indicating its former use for rabbit farming it is generally 'warren', the usual term in the post-medieval period. A number, however, are associated with fields or other features bearing variations on the older term, 'coneygarth':

examples include the mounds at Cold Aston (Gloucestershire) (in a field called 'Coneygres' on a map of 1752); Little Sodbury (Avon) (in a field called 'Conigre'); North Leigh, Oxfordshire (in a field called 'Coneygar Copse'); Rylstone; Portbury (Avon) ('Coneygar Hill'); Chatsworth (Derbyshire) (in an area called 'Cunygre' on Senior's 1617 survey). Some of these could be warrens first established in the sixteenth or seventeenth centuries but some at least may well be much older.

While the available evidence thus suggests that most surviving pillow mounds were built between *c.*1500 and 1850, as commercial warrens became a common feature of the countryside, some – and especially those attached to large mansions or within parks – are undoubtedly older. It is noteworthy that, in most cases, the latter come in small groups, or as single mounds, perhaps indicating warrens for domestic consumption rather than primarily for commercial production: although as we shall see there was probably no very close connection between the size of a warren and the number of mounds it contained.

THE FUNCTION OF PILLOW MOUNDS

While there is no doubt that pillow mounds were constructed to provide accommodation for rabbits, it is not immediately apparent why the creatures should have required this, nor indeed why warreners needed to build mounds of such regular and distinctive form. Why did they not erect mounds of amorphous or irregular shape? 'Burroughes' were evidently a common feature of the post-medieval landscape but, remarkably, no surviving agricultural text or treatise on estate management actually tells us anything in detail about them, although several refer in passing to their existence. We are therefore forced to speculate on their precise function, using the archaeological evidence and scraps of information from nineteenth-century writers, and from such documents as leases.

The primary purpose of the mounds was clearly to provide a body of loose, dry soil in which rabbits could burrow. Rabbits prefer to make their burrows on sloping ground – the sides of the mound – and they also need well-drained soil, failing to thrive in damp conditions. The ditches surrounding the mound would have helped to keep it dry: that this was their major purpose, and that they were functioning features rather than simply a side-effect of the mounds' construction, is evident from the fact that many were repeatedly re-cut, and from the way that most mounds are orientated with their long axes roughly at right angles to the contours. In some cases moreover, especially on Dartmoor, mounds have gripes or surface drains leading off from the perimeter ditches, clearly intended to drain water away, features which are perhaps original, perhaps later additions (*19*). But the perimeter ditches had another function in keeping the mounds dry.

19 A pillow mound on Dartmoor, showing the shallow gripes which have been dug to help drain water from the ditches surrounding the mound

On Dartmoor in the early twentieth century earth and peat were periodically dug out of them and piled on top of the 'buries', the warreners insisting on the importance of keeping the 'roof' intact. They tried, that is, to prevent the emergence of burrows on the upper surface, for these would have made the mound more prone to waterlogging (Haynes 1970, 148). The distinct layers of soil noted by excavators in a number of mounds, and the absence of obvious rabbit burrows within them, must similarly represent successive attempts to maintain the 'roof' and to ensure that the burrows remained deeply buried, close to or below the old ground surface and emerging at the sides rather than on the upper surface of the mounds. Elsewhere – at Shute Shelve, Axbridge (Somerset) and Castell Odo (Gwynedd) – the stone 'cappings' to the mounds discovered during excavation were also presumably intended to discourage burrows emerging there. In addition, leases suggest that brushwood and other vegetation was often laid on the surface of the mounds in the winter, and while this was partly to provide food for the rabbits it was also to help keep the mounds dry. One example, for the warren at Mildenhall in Wiltshire, drawn up in 1586, thus

20 A Dartmoor pillow mound, displaying the high-backed form and rounded ends typical of examples found in the uplands of England and Wales

gave the tenant the right 'to cutt frythe [brushwood] to stragge [cover] the berryes' when the weather was poor (Bettey 2004, 385). That for the warren at Tyttenhanger in Hertfordshire, dating to 1532, similarly refers to the tenant's right to take wood from the adjacent heath to 'cover, plash and lay the burrows' (HALS E.303/4:4, 101).

The distinctive, narrow, ditched form of the typical pillow mound makes immediate sense in these terms. Soil and subsoil dug from the ditch (or brought from elsewhere), as well as brushwood and other vegetation, could be spread without difficulty right across the mound's surface by men standing on either side. If the mound had been wider then they would have had to stand on its surface, breaking the 'roof' and exposing the burrows to the elements. Moreover, in lowland warrens, such regular maintenance would have been less important than in the damp uplands, and this may well explain why, on the whole, the mounds found in the latter areas tend to be higher, and have more rounded profiles, than those in the former, which generally approximate more closely to the neat, rectangular, flat-topped forms originally described by Crawford (*20 & 21*).

21 A pillow mound at Croydon-cum-Clopton in Cambridgeshire, with the low profile, flat top and neat, squared ends typical of examples constructed in lowland locations

In upland areas, where soils are often thin or waterlogged and the rainfall high, it might be necessary to provide purpose-built accommodation for most or even all of the rabbits on a warren. This explains why most of the larger groups of mounds are found in Wales, western England, and to some extent the north. In the south and east of the country, in contrast, mounds were less necessary. Here they were evidently often constructed only when new populations were being established on areas of heath, downland or other 'waste', or to house the most vulnerable members of the rabbit population – that is, the young, and the breeding does. The Middle English term *clapere*, which was originally used for rabbit warrens in general, seems from the later fourteenth century to have been applied in a more specialised sense, to special places where the does bred. John Lydgate's *Secrets of Old Philosoffies*, written in the early fifteenth century, thus describes how 'Yonge Rabbettys be to ther Claperys ronne', and it is probable that this term was employed for breeding mounds (Aitken 1894, 42).

Nevertheless, in dry lowland areas warrens were sometime provided with large numbers of mounds, even where the soils were deep and well-drained.

At High Beech in Epping Forest, for example, the group of 20 mounds was still infested with rabbits when Hazeldine Warren investigated it 1926. He described how 'the whole area [is] an exceptionally favourable one for them: it is all like a natural bank of dry Bagshot sand, and the rabbits burrow in the natural surface quite freely. ... The site would certainly be a rabbit warren even if the mounds were not there' (quoted in Crawford and Keiller 1928, 23). In such cases it was probably simply more convenient to house rabbits in pillow mounds than to let them develop their own burrow systems. On most warrens the rabbits were caught using some combination of ferrets, dogs and nets. Long nets or 'hays' were erected at night between the rabbit burrows and their food: concentrating the rabbits in a long, straight mound obviously facilitated such a procedure. But earthworks of this form would also have been helpful if rabbits were being bolted by ferrets into individual purse-nets, placed across the exit holes. In the case of a natural burrow system it can be hard to locate, and net, all of the exits: a proportion of the rabbits invariably escape, and so too can the ferret, subsequently becoming a nuisance on the warren. Burrow systems developing within the confines of a relatively narrow, relatively low mound, moreover, defined by ditches cut down to the subsoil, would have had few deep and exitless burrows from which rabbits would refuse to bolt, and from which ferret and prey might only be recovered after much digging. Rabbits would be particularly prone to bolt where simple artificial burrow systems were constructed within the mounds, at least until these were extended and complicated by the rabbits themselves. Here again careful maintenance was necessary, to ensure that the burrows did not spread beneath and beyond the ditches. There is some evidence that, when they did, warreners would break up the ground around the mounds by ploughing. A lease for a warren at Cobham in Surrey, drawn up in 1647, thus stipulated that the tenant should not destroy or dig down any of the rabbit burrows 'except outholes by ploughing of the ground' (Walker 1961, 88). Whatever the precise motives for building particular mounds, regular maintenance of the 'roof' and the ditches probably explains the remarkably neat and tidy appearance exhibited by many pillow mounds, as well as the 'unburrowed' layers which have been noted by excavators within them – both features which have, somewhat paradoxically, often been considered incompatible with their function as warrens. It also explains why leases frequently emphasise the importance of leaving the 'buries' in good condition at the end of a tenancy, as at Burderop Park in Wiltshire in 1696, where they were to be 'tenantable and not mangled or decayed' (Bettey 2004, 387).

Pillow mounds were thus built for a variety of reasons and there is therefore, unfortunately, probably little relationship between the number (and size) of mounds found on any particular warren, and the size of its population. Single mounds or small groups of mounds might represent 'clappers' for the breeding does, or pioneer accommodation, on a large warren: this is the probable explanation for the few mounds to be found, for example, on the great Breckland warrens in East Anglia. Alternatively, they might represent attempts to house a much higher proportion of the population on a small, domestic warren. Some small groups and single mounds might have had a rather different purpose. Rather than representing accommodation for effectively domesticated populations they may have been built to facilitate the small-scale, casual exploitation of scattered populations of essentially wild rabbits, by concentrating them in easily nettable mounds. At Hawkesbury in Avon local inhabitants thus informed Ordnance Survey archaeologists in the 1960s that a group of mounds had been constructed 'to attract rabbits'. This might, perhaps, explain why pillow mounds are so frequently located beside earlier earthworks: the latter, that is, might already have been occupied by rabbits, but dispersed across a wide area, in natural burrow systems which had all the disadvantages already described. Once constructed, the mounds would have provided appealing accommodation and would soon have been occupied. It is more probable, however, that in most if not all of such cases the pillow mounds represent 'pioneer accommodation' constructed for the first generation of colonists, when rabbits were being encouraged to take up residence in hillforts, or other earthworks.

3

OTHER FEATURES OF THE WARREN

ALTERNATIVE FORMS OF ACCOMMODATION

The kinds of ovoid or rectangular pillow mound discussed in the previous chapter were not the only form of shelter and accommodation specially constructed for rabbits on medieval and post-medieval warrens. On domestic coneygarths irregular mounds of earth, especially the upcast created by the excavation of fish ponds, were sometimes used, as at Higham Ferrars Castle in Northamptonshire, or (probably) Northill in Bedfordshire. Elsewhere, forms of rectangular or ovoid mound were employed which were larger than 'true' pillow mounds. Examples include the substantial bank at Sharpenhoe Clapper (Bedfordshire), excavated by Brian Dix in 1979, which is 58m long, 10-13m wide, but which ranges in height from 0.7m to as much as 2m (Dix 1983, 65); and the mound on Suttton Common in south-east Suffolk, nearly 16m wide, some 40m in length, and more than 2m high in places (Williamson 2005, 60). The latter is set within a circular enclosure within an extensive warren, and may have been a clapper mound – as too, presumably, was that at Sharpenhoe Clapper, to judge from its name. Secondly, on some warrens there were mounds of similar dimensions to pillow mounds, but of unusual shape. As already noted, pillow mounds can sometimes be conjoined – that is, laid out in such a way that they are joined end to end – and arranged as straight or curving lines, open polygons or squares. In some cases, the mounds themselves took such shapes. At Winterbourne near Newbury (Berkshire) for example a mound, now destroyed, formed three sides of a square, while slightly V-shaped mounds have been recorded, as at Ystradfellte (Powys) and L-shaped examples, as at Llanfair Clydogau (Dyfed) (*22*) (Austin 1988, 139; RCAHM 1982, 314-5). One noteworthy variant is the cross-shaped mound, a type of earthwork which antiquarians sometimes described as the 'embanked cross'. Examples have been recorded at Port Talbot (south Glamorgan), Newport and Haycastle (Dyfed), Chirbury (Shropshire), Banwell (Somerset), Swinton

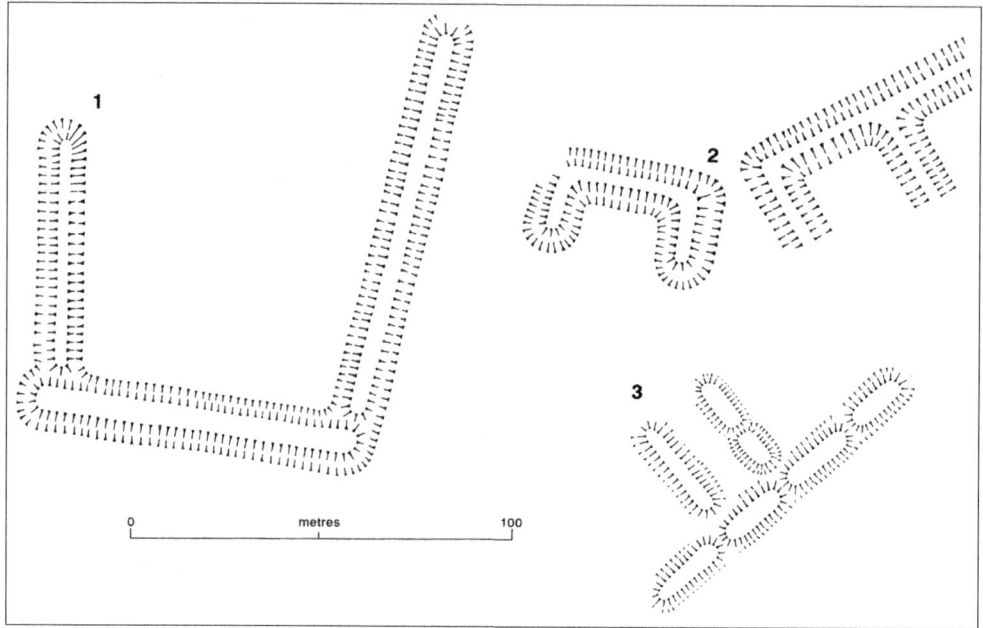

22 Conjoined pillow mounds and variant forms: 1 Hartfield, Sussex; 2 Winterbourne, Berkshire; 3 High Beech, Epping Forest, Essex

(Yorkshire) and elsewhere (*23*). There is no evidence that these fulfilled any special role and that at Port Talbot is located close to, and that at Chirbury lies beside, pillow mounds of normal form. The former mound, when excavated in 1852, was found to overlie examples of stone lines (RCAHM 1982, 334-5).

The most important variant form of pillow mound, however, is the round mound. Indeed, around a fifth of pillow mound groups include at least one circular example. Circular mounds can also, on occasions, occur in isolation, where they can easily be mistaken for small barrows. Most have diameters of 5-15m but some larger examples can be found (such as that now destroyed on Steeple Langford Cowdown, Wiltshire, recorded by Crawford in the 1920s) (Crawford and Keiller 1928) (see *68*). Round mounds are similar in general appearance to pillow mounds of normal form, in that most are flat-topped and display sharp profiles and well-defined ditches. Some examples are segmented, either with a single lateral groove or with two set right angles, meeting at the centre of the mound – christened by Crawford the 'Hot Cross Bun' form (Crawford 1927) (*24 & 25*). Like rectangular mounds, they sometimes have artificial burrows cut into the old ground surface beneath them: at Cefn Hirgoed in South Glamorgan an excavated example was found to overlie stone lines (RCAHM 1982, 339-40). These features clearly suggest that round mounds were used in the same ways as rectangular ones, and

OTHER FEATURES OF THE WARREN

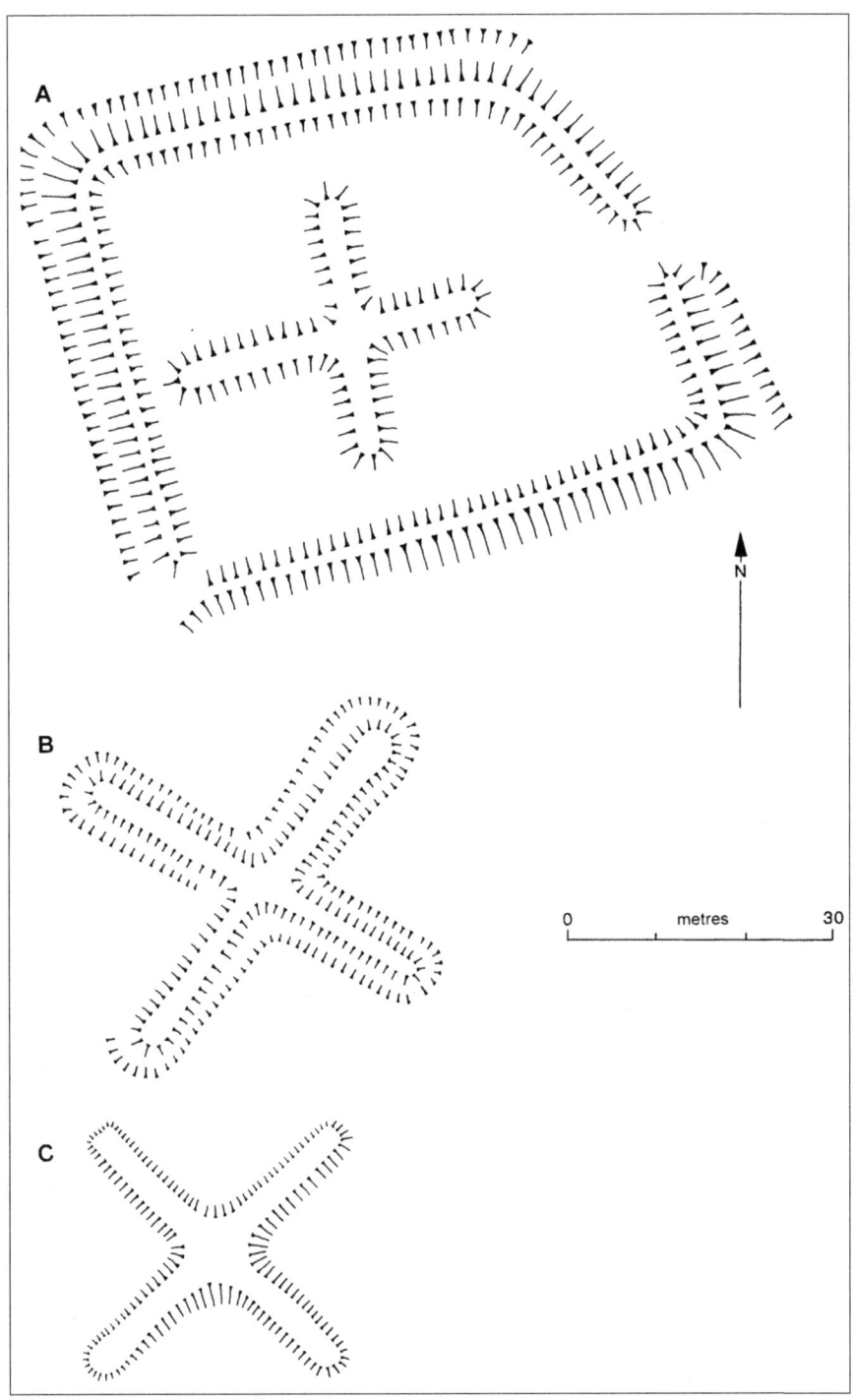

23 Examples of cross-shaped pillow mounds: A) Banwell, Somerset; B) Chirbury, Shropshire; C) Mynydd Brombil, Port Talbot, South Glamorgan

there are indeed a number of post-medieval documentary references to the use of circular mounds as rabbit accommodation, such as the 'round Coney berries' mentioned in an early seventeenth-century survey of the Duke of Hertford's park at Amesbury in Wiltshire (Bettey 2004, 383). It has, however, been suggested that some examples may have had a different purpose. The warren at Y Foel (Powys), excavated by Rob Silvester, contained only a single round mound, surrounded by at least 54 rectangular examples, and in contrast to the other excavated mounds in the group it displayed 'virtually no disturbance by rabbits' and contained no evidence for artificially constructed burrows. Instead, the centre of the mound contained traces of 'an almost vertically-sided feature, resembling a posthole' (Silvester 1995, 85). Silvester suggested that the mound may have been raised to provide stability to a pole surmounted by a platform supporting a trap to catch birds of prey. Certainly, there are documentary references to the use of mounds to support traps elsewhere, although not, apparently, elevated on poles. Daniel in 1801 reported how:

> The Norfolk Warreners use the following method to destroy Eagles, Kites, and other birds of prey : These birds are very shy, and like to settle where they can have an uninterrupted view for some distance ; a naked stump or hillock is their favourite resting-place ; the Warreners, therefore, raise mounds of Earth of a conical form in different parts of the Warren, and place steel traps upon the summit of these artificial hillocks (Daniel 1801, 354)

This said, there is little doubt that most circular pillow mounds were, indeed, used to accommodate rabbits, and were no different in this respect to mounds of normal, rectangular form.

Warrens were, as we have seen, often located in areas of earlier earthworks, which provided excellent accommodation for the rabbits. Indeed, the pillow mounds so often found beside hillforts, barrows and the like probably (as already noted) represent accommodation for pioneer populations which, it was anticipated, would subsequently colonise the loose soils of the adjacent earthworks. Many prehistoric earthworks have the name 'warren' or 'coneygar' applied to them. One of the most striking examples, noted by Taylor many decades ago, is the group of nine Bronze Age round barrows at Winterbourne Stoke (Wiltshire), which lies within an enclosure covering 2.2ha, defined by a polygonal bank $c.0.9$m wide and 0.7m high: the area is still described as 'The Coniger' (Taylor 1974, 108). There are several examples of hillforts bearing 'warren' names, including Warren Ring, Littlebury (Essex) and The Warren, Esher (Surrey). Later earthworks were also utilised by warreners. Redundant castles made particularly good warrens, especially if surrounded, in whole or part, by water-filled ditches,

OTHER FEATURES OF THE WARREN

24 A small, segmented circular pillow mound on Minchinhampton Common, Gloucestershire. The pattern of two lateral grooves, crossing in the centre, was christened the 'hot cross bun' form by O.G.S. Crawford

which provided a good boundary given the rabbit's strong aversion to water. The two sections of the north bailey of Kidwelly castle in Wales, for example, were used as a rabbit farm in the sixteenth and seventeenth centuries (James 1980, 8). Other earthworks used in this way include deserted medieval villages and old mounds of salt-working debris. Earthworks of all kinds might be adapted by warreners, in particular by having artificial burrows inserted into them. Examples include Juliberries Grave, a Neolithic long barrow in Chilham (Kent), which in the nineteenth century displayed clear signs of 'segmenting' (*Archaeologia Cantiana* 1889, 11); and the cairn on Wigber Low in Derbyshire, excavated by John Collis, which had two stone-lined burrow trenches inserted into it, probably during the early nineteenth century (*26*) (Collis 1983, 23, 103, 107). Early antiquarians sometimes expressed concern over the damage caused to ancient monuments by their use as warrens. In 1739 the Norfolk historian Francis Blomefield noted of the castle at Castle Rising how 'by the increase of these conies by the warren, and their breeding in the castle ditches and banks, the same are destroyed, and the walls are already in part, and the rest in danger of overthrowing' (Blomefield 1805, 51). Knox in 1855 similarly bemoaned the effects of the rabbit farms on the

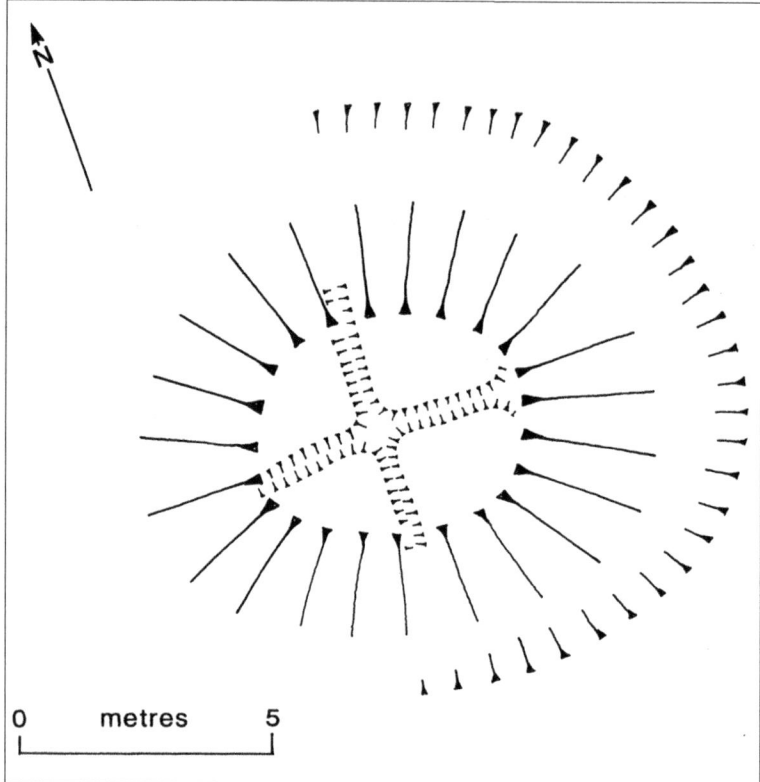

25 Plan of a segmented circular pillow mound on Minchinhampton Common, Gloucestershire

prehistoric dykes of the Tabular Hills in north Yorkshire: 'Such antiquities have ... been much defaced among rabbit warrens; as may be seen at the Scammidge war-dykes which were very strong fortification works' (Knox 1855, 115).

Mounds and other earthworks were not the only form of shelter and accommodation which might be provided on the warren. In some cases it appears that artificial burrows were dug into the subsoil and simply covered over with wood or turfs, bringing them more or less flush with the land surface, rather than being buried beneath mounds. While most of the warren slots excavated within Danebury hillfort by Cunliffe were probably covered by mounds, some were not. A number of examples had been excavated at the base of rather broader trenches, and were connected to the surface by holes bored through the solid chalk, diagonally to the surface (Cunliffe 1991, 14) (27). Warrens' slots revealed by aerial photography, and subsequently examined by geophysical survey and limited excavation, at Mount Down (Hampshire) likewise appear never to have been covered with mounds (Hampton 1981; Clarke *et al.* 1983). Another alternative was to shelter the rabbits in banks of low-growing vegetation, as on the Ashridge estate (Hertfordshire), on the thin chalk soils of the Chiltern escarpment.

OTHER FEATURES OF THE WARREN

26 A stone-lined rabbit burrow inserted into the Bronze Age cairn on Wigber Low, Derbyshire, probably in the nineteenth century, revealed by excavation

Here, within an area described as 'Box Warren' in a document of 1656 (BRO Ashridge I 62/2), a number of strips of box, around 15m wide, still survive (*28*): some are planted on top of earlier lynchets. The strips are shown, much as they are today, on an estate map of 1762 (HALS AH 2770). There are hints of similar arrangements elsewhere, as at Dorking in Surrey, where a manorial survey of 1580 describes 'the lodge and warren of cunneys with a close grown with box containing 12 acres' (Ettlinger 2000, 10). Sometimes such banks of vegetation were surrounded by a wall or bank, as on Headland Warren in Dartmoor, where small enclosures, covering between a quarter and two acres (*c*.0.1-0.8ha), were thickly planted with gorse to accommodate the rabbits (Haynes 1970, 162).

BOUNDARIES

Some warrens, but by no means all, were enclosed by walls, banks or fences. This was partly to protect the rabbits from predators but mainly to prevent them straying onto neighbouring properties, where they might be lost to the

27 An unusual form of artificial burrow, excavated within the hillfort at Danebury. It consists of a narrow slot, dug into the chalk at the base of a broader trench. From its sides, burrows have been bored through the chalk, running diagonally to the surface. The complex was probably never covered by a pillow mound

warrener or cause damage to crops. In addition, physical boundaries helped to define the legal area of the warren, thus making it easier to prosecute poachers; and prevented wild rabbits from entering the warren, an important consideration where warrens specialised in the production of special varieties of rabbit – black, or silver-blue. As with other aspects of the warren, moreover, it is possible that the expense and effort involved in the construction of boundaries also served to express the wealth and status of the warren's owner, at least in the Middle Ages.

A number of factors decided whether warrens were open to the outside world, or enclosed. One was the kind of land use in the surrounding areas. Rabbits would not, in normal circumstances, make strenuous efforts to leave the warren: but a shortage of grazing resulting from drought, or from severe winter weather, would encourage them to exit in numbers in search of food (Sheail 1971, 47). Where warrens abutted on open heaths or moorland, warreners were less concerned about escape than when they lay next to arable land. Rabbits were generally loath to range into inhospitable territory where they could do little damage anyway. On the other hand, warreners might be more motivated to construct a boundary where two warrens in different ownerships lay in close proximity, in order to avoid disputes over the ownership of particular rabbits, and especially where the genetic purity of some special breed – black, or silver-

28 Box Warren, Ashridge, Hertfordshire. The narrow strips of box, probably planted in the seventeenth century, provided shelter for the rabbits

blue – needed to be maintained. But the main variables deciding whether or not physical boundaries were erected were the size of the warren, and time: in essence, the later in time we come, the more likely it was for warrens to be enclosed; and smaller warrens were in general more likely to be enclosed than larger ones. As Harting put it in 1898:

> The larger the feeding area, of course, the better, and the less need is there for enclosure … since the rabbits have less incentive for straying, and the very openness of the ground gives greater security, for it makes it more difficult for an enemy to approach unseen. It is naturally otherwise when the warren is confined to a comparatively small area, for to prevent them from straying in search of 'fresh woods and pastures new', it becomes necessary to confine them within stone walls or a rabbit-proof fence, which may serve the double purpose of preventing the rabbits from getting out, and other creatures from getting in (Harting 1898, 59)

Some of the larger warrens were enclosed, at least in part, even in the early Middle Ages. A *fosse* is thus recorded at Lakenheath (Suffolk) in the early fourteenth century (Bailey 1989, 131), while witnesses in a court case at Methwold (Norfolk) in the 1580s were uncertain about when the 'olde banks that lyeth about the skirts of the warren were first made', suggesting that these were then already of some antiquity (TNA: PRO MPC 75). But so far as the evidence goes physical boundaries became more common in the post-medieval period, and especially in the seventeenth and eighteenth centuries (Sheail 1971, 44-5), perhaps because stocking levels on many warrens were increased with the use of fodder crops, particularly turnips. In overcrowded conditions rabbits suffered from stress and the younger members of the colony, in particular, were more likely to stray.

Warrens could be bounded in a number of ways. Some examples, and especially the smaller ones, were fenced. At Kingsclere in Hampshire in 1783 the landlord provided the warrener with both timber and nails to construct a substantial fence, while at Driffield in Yorkshire in the eighteenth century wooden palings were used along part of the boundary (Sheail 1971, 45-7). Wooden fences were expensive, however, because they needed constant maintenance and replacement. In areas of heathland and chalk downland warrens were thus usually enclosed by banks of turf, a relatively cheap and durable material, although one easily burrowed through by rabbits. Such banks were 1m-1.5m in height and were usually topped with faggots of furze or gorse, or thorn, held in place by a capping of turf, which overhung the inner face of the bank; or, more rarely, by live gorse or thorn bushes (*29*). Occasionally a projecting capping of stiff reeds was used. The inner face was sometimes, although perhaps rarely, lined in places with flint or other available stone, to deter burrowing, as on Thetford Warren in Breckland. Such banks used a great deal of pasture: indeed, it has been calculated that in the case of the Breckland warrens a bank *c*.1.3m high would require more than 20sq. m of turf for every metre of its length (Sussams 1996, 116). Some examples had, and often still have, an asymmetrical profile, with the side facing the inside of the warren being more vertical than that on the outside.

Where warrens were numerous boundary banks were, and in some cases still are, a prominent feature of the landscape. Some of the Breckland warrens, for example, were enclosed by banks as much as 20km in length. Moreover, some had, for all or part of their circuit, two parallel banks, one perhaps added at a later stage, as an added deterrent to escapees. Where (as was often the case) two warrens abutted on each other there might be three or even four parallel banks running across the heath, as for example where the boundaries of Brandon Warren and High Lodge Warren in Santon Downham ran next to each other for nearly 1km.

Where stone was freely available – mainly in upland areas like Dartmoor, but also to some extent on the Cotswolds and Mendips – drystone walls were

29 One of the boundary banks of High Lodge Warren in the Suffolk Breckland, revealed by recent felling in a Forestry Commission plantation. The bank has slumped and spread over time, but still displays the slightly asymmetrical profile characteristic of such features

used to define the boundary. These provided better barriers to fugitive rabbits than earthen banks and so there was usually only a single perimeter wall, rather than the multiple banks often seen in heathland or downland areas. The walls were normally 1.5-2.5m in height and in some cases – as at Wood Hall Warren, Carperby, in the Yorkshire Dales (*30*) – had an overhanging coping, projecting out from the wall face (Dennison 2004, 141). The walls at this remarkably well-preserved warren – the details of which were recorded with exemplary thoroughness by Ed Dennison in 1996 – also display a number of deliberately curved rather than sharply angled corners, probably to make it difficult for rabbits to scramble over them (Dennison 2004, 141). Some warrens, such as those in the Tabular Hills of North Yorkshire, had boundaries of both types: turf or stone walls were used on the more level terrain, but stone walls alone on the sides of the valleys (Harris and Spratt 1991, 183). Wire netting began to be employed on some warrens in the 1850s, usually in limited lengths to firm up particularly vulnerable boundaries. It was usually sunk into the ground to a depth of 0.5m

30 The boundary walls of Wood Hall Warren, Carperby, in Wensleydale have an overhanging coping to deter escape

or so, to prevent the rabbits from burrowing underneath, which it achieved with considerable success – but it was very expensive, and normally did not last very long (Sheail 1971, 46; Harris and Spratt 1991, 183).

Sometimes walls or banks were built along the top of some earlier earthwork of appropriate form. The western boundary of Beachamwell Warren in Norfolk was thus defined by the Dark Age linear earthwork known as the Devils Ditch, while Snainton Dyke on the Tabular Hills in north Yorkshire has a turf wall running along its crest which seems to have formed the eastern boundary of High Scamridge Warren (Harris and Spratt 1991, 193). Warrens also, whenever possible, used natural watercourses as part of their boundaries. Most of the Dartmoor warrens included at least one length of stream or river along their perimeter. These made reasonable barriers, for rabbits are averse to water, but they can swim and will do so if desperate to escape. Driffieldgreets Warren in Yorkshire was bounded on one side by a stream but escapes were frequent and the boundary here eventually had to be defined by a paling fence (Sheail 1971, 47).

OTHER FEATURES OF THE WARREN

ENCLOSURES AND INTERNAL SUBDIVISIONS

Many warrens had internal subdivisions, or contained discrete enclosures defined by walls or banks. These had a variety of functions. Most were to allow parts of the warren to be cultivated, either periodically – as part of a system of 'convertible husbandry' – or more specifically and permanently for the production of fodder crops. Some, however, were to segregate some section of the warren population, usually the breeding does.

Small, discrete enclosures for cultivating fodder survive on a number of warrens. Many lack clearly defined, permanent entrances. It was hard to make gates rabbit-proof, so the perimeter wall or bank was evidently taken down and reassembled whenever the interior of the enclosure needed to be accessed. Good examples survive on Lakenheath Warren in the East Anglian Breckland, where there are four enclosures, almost square in shape and each covering 4-6ha, surrounded by low banks around 0.6m in height (Crompton and Taylor 1972). They still contain slight plough-ridges, showing that they were once under cultivation (*31*). Similar enclosures can be found within warrens located in high moorland areas, on Dartmoor or in the Brecon Beacons, where they are defined by dry stone walls. Particularly good examples survive, in ruinous state and again without defined entrances, at Ystradfellte and Cray (Powys). These also contain slight traces of ploughing which are particularly visible from the air.

Subdivisions of warrens (as opposed to discrete enclosures) are rather more difficult to interpret as in certain cases they may relate to some later stage of landscape history, when the warren ceased to operate or was reduced in scale, and some or all of its interior was cultivated as normal farmland. Many of the large Breckland warrens contain internal banks which might relate to fodder cultivation or convertible husbandry, but which could just as easily relate to the destruction or contraction of the warren in question. Nevertheless, in some cases the evidence clearly indicates that divisions have something to do with the functioning of the warren itself. The warren at Chatsworth (Derbyshire), now incorporated within Chatsworth Park, is shown on Senior's detailed survey of 1617 as entirely undivided (Senior 1617; Barnatt and Williamson 2005, 48). But it now contains earthworks of straight-sided field boundaries, evidently post-medieval in date although earlier than some of the pillow mounds there (Barnatt and Williamson 2005, 81-3). These banks were presumably made to facilitate the periodic cultivation of parts of the warren, for the documentary evidence makes it clear that the latter continued to function, without interruption, into the 1750s, when it was destroyed and its area absorbed directly into the new landscape park. It is moreover noteworthy that while signs of medieval arable farming – in the form of ridge and furrow and strip lynchets – survive across much of the area of the present park at Chatsworth they are largely absent from the area of the former warren, presumably because later cultivation has here ensured that they have been

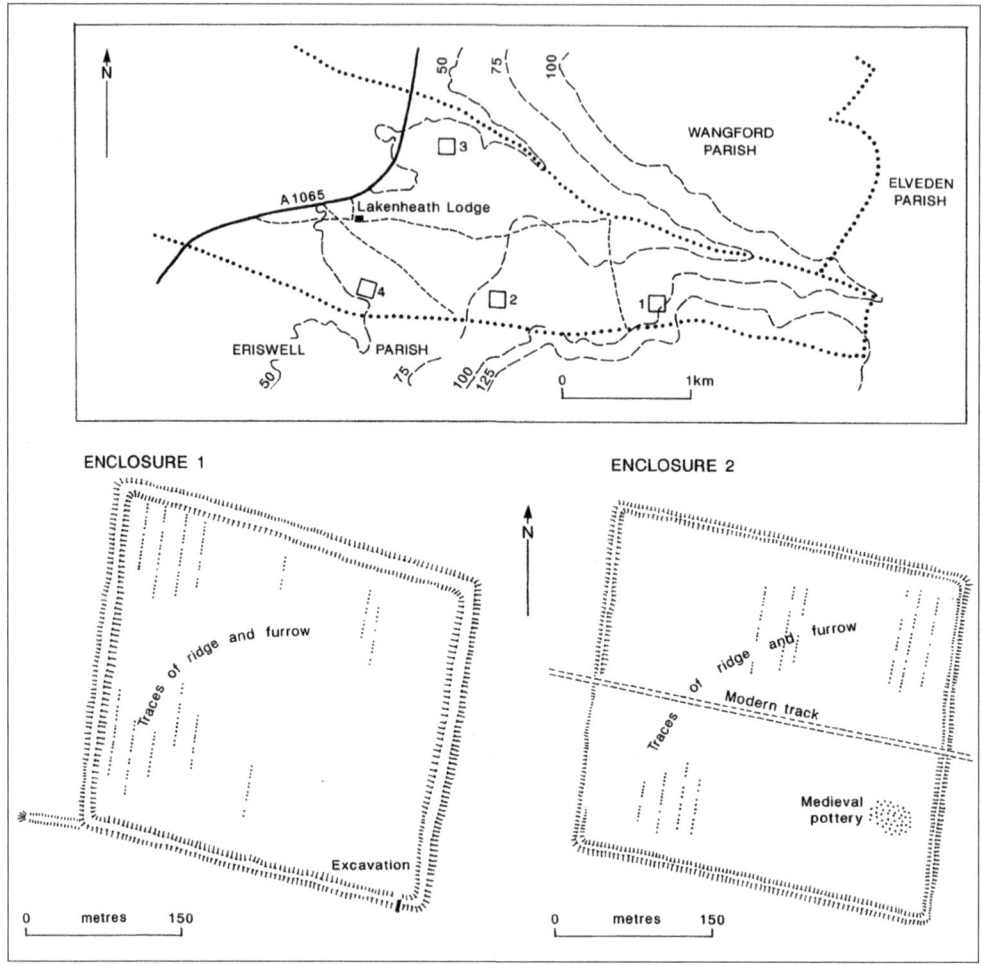

31 Enclosures on Lakenheath Warren in the Suffolk Breckland, defined by low earthwork banks. They contain faint traces of ploughing and were probably used for the cultivation of fodder crops. There are no obvious entrances, presumably because no form of gate was considered to be sufficiently rabbit-proof. Sections of the bank must have been taken down, and reconstructed, as necessary (after C. Taylor)

levelled. The warren's subdivisions may, however, also have served another purpose. The estate records indicate that its area was also grazed by other livestock – cattle and horses, according to the one surviving Joyst Book, for 1745 (Chatsworth Archives AS 1408). The division of the warren into fields might also thus relate to the management of grazing by livestock other than rabbits, and the same may be true in other cases.

At a number of places rectangular or sub-rectangular enclosures, defined by banks or walls, surround single pillow mounds, or small groups of mounds, of round or rectangular form, as at Llanfair Clydogau in Dyfedd or Friarhead near

Flashby in North Yorkshire (Austin 1988, 137-8; Villy 1912, 340) (*32*). In the former case the mound, when excavated, was found to overlie artificial burrows, capped by lines of stones, of the kind frequently encountered beneath mounds in upland locations. Such enclosures were presumably intended to provide protection to breeding does and young rabbits living in 'clapper' mounds, which were particularly vulnerable to predators, and to attacks by adult males: Henderson has described how stone walls and earthen embankments were 'used to construct smaller internal breeding ... enclosures within the larger territory of the warren' (Henderson 1997, 105). It is likely that in some cases such enclosures (rather than the mounds within them) were themselves termed 'clappers'. In 1551 the lord of the manor of Sevenhampton in Wiltshire described how he had made 'vii or eight severall berryes in Clappers' on a disputed area of land (Bettey 2004, 383). It is noticeable that such enclosed mounds sometimes occur in warrens where pillow mounds of normal, unenclosed form are completely absent, as on Knettishall Heath (Suffolk); and that they are sometimes found close to the warrener's house, as probably at Llanfair Clydogau (Dyfed), presumably reflecting the particular attention which needed to be paid to the breeding does and their young.

Even where warrens were entirely open to the surrounding countryside, they might include one of these small or medium-sized enclosures, containing one or more mounds. This is presumably how we should interpret sites like Wanborough (Wiltshire) (*33*). Rather than representing the entire area of the warren the enclosed ground here, and its mounds, was probably only a 'clapper' area. The Wanborough enclosure is fairly extensive and contained only two mounds. Often the enclosures were smaller and/or more densely filled with mounds. The Buries near Repton (Derbyshire) is a rectangular earthwork measuring *c*.52m x 38m, on slightly raised ground above the Trent floodplain, which contains three rectangular and two circular mounds (Guilbert 2004, 248). A similar earthwork survives, although less well preserved, at Sawley in the same county (Guilbert 2004, 247), again occupying a raised area above a floodplain. The silty, largely stoneless soils found in such locations made them suitable for rabbits, but the high water table and dangers of flooding would have required the provision of particular protection for the young. The site called 'Newark Camp', Hempstead, just outside Gloucester, may be a similar case. It is broadly comparable in size and layout, and likewise occupies ground raised slightly above a floodplain. But such breeding enclosures within large or open warrens did not necessarily contain pillow mounds. The example at Winterbourne Stoke (Wiltshire), covering just over 2ha and containing a small Bronze Age barrow cemetery, has already been noted. Others may have lacked mounds of any kind, like the kite-shaped enclosure at Stapleford (Wiltshire): this was originally interpreted as a late Roman stock enclosure but was identified by Christopher Taylor as a rabbit warren on the basis of documentary evidence (Taylor 1967, 306). In such cases, the breeding does may have been accommodated in wooden hutches (Sheail 1971, 59).

RABBITS, WARRENS & ARCHAEOLOGY

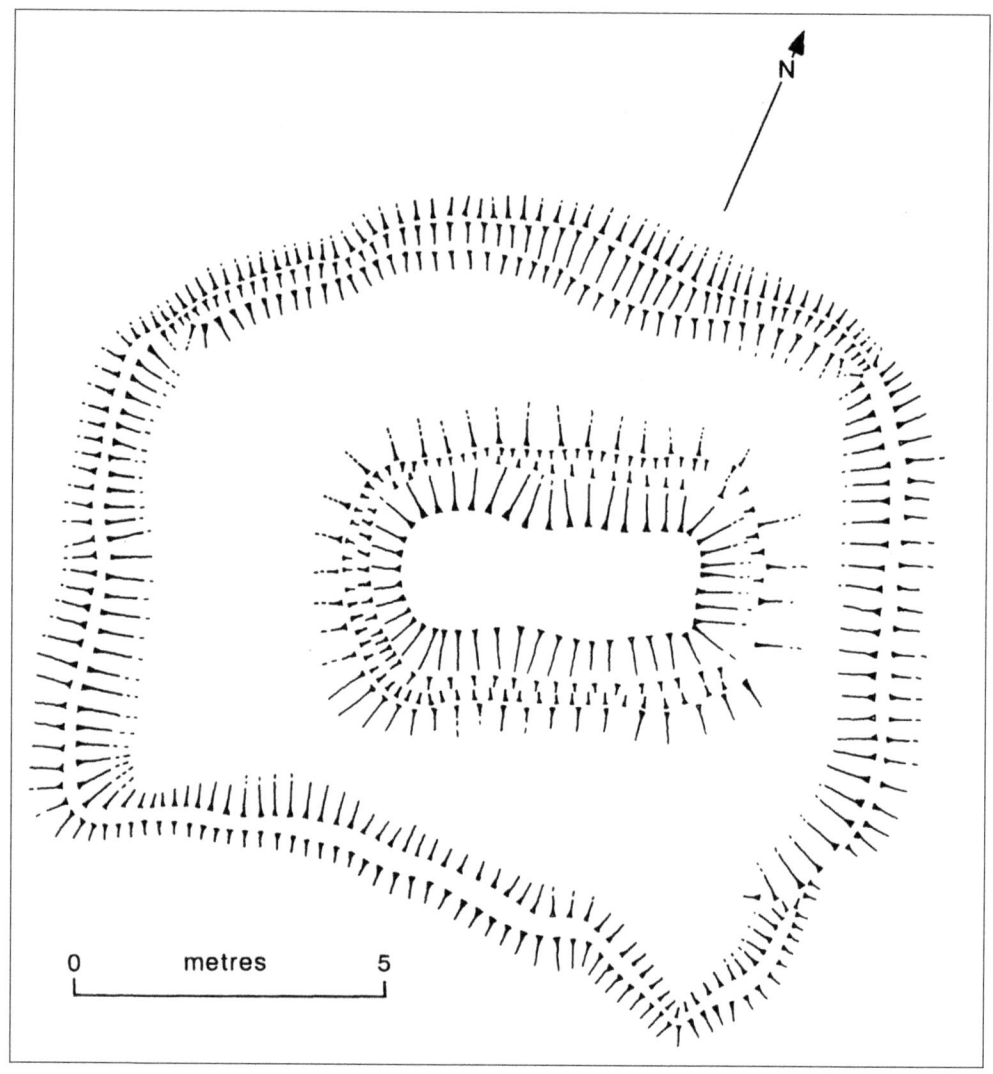

32 A sub-rectangular enclosure surrounding a pillow mound at Llanfair Clydogau in Dyfed. Mound and enclosure together probably represent a 'clapper', accommodation for breeding does and young rabbits (after D. Austin)

TRAPS

As we have seen, rabbits were usually caught by using some combination of dogs, nets and ferrets. A long net might be erected between the rabbits and their burrows, usually at night, and the animals driven into it by dogs, usually lurchers or tumblers. Alternatively, ferrets might be introduced into the burrows, and the bolting rabbits caught in nets placed at the various entrances. Both these

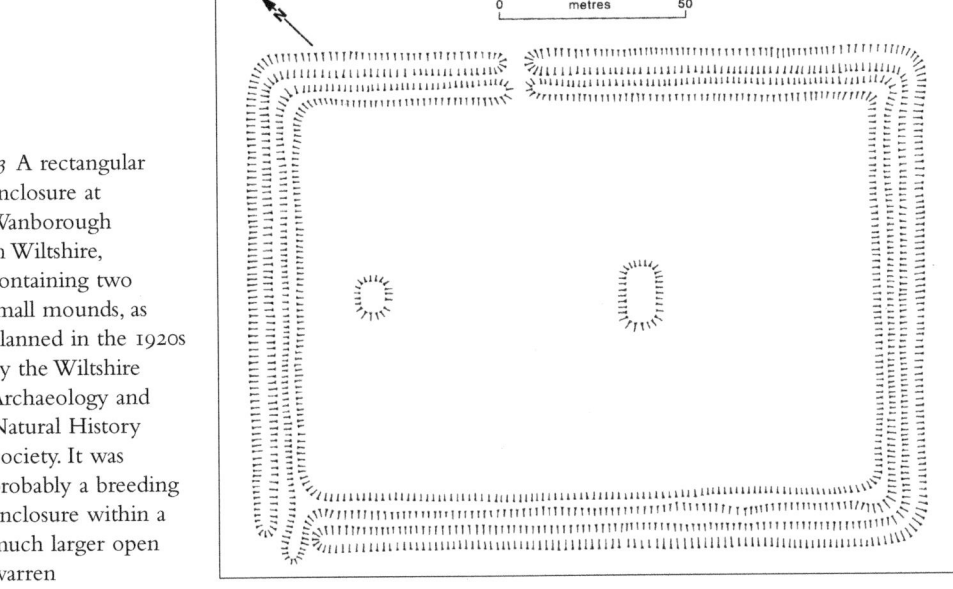

33 A rectangular enclosure at Wanborough in Wiltshire, containing two small mounds, as planned in the 1920s by the Wiltshire Archaeology and Natural History Society. It was probably a breeding enclosure within a much larger open warren

methods were probably facilitated by the construction of pillow mounds. On a few warrens, however, another method was used: the rabbits were caught in *types* or tip traps. Their operation was described by Daniel in 1801:

> The Tipe or trap ... consists of a large pit or Cistern, covered with a floor, with a small trap door, nicely balanced, near its centre, into which the Rabbits are led by a narrow Meuse. It used to be set by a Hay-stack, but since turnips are now grown for winter food, in an enclosure within the Warren, the trap is placed within the wall of this inclosure. For a night or two the Rabbits are suffered to go through the meuse, and over the trap, that they may be familiarized to where the turnips are grown, after that the trap door is unbarred, and the number wanted are taken (Daniel 1801, 351)

The *meuse*, or *muce*, was a narrow wooden tunnel which ran through the wall. The trap door was set in its floor, and for most of the time was wedged shut. When the wedges were removed, the rabbits would fall into the trap, usually surviving their short descent alive. A larger wooden covering to the pit prevented any escape: this could be easily removed, to allow the rabbits to be extracted (Harris and Spratt 1991, 185-93; Doughty 1965, 17-18; Dennison 2004, 142-3 (*34*)). While, as Daniel notes, tip traps were often (and perhaps originally) placed in the walls of fodder fields, in most cases they were located beside the walls of small, purpose-built enclosures in which fodder was not grown, but rather placed in piles.

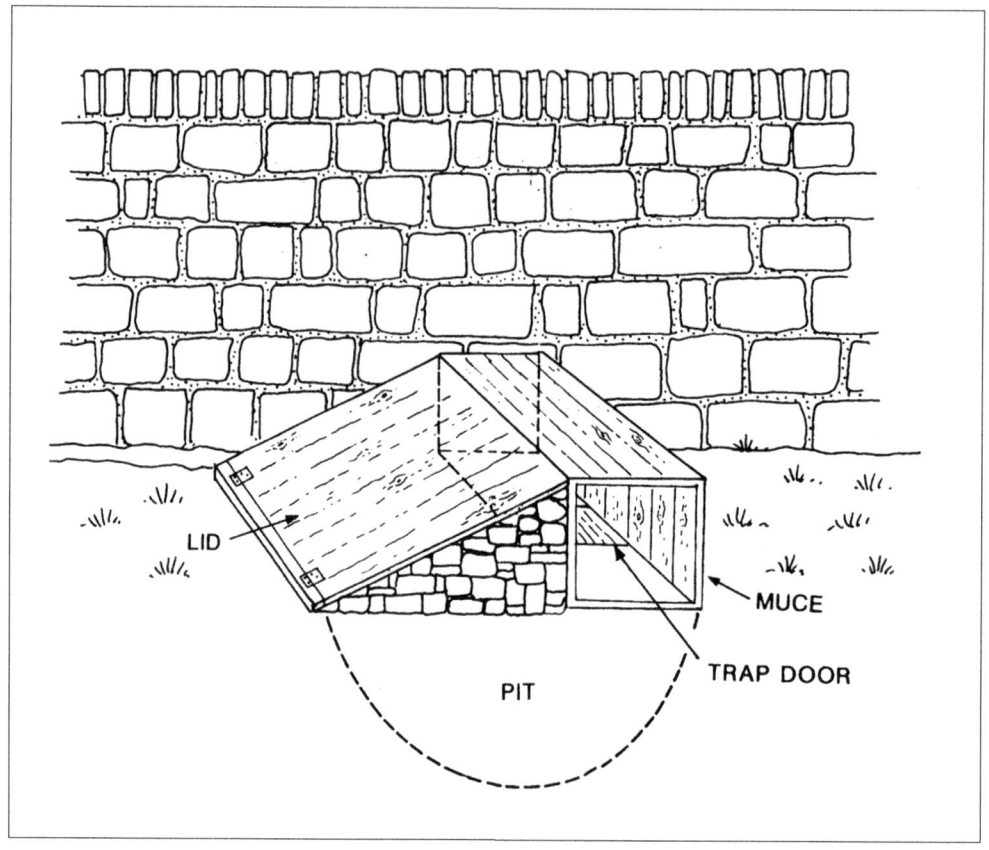

34 Diagram of a typical tip trap. A narrow wooden tunnel or muce runs through the wall and across the top of the pit. Here there is a small trap door in the tunnel floor, which is wedged shut for a time so that the rabbits can reach fodder. When the wedges are removed the rabbits fall into the pit, from which they can be removed via the larger wooden trap door (after A. Harris and D. A. Spratt)

Large numbers of rabbits would be trapped by these devices. There are reports of four, five or six hundred being taken each night in a single trap, and in one case (at Driffield Warren) allegedly as many as 1500 (Daniel 1801, 351; Doughty 1965, 18).

The remains of many 'types' survive on the Tabular Hills in North Yorkshire, within the former warrens which are now buried beneath Forestry Commission plantations (Harris and Spratt 1991). They take the form of circular pits, 1m deep and around 1m in diameter, lined with dry-stone walling, which slope outwards slightly towards their base. Most are located beside the perimeter banks or walls of enclosures which range in size from 5-6m square to as much as 1ha, the latter presumably representing fields in which turnips were actually cultivated. They are also found beside field walls outside the major warrens, indicating small-scale trapping carried out in 'farm warrens'.

Tip traps were mainly a feature of the north east of England. As well as being used in the warrens on the Tabular Hills, they were employed on the Lincolnshire Wolds, where they were almost always placed near the centre of very small turf-walled enclosures, around four metres square (Doughty 1965, 17-18). They were also a feature of some of the warrens on the Yorkshire Wolds. No examples appear to survive in recognisable form in either area (Harris 1970, 431), but they are known from elsewhere in the North East, most notably at Wood Hall Warren at Carperby in the eastern Pennines (Dennison 2004, 142-3). Here they are set, not within small enclosures, but against the various drystone walls which subdivide the area of the warren (35).

Tip traps are only known from a handful of places outside the North East, most notably on a small number of warrens in the Brecon Beacons, at Traianglas, Cray and Ystradfellte (Powys) (RCAHM 1982, 315). Here they were often rather larger than those on the Tabular Hills, up to three metres in diameter and usually tapering towards the base rather than the top. Once again the traps were set within the walls of small enclosures. Those at Ystradfellte were quadrilateral in shape, typically 20m in length, 13m wide at one end and tapering to 6m at the other. This method of trapping was also introduced into at least two Breckland warrens, Thetford and Santon Downham, in the nineteenth century (Clarke 1937, 116). Here the pits were circular, around three metres deep, and lined with chalk and flint to prevent the rabbits from making their escape by burrowing through the soft sandy soil. Unlike the northern examples, however, these traps seem to have been set in the open rather than within enclosures or beside field walls. Their iron lids were covered with hay, on which the rabbits would be encouraged to feed. We only know of them from written accounts: no remains have so far been discovered beneath the Forestry Commission plantations which now cover the area.

It is likely that tip traps were a relatively recent development in the long history of warrening in Britain. Certainly, most of the Yorkshire and Lincolnshire warrens in which they were used appear to have begun life in the eighteenth or nineteenth centuries, and the three warrens in the Brecon Beacons in which they occur are all of nineteenth-century date. William Marshall, writing in 1788, described pit trapping as 'a more modern' method of catching rabbits than the use of nets and ferrets (Marshall 1788, 266). Tip traps may only have come into use as the amounts of fodder available increased in the course of the eighteenth century. However, rather simpler methods of trapping with pits may have been used in earlier periods: there are a number of sixteenth- and seventeenth-century court cases concerning warrens which describe the making of 'falls', presumably some kind of pit trap (see the account of the dispute over Cawston Heath in Norfolk, below pp.161-2). 'Falls' are also referred to in a number of early warren leases.

35 Example of a tip trap set against an internal wall on Wood Hall Warren, Carperby, Yorkshire

Traps were also used to catch the various vermin that preyed upon the rabbits – polecats, wild cats, weasels, foxes, rats and stoats. In most cases these were made of wood, and have left little if any archaeological trace, although they are frequently referred to in leases. One drawn up in 1634 for the warren at Hertingfordbury in Hertfordshire, for example, instructed the tenant to leave at the end of his term 'sufficiente and conveniente Trappes, Doggestalles, Hutches and Latches' on the warren (HALS D/EP T264). But on the Dartmoor warrens stone vermin traps were constructed and a number of these survive *in situ*, albeit in fragmentary form. These have been discussed in some detail in an important article by Haynes (Haynes 1970), although fewer examples remain intact, apparently, than when he carried out his survey work in the 1960s.

The Dartmoor traps were constructed with five large, flat stones. A heavy rectangular base stone, placed on the ground surface, supported three uprights. One of these ran the full length of the trap. The others, which were smaller, formed the opposite side, leaving a gap in the centre (*36*). A heavy flat cap stone was laid on top of these, thus creating a square-sectioned tunnel of stone with openings at either end, and in the middle of one side. The latter held a trip

OTHER FEATURES OF THE WARREN

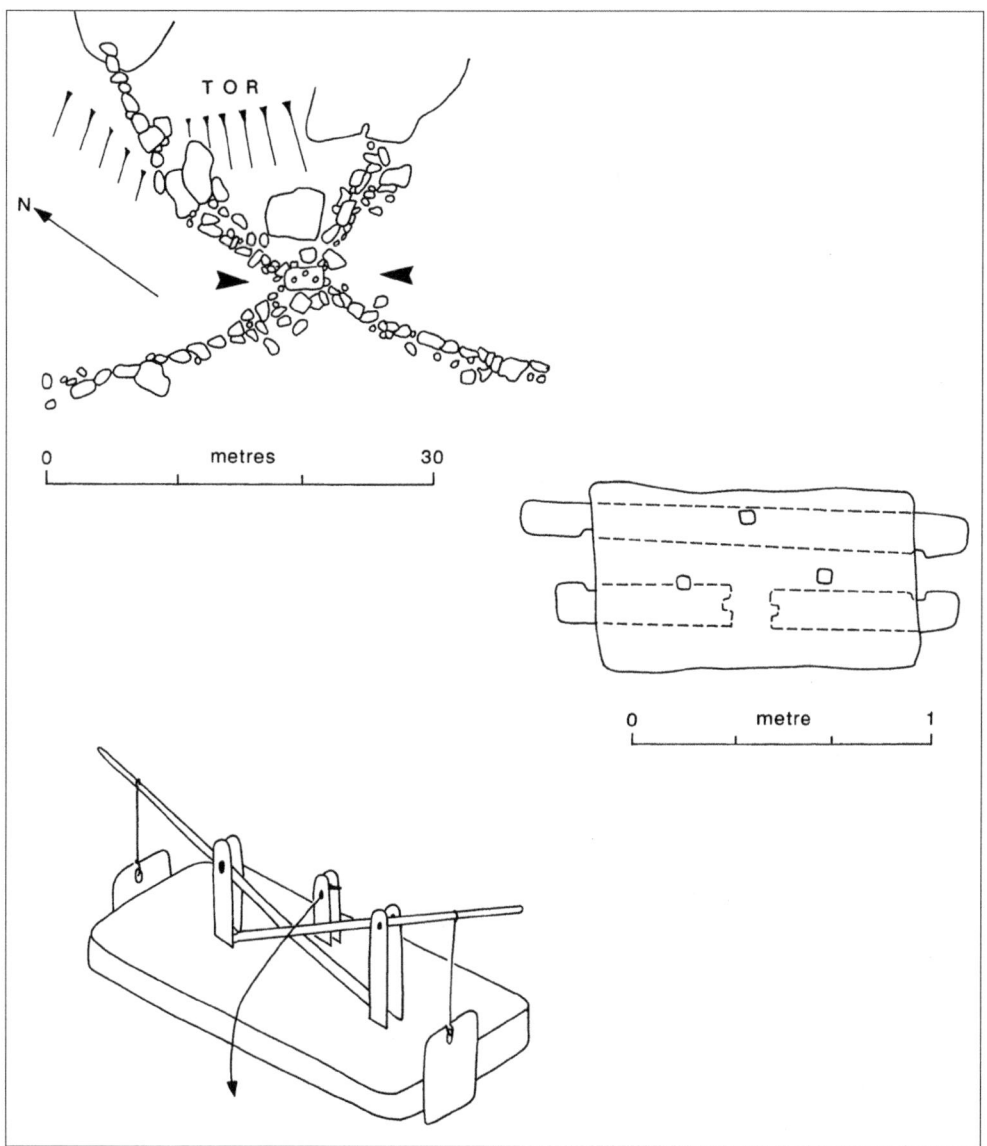

36 Remains of a typical stone vermin trap on Dartmoor, as planned by R. Haynes. Plan of trap and associated funnel wall; detail of the trap lid; and reconstruction of trip mechanism

mechanism, and the ends were closed by pieces of slate which, held in grooves in the side stones, could be dropped and lifted with comparative ease. The cap stones, which can still be found in some places, have two or more holes drilled in them, usually an inch and a half in diameter and the same deep. These seem to have held small upright wooden posts which were connected by wires to the slate shutters closing each end of the trap. When a rat, stoat or weasel ran through the 'tunnel' it would step on a plate attached to the trigger passing through the side. This released a small block of stone to which were attached the other ends of the wires. The slate shutters, no longer held up by the wires, fell under their own weight and the predator was neatly trapped (Haynes 1970, 148-50).

The traps were usually unbaited. The animals, seeking their prey, were cleverly funnelled towards them by low walls of stone and earth, generally $c.0.6$m or less in height. These were arranged as two opposed Vs which were separated by a small gap, where the trap was placed. The whole arrangement would be positioned on one of the natural access routes into the warren and in such a way that various large natural or man-made obstructions, such as stone outcrops or ancient walls, also served to encourage predators to pass along that particular route (Haynes 1970, 151-2). Large numbers of such traps survive, in varying states of decay, on the Dartmoor warrens, but mainly on those which were established before the early nineteenth century. Later warrens either lack them entirely, or have them only in small numbers. Most of the traps are thus probably of seventeenth- and eighteenth-century date: they perhaps, as Haynes suggested, fell from favour in the course of the eighteenth century as gin traps and shotguns came into widespread use.

Almost identical wooden versions of such traps, usually described as 'hutches' in early documents, are illustrated in a number of eighteenth-century game-keeping manuals (Haynes 1970, 150), and examples on Hertfordshire warrens were described by Perh Kalm, a Swedish tourist who came to England in 1748 (Lucas 1892). These were constructed of 'four boards, like a long box. At each end hangs a perpendicular board, like a door, which by specially contrived arrangement above the trap … can be hoisted up so that the entrance stands open. In the middle of the trap an iron pin or a little wooden rod goes cross-wise'. When this was pressed down, 'a pin on the outside slips loose and the boards at both ends fall down' (Lucas 1892, 158). Kalm thought that they were designed to catch rabbits and while there is little doubt that he was mistaken, rabbits were doubtless sporadically caught in them. Indirect evidence for the former existence of such traps survives on a number of warrens, in the form of the low walls of earth and/or stone built to funnel the vermin towards them. At Llanfair Clydogau in Dyfed three such features were surveyed and recorded by David Austin and his team, each comprising two chevrons laid apex to apex but separated by a narrow ($c.1$m) area of flat ground, where the trap would have been positioned (*37*) (Austin 1988, 141,155). At least two examples exist on Minchinhampton Common, again consisting of two opposed chevrons defined by low ($c.0.2$m) earth banks, this time separated by $c.0.5$m (*38*). Other examples are reported from Dolebury Warren (Somerset) (Allcroft 1908, 690-1), Avebury (Wiltshire) and Worlebury (Somerset) (Haynes 1970, 155). Many others doubtless await discovery and recognition.

OTHER FEATURES OF THE WARREN

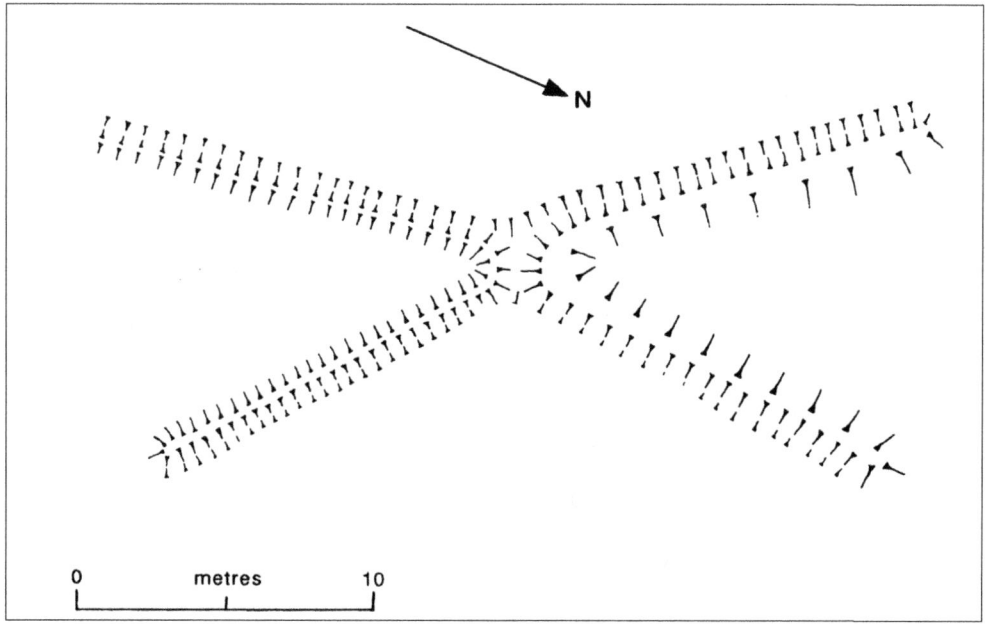

37 Even where vermin traps themselves have not survived, the distinctive funnel walls leading to them often remain. This example was planned during a survey of the warren at Llanfair Clydogau (Dyfed) (after D. Austin)

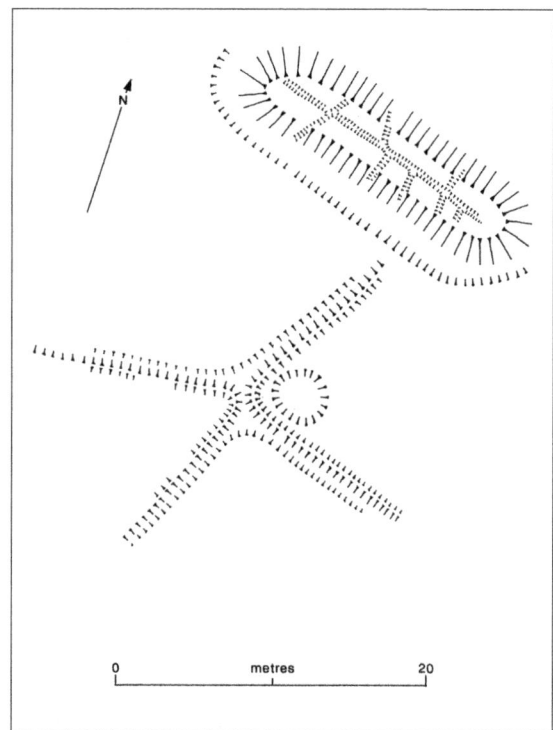

38 Characteristic funnel walls, arranged as opposed chevrons, marking the site of a vermin trap on Minchinhampton Common, Gloucestershire. The trap lies beside a typical segmented pillow mound. The pit beside the trap is a later feature

39 The fifteenth-century warren lodge at Thetford in Norfolk, the best-preserved medieval lodge in England. As well as serving to house carcasses and equipment, and providing accommodation for the warrener, this elaborate building may also have been used by its owner, the Prior of Thetford, while on recreational hunting trips. The Priory lay only $c.2.5$km to the south-east

WARREN HOUSES AND LODGES

Lodges or warren houses provided accommodation for the warrener and a place to keep carcasses and skins, as well as all the nets, traps, and other equipment required on the warren. In some cases, as already noted, they may also have been used by the warren's owner as a base for recreational hunting, at least in the period before the mid-seventeenth century. Relatively few medieval lodges survive today in recognisable condition. The best preserved are in the East Anglian Breckland. Thetford Lodge was erected by the Prior of Thetford to serve Westwick Warren in the early fifteenth century and is now in the care of English Heritage (39). What survives is the roofless shell of the medieval core: early illustrations show that many additions were made to this in the course of the post-medieval period but these were destroyed by fire in 1935. It is a well-built tower house constructed of local flint with some brick and limestone dressings. In plan it is rectangular, measuring 8.5m x 5.7m, and it originally had two floors, each with a single room, which were connected by a staircase in the south-west corner. The upper floor probably provided accommodation for the warrener while the lower was used to store carcases and equipment, although both were equipped with a fireplace, that on the lower floor presumably to provide the heat necessary for drying skins. What is striking is that the building was apparently designed with serious defence in mind. Not only does it have small windows, with those on the ground floor narrower than those above – little more than arrow slits – but above the single entrance is a *meurtriere*, a hole for dropping missiles onto attackers. These features perhaps indicate the high value of rabbit skins and the fact that attacks from armed intruders were expected. But the building may also have served as an expression of the power and status of its owner, for it was probably used as a hunting base by the Prior of Thetford – the Priory was conveniently located a mere 2.5km to the south-east.

The lodge at Mildenhall in Suffolk, some 14km to the south west, is broadly similar in size and shape, but probably slightly later in date, and is less overtly defensive in appearance. It is also less well preserved, although it has recently been extensively repaired under the auspices of the Friends of Thetford Forest and the Forestry Commission, with Heritage Lottery Fund support. It is again a small tower house, built of flint with some brick and stone, rectangular in plan and measuring 6.4m x 7.5m. It also had two floors: the upper one was supplied with a fireplace and once again presumably provided accommodation for the warrener, with the ground floor being used for storage. Traces of a number of other warren lodges of medieval or early post-medieval date survive in Breckland. One – Langford Warren Lodge in Ickburgh – now consists only of a stump of masonry walling, but fragments of others at Methwold, Lakenheath, Eriswell and Santon also remain, incorporated into later cottages or farm buildings. So far as it is possible to tell, most of these also seem to have taken the form of small tower-like buildings.

Only a handful of early lodges are known from elsewhere in England, and most are of similar form. Norton Tower at Rylstone (Yorkshire) is of late fifteenth- or early sixteenth-century date. Measuring 10m x 15m in plan, it was slighted in 1569 and consequently reduced to a ruined single storey. It may have served in part as a deer park lodge but it lay in the centre of a warren, for several pillow mounds remain around it, and it presumably also functioned as a base for warrening. Documentary and cartographic evidence suggests that many other medieval and early post-medieval lodges were well-built tower houses. The lodge for Dorking Warren, for example, was rebuilt in the 1380s at a cost of £4 as a timber-framed, plastered building with a roof of Horsham stone, brought all the way from Reigate Castle (Ettlinger 2000, 5). The most famous and remarkable surviving example of an early lodge, however – although one of highly idiosyncratic form – is the unusual building erected at Rushton in Northamptonshire in the 1590s

40 Sir Thomas Tresham's unique three-sided warren lodge at Rushton, Northamptonshire. This bizarre building, a statement of its owner's adherence to the Catholic faith and presumably used as a place of meditation and retreat, nevertheless served as a working warren house

by the wealthy Catholic recusant Sir Thomas Tresham (Isham 1970) (*40*). It was located within the rabbit warren a short distance from Rushton Hall and is discussed in more detail in Chapter 6, for it was in part intended as a place for meditation and retreat, loaded with symbolism relating both to Tresham's name, and to his belief in the Trinity and the Tridentine mass. It is, in typical fashion, a tower-like building: but it has three sides, each 33ft long and with three gables; three storeys; and a three-sided chimney. There are numerous similar numerical references in its structure and ornamentation. It was not simply a folly, however, for it is referred to as the 'Warryners Lodge' in the estate accounts and its overall structure was similar to that of the buildings already discussed, with a single room on each floor, accessed by a spiral staircase located in one of the corners. The half-basement presumably provided a suitable place for storing carcases but on each floor the corners of the triangle are sealed off as separate chambers, so that each room is hexagonal in plan. This multiplicity of storage spaces may have been intended to allow rapid conversion of the building from working lodge, to place of retreat and meditation.

Tower-like, or at least relatively tall and narrow, warren lodges continued to be constructed in some places into the seventeenth century. The tall central

41 The lodge in the centre of Minchinhampton warren in Gloucestershire is now a public house, but still bears an appropriate name – the Old Lodge Inn

section of the pub now known as the Old Lodge, in the middle of the vast warren on Minchinhampton Common (Gloucestershire), is thus probably of early seventeenth-century date (White 2002, 30) (*41*). A particularly late example is the building known as Warren Cottage, which stands next to the group of 17 pillow mounds in the middle of Hatfield Forest in Essex, which was built in the 1680s (Rackham 1989, 181-4). Once again this is a tall building in proportion to its ground plan – 9m x 4m – which originally had a single room on each floor, connected in this case by an external stair turret (*42*). The latter is a somewhat archaic architectural feature, as are the building's elaborate patterned brickwork and the massive external chimney stack, and it is possible that the lodge was a consciously old-fashioned structure. Its builder, Sir Edward Turnor, was attempting to revive the warren here after a period of disuse and the lodge may have keen intended to assert, in symbolic form, what Turnor saw as his traditional rights over those of the local commoners (Rackham 1989, 183-4).

Many medieval and early post-medieval warren lodges were thus elaborate, well-built structures which served as statements of status and in some cases – as at Rushton and perhaps Thetford – as places which their owners could visit, for hunting or other reasons. The fairly standardised and repetitive form of a tall

42 Warren Cottage, Hatfield Forest, Essex. Although built as late as the 1680s, this building still displays the relatively tall form, and flamboyant use of materials, associated with traditional warren lodges

tower may in part be explained in symbolic terms. Such a form, which mirrored that of traditional deer park lodges, served to stamp authority over the landscape – warrens were often contentious symbols of lordly appropriation. But it probably also has a practical explanation, in that such a building provided the warrener with extensive views across his domain. He could thus keep an eye on his stock, observing the intrusion of poachers and, perhaps, the effects on the rabbits of the arrival of predators like foxes or stoats. In this context, it is noteworthy that many of these buildings were constructed in commanding positions, with wide views across the surrounding landscape. Indeed, on the largest warrens there might be two or even more separate lodges, although always standing at a distance from each other, so that the entire area of the warren could effectively be kept under surveillance. Nineteenth-century maps show that Lakenheath Warren in the East Anglian Breckland, for example, had a lodge, a building called the Grotto Lodge, and a Warren House (WSRO MS E3/18/11.2).

Not all warren houses, however, were well-built tower houses, even in the Middle Ages. The warren at Llanfair Clydogau (Dyfed) was excavated by David Austin in 1979 and, as already noted, radiocarbon dates obtained from burnt

43 Ditsworthy Warren House, Dartmoor, is typical of later warren lodges, in that it looks little different from other local farms. The particularly high enclosing walls, however, were presumably intended to keep rabbits out of the garden and yards

material beneath one of the pillow mounds suggest that the first phase of the enterprise dates to the fourteenth century. Associated with this are a number of small, rectangular buildings, represented by low banks with rounded corners, typical of 'the class of platform houses frequently associated with hafotau', that is, seasonally occupied upland farms (Austin 1988, 135). Excavation of three of the four buildings showed that they had simple earth floors. At Danebury, similarly, the warren lodge excavated by Cunliffe, which was probably of sixteenth- or early seventeenth-century date, was described as 'a simple affair built of cob walls on a flint and cob base … . The floor was of flint rubble. There was little evidence of comfort …' (Cunliffe 1983, 186). House platforms associated with a number of other early post-medieval warrens likewise imply lodges that were little more than simple cottages, like the small platform, 14m x 9m, associated with the group of pillow mounds at Lydiard Millicent (Wiltshire). Some of the buildings associated with the seventeenth-century warrens on Dartmoor similarly appear to have been poorly built long houses (Haynes 1970, 155-64). Later post-medieval examples, moreover, both here and elsewhere, simply resembled other small farm houses in the locality. While outhouses and sheds were needed for storing fodder, especially once turnips had come into widespread use, such structures are not obviously different from those erected on ordinary farms in the eighteenth or nineteenth centuries. In most cases eighteenth- and nineteenth-century warren houses thus proclaim their former function — if at all — only through their name (and even this can be misleading: 'Warren Farm' can just as easily refer to a building erected on a new site after a warren was destroyed, or even to a farm which existed close to a warren). Nevertheless, in some cases associated features do survive to indicate the special role of otherwise undistinguished buildings. Some of the Dartmoor warren houses, for example — such as those at Trowlesworthy and Ditsworthy — not only have stone-walled fields for growing fodder, and garden yards enclosed by high walls to keep the rabbits out, but also special enclosures for keeping the warren dogs, again enclosed by high walls, which have overhangs to prevent escape (*43*).

The essentially utilitarian character of later warren houses reflects the gradual decline in the status of the rabbit from a rare delicacy, and a source of fur to trim the robes of the wealthy; to a food for the poor, and a raw material for felt hats. While many early lodges were thus places for lordly retreat and recreation, and objects of elite display, eighteenth- and nineteenth-century warren houses were purely functional. Comparing Ditsworthy Warren House (*43*) with the lodges at Rushton (*40*) or Thetford (*39*) makes the point forcibly.

4

THE LANDSCAPES OF WARRENING

Rabbit warrens were widely scattered across medieval and post-medieval England, close to high-status residences, in deer parks, and on areas of common land. But there were districts in which, from late medieval times, substantial concentrations of large, commercial rabbit farms developed and where, in some cases, contiguous warrens covered many hundreds of hectares, without interruption (*44*). These concentrations reflected particular environmental factors – the existence of large tracts of ground which could not otherwise be used profitably by their owners, especially in times of agricultural recession – as well as the presence nearby of suitable markets, or the existence of good transport links to ones more distant. Warrens also flourished where population densities were low and/or where landlords were particularly powerful, for their establishment was invariably opposed by local people because of the damage wrought to crops and pastures by escaped rabbits. Indeed, within suitable districts warrens tended to cluster together because the damage caused by rabbits meant that neighbouring areas could not easily be used for much else. In the later eighteenth century it was thought that land at Allerston on the Yorkshire Wolds 'must by the vicinity of the neighbouring Warrens, lose most of its produce, if not converted into a Warren' (Harris 1970, 436). Similarly, when in 1782 the future of Stanford Farm in the Norfolk Breckland was being debated, it was stated that because it was bordered by the warrens of Wretham and Sturston, it was likely that 'the greater part of it will be made a rabbit farm' (Wade Martins and Williamson 1999, 42).

THE WARRENS OF WESSEX, THE COTSWOLDS AND MENDIPS

Even a cursory examination of the distribution map of pillow mounds presented on page 35 shows that the highest concentrations, other than on the high moorlands of Wales and western England, are to be found on the chalklands of Wessex, on the

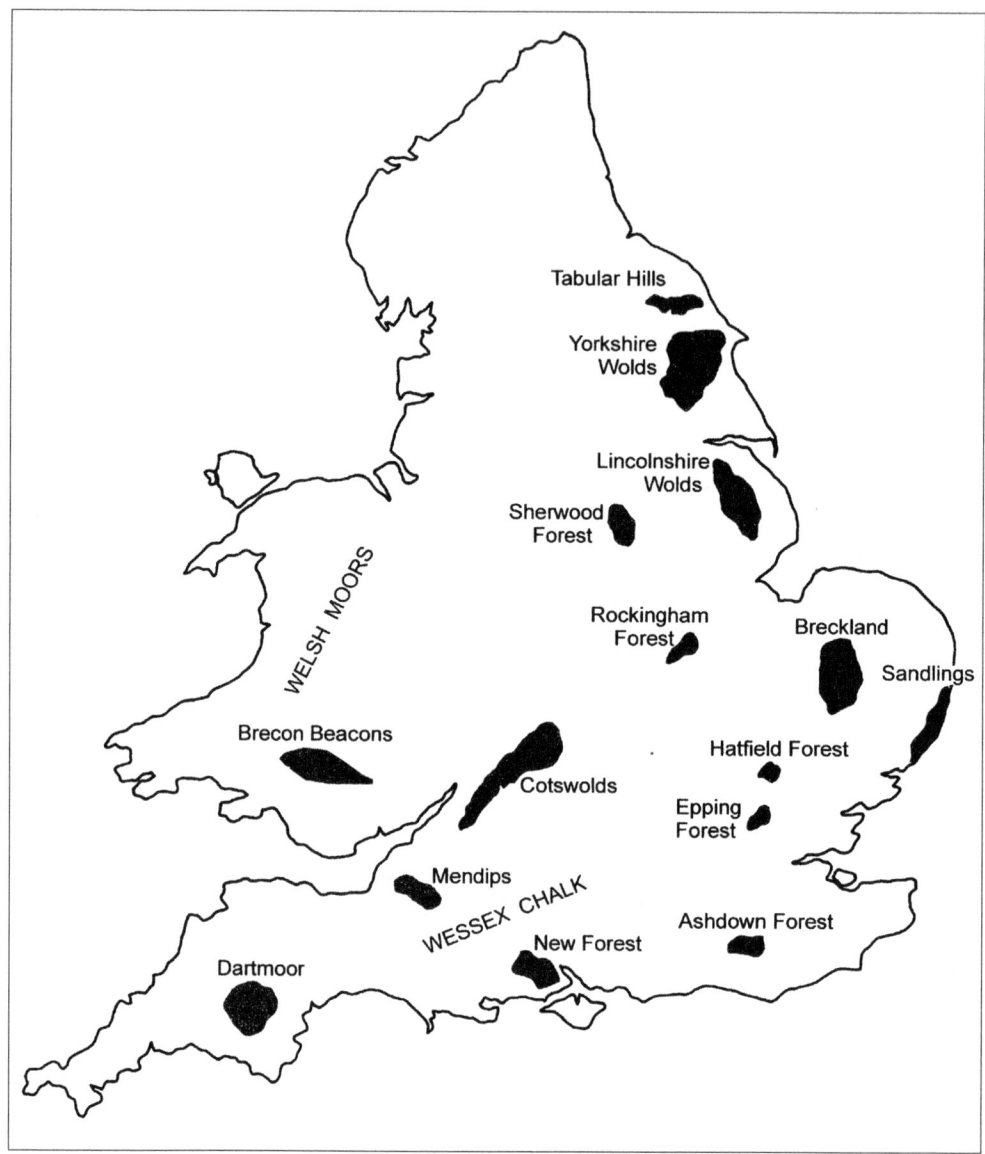

44 Map showing the principal areas and districts discussed in the text

Mendip Hills, and on the Cotswolds, especially the southern Cotswolds. While, as we have seen, the distribution of surviving mounds provides a poor guide to the overall distribution of warrens, these concentrations nevertheless clearly attest the importance of rabbit-production in the post-medieval economies of these areas.

The Wiltshire warrens have been the subject of an intensive study by Joe Bettey (Bettey 2004). Large warrens, producing for the market, had existed in the county since the fifteenth century but 'the rapid expansion of population and the growth of towns during the seventeenth century greatly increased the demand for the relatively cheap meat provided by rabbits', as well as for their fur (Bettey 2004, 381). While some warrens, like that at Lydiard Millicent, were on low-lying, heavy ground the vast majority were on the chalk downland, where thin soils and often steep slopes made other forms of land use problematic. The former factor explains why a large number were placed beside or within hillforts or other early earthworks, which provided better opportunities for burrowing than would otherwise be presented by the environment, and why most were equipped with pillow mounds. Many were provided with lodges and some, although by no means all, were enclosed with banks of turf, or fences. Many of the rabbits were sold in local markets, but significant numbers went, via dealers, to London and other distant towns. The warrens varied in size but most were relatively small compared with those located in more marginal areas of the country, such as the East Anglian Breckland or the Tabular Hills of Yorkshire, which frequently extended over 500 acres (*c*.200ha) or more. The warren at Easton Royal covered 150 acres (60ha) in 1608; that at Durley extended over 150 acres (60ha) in 1624; Ashcombe covered 265 acres (107ha) in 1594; and Hippenscombe Warren, 160 acres (65ha) in 1698 (Bettey 2004, 385-9, 391). Although the downland soils were thin, the grazing was valuable for the sheep flocks, which were economically important not only in their own right but for the manure they provided for the arable land, on which they were systematically folded by night (Kerridge 1967, 43-51). The arable open fields were usually extensive and villages often substantial, and filled with litigious and recalcitrant yeomen, like those who in 1671 occupied the Earl of Pembroke's warren at Aldbourne and damaged his lodges (Bettey 2004, 389). In such circumstances, large warrens were difficult to sustain, and these same factors presumably explain the early decline of the Wiltshire warrens, which began in the later seventeenth century. Bettey has discussed the long-standing dispute over Hippenscombe Warren which culminated in a court case in 1709, in which witnesses described the damage done by escaped rabbits to crops and grassland:

> Soon after 1710 the rabbits were evidently destroyed and the property was described as 'all that the Warren knowne by the name of Hippenscombe Warren sometime stock'd with Conyes'. A similar process led to the abandonment of the majority of Wiltshire warrens during the eighteenth century as the price of grain and other agricultural products increased, so that by the end of the century very little remained of what had been an important and lucrative trade (Bettey 2004, 391)

Adjoining areas of chalk downland in central-southern England seem, on the present evidence, to have a broadly similar history. Most of the larger warrens on

45 Aerial view of the former warren on Minchinhampton Common in the Gloucestershire Cotswolds. This is one of the largest surviving groups of pillow mounds in England, and includes both round and rectangular examples. Many are 'segmented' – that is, cut by shallow surface grooves. The building at the end of the track is the former warren lodge, now a public house. The warren was probably established on the common in the early seventeenth century

the chalklands of Dorset, Hampshire and Berkshire appear to have originated in the sixteenth and seventeenth centuries, and most seem to have been relatively modest enterprises. In these districts, too, warrens appear to have begun to decline at an early date, before the end of the seventeenth century – like that at Danebury, described in 1678 as 'anciently and till since the memory of man a warren' (Cunliffe 1983, 184).

In the Cotswolds warrens had existed close to major elite residences, and in deer parks, since medieval times but the main period of expansion again seem to have been in the later sixteenth and seventeenth centuries when, among others, the great warren at Minchinhampton Common, with its numerous pillow mounds and warren lodge, was established (White 2002, 41) (45 & 46). Warrens in this district, and especially towards the southern end of the hills, were often larger than on the Wessex chalk, reflecting the poorer quality of the land and the presence in some places of extensive commons. Many probably supplied the substantial Bristol market. Pillow mounds were a common feature on this relatively high and often wet land. In this district, however, warrening seems to have gone into decline slightly later than on the Wiltshire chalklands, as prices for more conventional commodities rose, and new agricultural techniques were adopted, in the decades after 1750. Either way, few examples seem to have survived far into the nineteenth century. On the Mendip Hills, likewise, the later sixteenth and especially the seventeenth century saw an expansion of warrens, and it is probably in this period that those at Dolebury, Charterhouse, West Cranmore, and Shute Shelve were first established (Aston and Bettey 1998, 134-5). In 1660 the commoners of Mendip petitioned the Lord Chancellor over the proliferation of warrens in the area (Bettey 2004, 391). Most were fairly extensive and, like those in the Cotswolds, were generally located on open common land, often close to earlier earthworks (especially hillforts like Dolebury or Bury Hill near Bristol), and most were well provided with pillow mounds. Some continued to operate right through the eighteenth century – Rowberrow Warren was still being let for over £65 per annum in the 1790s, and producing several hundred couples of rabbit a year (Aston and Bettey 1998, 135). But in general, as in the Cotswolds, warrening appears to have declined in importance in the later eighteenth century and few warrens seem to have operated much beyond 1800, as large-scale land improvement schemes and enclosure replaced areas of rough pasture with improved grass and arable land (Williams 1971).

WARRENS IN LOWLAND FORESTS

Across much of England to the east of Wessex pillow mounds, and other archaeological evidence for warrening, are thinly scattered, but nevertheless

46 Low earthworks of a vermin trap within Minchinhampton warren

with a number of distinct clusters. Several of these correspond to 'forests': areas over which, in medieval times, special laws preserved deer stocks for the royal hunt (Rackham 1986, 129-31). Forests were generally located in areas of poor soil – heavy clays, or acid sands – on which extensive reserves of woodland had survived into the Middle Ages. At the core of any forest was a series of wood-pasture commons, but the legal 'forest' extended far beyond these, embracing villages and extensive tracts of normal agricultural land. Warrens came to be concentrated, mainly in the post-medieval period, on these 'cores' of common land, often after they had been enclosed, disafforested, and taken into private ownership. Those in the forests of Ashdown and St Leonards in Sussex have been discussed by Tebbut (1968). They are characterised by particularly long pillow mounds, mostly more than 50m and in some cases over 200m in length. The few surviving lodges, much altered, resemble well-built farm houses of seventeenth- and eighteenth-century date. Rabbit farming probably first began on a large scale in the area in the sixteenth century, after over-grazing stripped large areas of trees, and large warrens certainly existed here by the seventeenth century: at Hartfield two separate groups of pillow mounds are located in areas described as 'The Warren' and 'Warren Lodge' in a parliamentary survey of 1646. But the industry appears to have expanded significantly after the partial enclosure of

Ashdown Forest in 1693. By the end of the century 3000-4000 acres (1200-1600ha) of the forest were occupied by warrens (Short 1984, 271). In Sherwood Forest in Nottinghamshire, similarly, the heyday of rabbit farming was in the later seventeenth and eighteenth centuries, again following the progressive sale and enclosure of portions of the Forest. Particularly extensive warrens existed at Clipston, Oxton, Blidworth, Calverton and Newstead (Mingay 1984, 106). Here, in contrast, virtually no upstanding archaeological evidence for warrening remains in the landscape, due to the progressive reclamation and 'improvement' of the area in the course of the nineteenth century, when the industry ceased.

In other forest districts warrening seems to have been on a smaller, but nevertheless significant scale. Warrens existed in the New Forest, especially on Rockford Common in Ellingham where one of the pillow mounds, excavated in the 1960s, was found to overlie a post-medieval enclosure bank. A number of groups of pillow mounds are also known from Rockingham Forest (Northamptonshire). That at Rockingham itself is mentioned in 1616 but others, such as that at Great Oakley, were established in the mid- or late seventeenth century (Moore-Collyer 1997, 154). Warrens are also known from Savernake Forest in Wiltshire; from Cranbourne Chase; from Hatfield Forest in Essex, where a large group of pillow mounds and the warren lodge remain, the former probably dating to the 1640s and the latter to the 1680s (Rackham 1989, 163-4, 183-4); and from Epping Forest, where a large group of pillow mounds survives at High Beech. The importance of rabbit farming in the Essex and Sussex forests probably reflects the proximity of the London market. In all of these areas, to judge from the available evidence, the heyday of warrening was the seventeenth and eighteenth centuries. Only a few warrens, most notably that at High Beech, seem to have continued operating far into the nineteenth century (Warren 1926, 221).

THE WARRENS OF THE WOLDS

Sherwood Forest is not the only area in eastern England where an important post-medieval warrening industry has left virtually no archaeological traces. Perhaps even more striking in this respect are the chalk Wolds of Lincolnshire and Yorkshire. There were some commercial warrens on the Lincolnshire Wolds by the later sixteenth century — a lease for the warren at Brumby, dated 1616, refers to its existence in 1568 (Doughty 1965, 15). But the main period of expansion appears to have been the later seventeenth and eighteenth centuries (Mingay 1985, 125), and by c.1800 there were around 43 extensive warrens in the district, some specialising in silver or black rabbits, stocked at a density of around five or six per acre (Doughty 1965, 16). Many of the skins were sent to London, once they had been dressed, an activity concentrated in and around the town of Brigg. Some of the silver furs were destined for the China market.

The warrens were enclosed by sod walls, capped with gorse and stabilised with 'kidds', wooden stakes placed at *c.*1m intervals. There are no pillow mounds surviving in the area and none appear to be referred to in documents but, on analogy with other warrens in the east of England, some 'clapper' mounds may well have existed. By the later eighteenth century 'types' were widely employed to catch the rabbits, set in sod-walled enclosures around 10m sq and with pits 1.2m deep and the same square. In addition, trapping banks were employed. A stretch of bank was built roughly parallel to the perimeter bank, low enough for a rabbit to jump but with holes provided in the base to allow for easier access. This converged with the outer wall at one end, the other end of the narrow compartment thus formed being closed with a rabbit-proof gate. The space was baited with food and the rabbits became accustomed to reach this through the holes provided: the holes were then closed off, so that the animals were obliged to jump the inner wall. The narrowness of the compartment prevented them getting enough of a run to clear the wall, however, so they were trapped: the warreners then entered through the gate and drove the rabbits to the end, where they could be netted (Doughty 1965, 17-18).

The warrens on the Yorkshire Wolds, to the north of the Humber, were similar in character. Here too, commercial warrens had existed since at least the sixteenth century but the great period of expansion was from the later seventeenth century: in the words of Harris, who undertook a detailed study of the subject, 'most of the warrens known to have been in existence about 1750 had been planted during the previous fifty or sixty years' (Harris 1970, 437). Few were created after *c.*1760, presumably because the price of grain was by then rising again. The warrens covered a vast area of ground. Even in 1808, when the attack on them was already well underway, over 10,000 acres (*c.*4000ha) were devoted to more than 20 warrens (Harris 1970, 429). There was probably a higher proportion of unenclosed warrens here than on the Lincolnshire Wolds to the south of the Humber, and on many the grazing was shared with the sheep flocks (Harris 1970, 439).

From the mid-eighteenth century tip traps came into widespread use in the area, often placed beside enclosures within the warren in which turnips were cultivated. Profits came, as usual, from both the meat and the fur: 'the Rabbits supply the markets of Hull, York, and the neighbouring Towns, and the skins are sold to the Furriers at Stanford Bridge, and Malton, who sell their wool to the Hat Manufactories of London and Manchester' (Daniel 1801, 346). Most of the warrens were stocked with grey rabbits, but silver ones were also being kept in a number of places by the end of the eighteenth century.

In both districts the majority of the warrens were on the highest ground, often where reserves of common pasture were particularly extensive, where depopulated or shrunken villages existed, or where early enclosure had taken place. They were relatively rare in places where large villages, farming extensive common fields, could be found, because of the opposition of the tenants to the destruction the rabbits caused to crops. And, as in other areas, warrens tended to cluster together and share common boundaries: the existence of one warren encouraged the creation of another because the effects of escaped rabbits made it difficult to use land in any other way. This presumably accounts for the creation, on the Yorkshire Wolds, of the three great adjoining warrens of Cottam (established in 1732); Cowlam (1743); and Croom (1744), which together covered an area of nearly 4000 acres (*c.*1600ha) (Harris 1970, 435-8).

On both the Yorkshire and the Lincolnshire Wolds warrens began to be abandoned at the end of the eighteenth century. With the advent of new agricultural techniques, the thin chalk soils could be improved sufficiently to produce a reasonable crop. 'Land ploughed, marled and manured made more per acre than it could as a rabbit warren. Few of the warrens listed in the early nineteenth century directories were recorded in the 1880s' (Beastall 1978, 144). Changing social perceptions added to the weight of economic and agrarian imperatives. 'In time, as agricultural improvement became widespread, rabbit warrens were looked upon as an affront to a well-conducted neighbourhood' (Harris 1970, 430). Throughout the Wolds, the ploughs of the improvers levelled the warren walls, types and specialised enclosures with peculiar thoroughness. When Eastburn Warren near Driffield was destroyed in 1849-50, six miles of warren walls were levelled, and 20 miles (32km) of new hawthorn hedge planted; the warren house was replaced by a farm and the rough pastures by arable fields. Virtually no trace of the industry now survives on either the Yorkshire or the Lincolnshire Wolds.

THE TABULAR HILLS IN NORTH YORKSHIRE

In contrast to the situation on the Wolds, the important rabbit farming industry on the Tabular Hills – the low limestone range running across the southern flank of the North Yorkshire Moors – has left extensive traces, which have been discussed in some detail by Harris and Spratt (Harris and Spratt 1991). Most of the warrens here were located towards the eastern end of the hills, where the headwaters of the river Derwent have cut numerous valleys, some now dry, creating undulating ground where the alternating beds of limestone and sandy, calcareous grit provided excellent conditions for rabbits, although some warrens were located on other formations. No less than 15 extensive warrens existed in

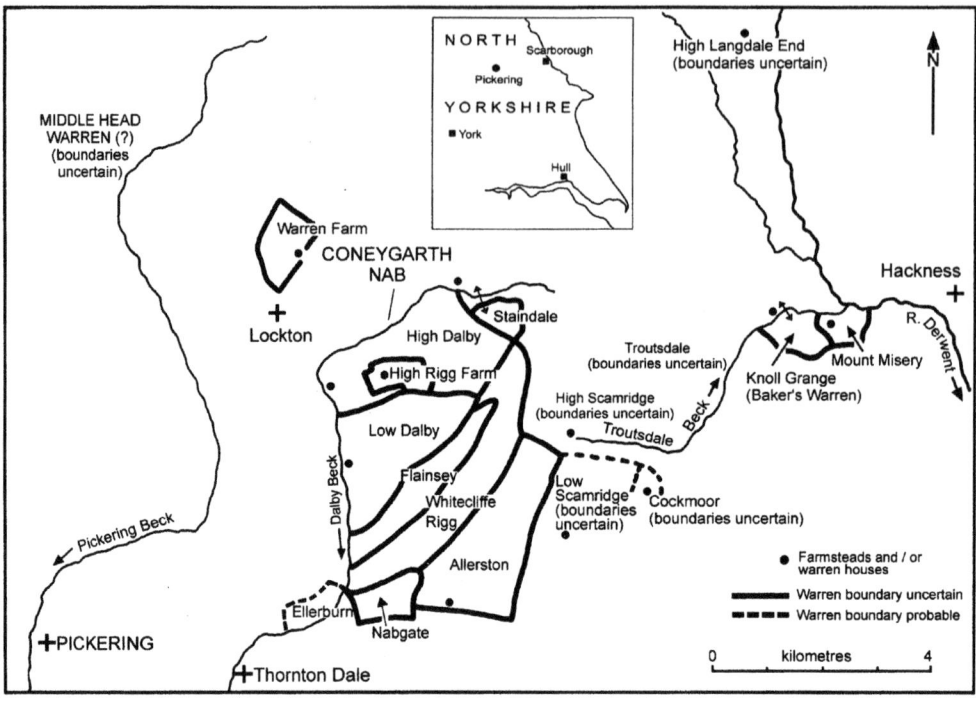

47 The tight cluster of rabbit warrens at the eastern end of the Tabular Hills in North Yorkshire. The conversion of one place into a rabbit farm tended to encourage similar use of neighbouring areas (after A. Harris and D.A. Spratt)

this area (*47*). None, however, were to be found on the higher ground of the Moors proper, to the north, where the land was considered too wet for rabbit farming to be a serious proposition (Harris and Spratt 1991, 178).

The warrens eventually came to form part of a distinctive belt of moorland and pasture which, by the early nineteenth century, occupied some 6000 acres (2430ha) of land. But the industry developed gradually. While there are scattered references to warrens in the late Middle Ages, and a few extensive examples existed in the sixteenth and seventeenth centuries, it was only in the course of the eighteenth century that warrens became numerous in the district, as areas of common pasture were enclosed; as larger units of landholding, suitable for warrens, were created; and as landowners in the early and middle decades of the century sought more profitable uses for this land, at a time of agricultural depression (Harris and Spratt 1991, 196-201). William Marshall, writing in 1788, believed that rabbit farming was still being held back by the strength of local property rights and the intermixed pattern of landholding in the area (Marshall 1788, 265): further new warrens were created in the course of the nineteenth century, as estate consolidation and enclosure continued apace. Warrens made good use of this relatively marginal land, even as the prices for more conventional agricultural produce recovered in the late eighteenth century, and remained buoyant for most of the nineteenth. There was sufficient grazing, supplemented to some extent with cultivated fodder, for the warren at High Dalby (for example) to carry between two and four rabbits to an acre (5-10 per hectare) through the winter, while that at Low Dalby could over winter carry 4-6 per acre (10-15 per hectare) (Harris and Spratt 1991, 204). Harris and Spratt have estimated that the largest warrens in the area may have been producing as many as 16,000 rabbits in an average year, and that by the early nineteenth century more than 54,000 rabbits were being produced annually in the area as a whole (Harris and Spratt 1991, 204). Many of the warrens continued to operate into the later nineteenth century (in marked contrast to those on the Wolds to the south): there was still a breeding stock of 590 couples at High Dalby in 1899. The warreners were fortunate in being close to large urban markets, and in particular to the towns of Melton, Whitby, Scarborough and York, where there were important hat-making industries, although skins were also sent as far afield as Manchester and even London. Some of the warrens survived into the early twentieth century, when they were purchased by the Forestry Commission and planted up.

The archaeology of the Tabular Hills' warrens, which mainly survives within the Forestry Commission plantations, displays a number of interesting features. There was a distinction, as Harris and Spratt note, between 'farm warrens' – on which rabbits were encouraged on small areas of rough land, and trapped on a fairly casual basis as a supplement to farm incomes – and the extensive commercial warrens of more normal form, which could cover anything up to 1800 acres (728ha). Only a small number of these were equipped with pillow mounds – probably no more than three (those at Hutton Nabb, Spaunton Moor, and Levisham Moor) (Hayes 1983; Harris and Spratt 1991, 78). More noticeable are the boundaries, which can be traced for all or most of the way around 12 of the 15 former warrens at the eastern end of the hills. Several used the Dalby Beck as their western boundary, but otherwise they were defined by a mixture of turf banks and stone walls, with a combination employed on the level areas, but walls alone on the steeper slopes. Many sections of wall survive to a height of around 1.3m, and are of rather simple drystone construction, without throughstones or coping stones. The turf banks also survive in many places, to a height of around 1.3m, and are now as much as a metre wide at the base. As elsewhere, they were usually capped ('brushed') with heather or gorse. The most important and distinctive feature of the warrens, however, is the large numbers of tip traps or 'types' of the kind already discussed (above, pp.74-7). Most were placed inside enclosures of various sizes (*48*) but some, associated with farm warrens, were set

RABBITS, WARRENS & ARCHAEOLOGY

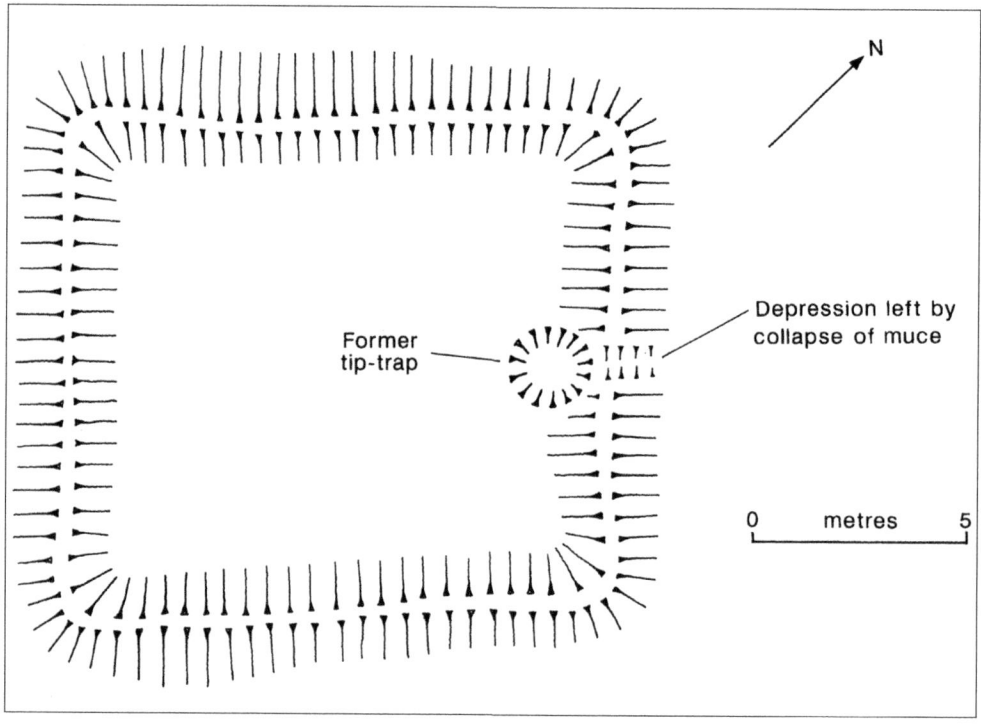

48 Earthworks of a small 'type' or tip trap enclosure in Dalby Warren, North Yorkshire. The turf walls are now represented only by low banks. The position of the 'muce' is marked by a slight depression and that of the tip trap itself by a shallow pit

beside field walls. The most extensive warrens, such as High Dalby, might have as many as 19 individual types.

The surviving warren houses are eighteenth- and nineteenth-century buildings, little different from farm houses. The rabbits were usually sold to middlemen immediately after they had been caught so 'there was no need to provide extensive storage for carcasses, though it might be needed on occasion for skins': as a result 'no special buildings are to be found at the warren houses, even when these retain outbuildings of any age' (Harris and Spratt 1998, 190).

THE WARRENS OF BRECKLAND AND THE SUFFOLK SANDLINGS

The Breckland warrens have been the subject of much excellent historical research, and of some important, although more limited, archaeological investigations: the works of Sussams (1996, 95-7, 113-17); Bailey (1988 and 1989); Crompton and Taylor (1972); Crompton and Sheail (1975); and Sheail (1971) are of particular

THE LANDSCAPES OF WARRENING

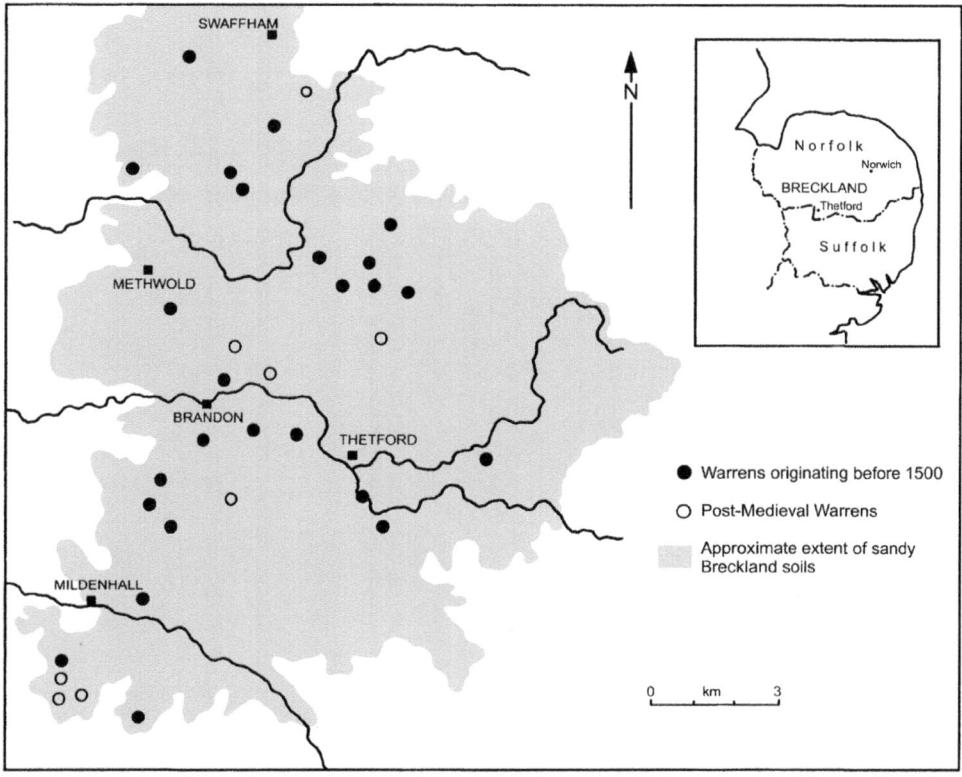

49 The location of the principal warrens in the East Anglian Breckland (after G. Crompton and J. Sheail)

note, as is the unpublished research of Anne Mason, some of which is used here. In addition, W.G. Clarke described the operation of the Breckland warrens in their last days, in the 1920s and 30s (Clarke 1937, 108-117). The warrens of the Sandlings – that is, the long stretch of heathland extending down the coast of Suffolk – have left fewer remains, and have received less historical attention, but have been discussed by Bailey (1989) and, briefly, by myself (Williamson 2005, 58-61). The most important outstanding items on the research agenda are the need to ascertain the boundaries of the warrens, and to plot surviving remains of boundary banks, although the latter has been done for particular warrens (Rackham 1986; Figure 51). Establishing the boundaries of the warrens is made difficult by the fact that their extent clearly changed over time. Figure 49 shows the numbers, and general distribution, of warrens in Breckland: as Crompton and Sheail have noted, they were concentrated 'in the areas of deeper sands marked by a dominance of *Carex arenaria* [sand sedge]' (Crompton and Sheail 1975, 303). Figure 50, an extract from William Faden's 1797 map of Norfolk (digitally remastered by Andrew MacNair), showing the area to the north of Thetford, gives some indication of

RABBITS, WARRENS & ARCHAEOLOGY

50 An extract from William Faden's 1797 map of Norfolk, redrawn by Andrew MacNair, showing the remarkable density of rabbit warrens in the area to the north of Thetford in the East Anglian Breckland the phenomenal number of warrens in this district and the way that they formed contiguous clusters, extending over many hundreds of hectares.

In contrast to the other districts so far described, large-scale commercial warrening appears to have begun in these dry, sandy districts of East Anglia in the early Middle Ages. In Breckland, Brandon Warren, owned by the Bishops of Ely, was established before 1252; the Prior and Convent of Ely had a *cuniculum* at Lakenheath by 1300; and the Abbey of Bury St Edmunds had a warren at Mildenhall by 1328 (Bailey 1989). On the coastal heaths of the Sandlings there were warrens at Dunningworth by 1274, at Iken by 1392, and within the deer park at Staverton from *c.*1322: Blythbugh and Walberswick Warrens had also probably been established by the end of the fourteenth century (Bailey 1989). Some of the Breckland warrens may already have covered more than 1000 acres (405ha) by the early fourteenth century (Sussams 1996, 96), but their area seems to have increased significantly during the agricultural depression of the later fourteenth and fifteenth centuries, in part at the expense of arable land. At Mildenhall in 1425 William Gayton was awarded 18 acres (*c.*7ha) of arable in compensation for land which 'now lay within the warren' (WSRO BE 18/451/4) while in Brandon an area of arable infield, called Oxwickfield, abandoned after the Black Death, had been absorbed within the warren by 1566 (Bailey 1989, 236). Further expansion of warrens on the East Anglian heaths may have accompanied the next major period of agricultural depression, in the late seventeenth and early eighteenth century: on the Rous estate in the Suffolk Sandlings for example 150 acres (60ha) of former arable were converted to a warren in 1700 (ESRO HA 11 L9/22). By the late eighteenth century some of the largest warrens in England could be found in the region, and especially in Breckland. Mildenhall Warren covered 1056 acres (427ha) at the time of enclosure in 1807, while Lakenheath extended over more than 2300 acres (931ha) (WSRO Q/R124; Sussams 1996, 115-6). Stanford, which was considered a modest enterprise, nevertheless covered 537 acres (213ha) in the 1820s (NRO WLS LXI/23 436 X 6). From at least the sixteenth century some of the warrens in the area specialised in black rabbits; silver blue rabbits were introduced into Thetford Warren from Lincolnshire in the early nineteenth century (Clarke 1937, 108; 116).

Few pillow mounds survive in Breckland – only eight probable examples are recorded in the Norfolk and Suffolk HERs – and a mere four are known on the Sandlings Warrens, including the substantial and slightly atypical example on Sutton Common (above, p.59; *51*). The latter is set within a circular enclosure and is almost certainly a 'clapper' mound, and most of the other examples in the region were likewise probably constructed as special accommodation for the young and breeding does. Yet it remains possible that mounds may once have been rather more common on the East Anglian heaths than surviving numbers suggest. The fine map of Methwold Warren in Norfolk, surveyed in 1699, shows

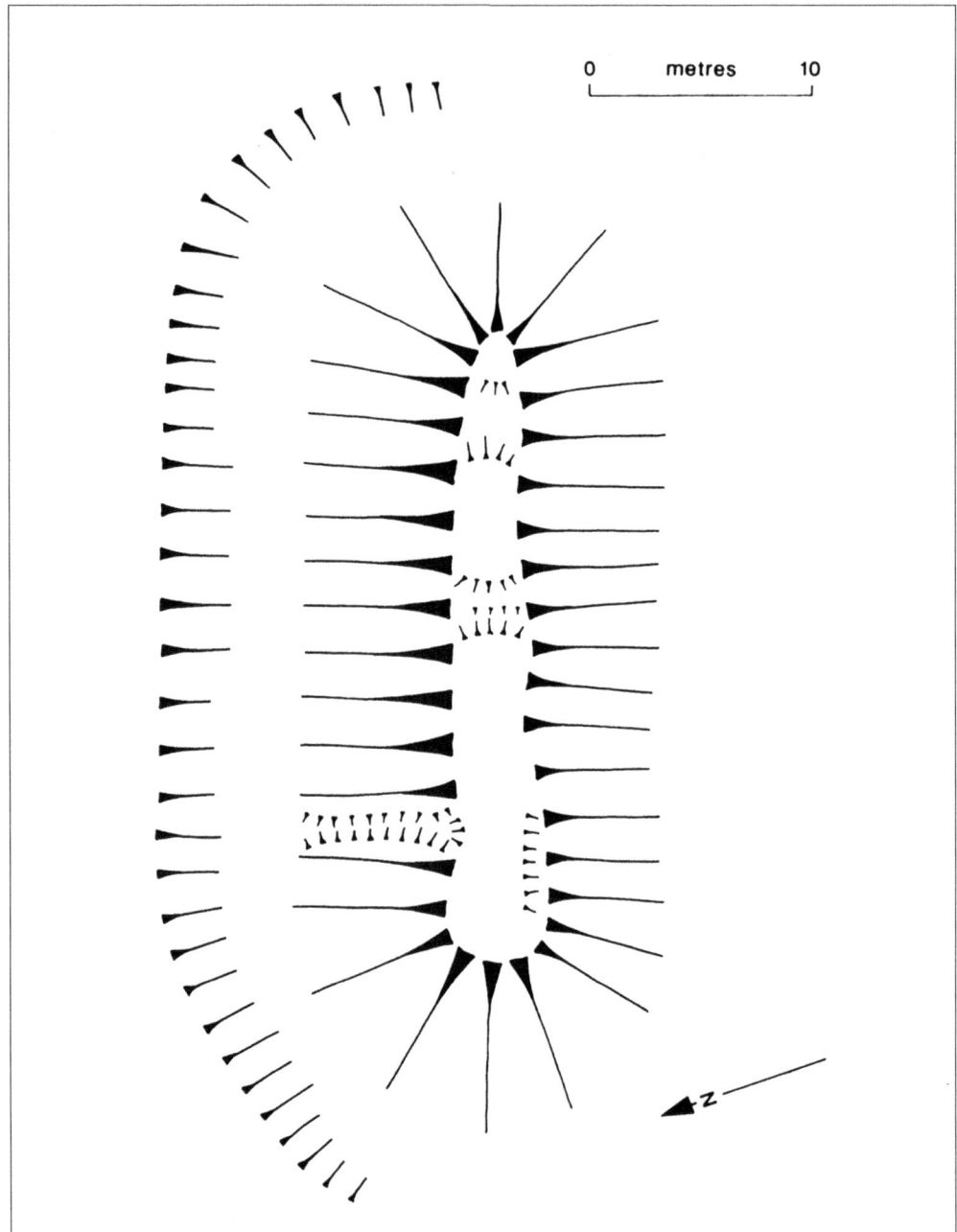

51 The East Anglian warrens can boast few pillow mounds. Those that do exist probably served as 'clappers', or as accommodation for pioneer populations. This example, on Sutton Common in south-east Suffolk, is unusually large for a pillow mound, standing nearly 2m high in places

52 Mildenhall Warren Lodge, Suffolk, was probably built in the later fifteenth or early sixteenth century

what appear to be a number of examples, although these may be representations of natural sand dunes (NRO MC 656/2: Figure 6). Local leases sometimes refer to warren mounds. That for Walberswick Warren, for example, drawn up in 1611, bound the tenant to 'make burrows for the said coneys' (ESRO HA30: 50/22/1, 4). As in other regions, existing earthworks, especially Bronze Age round barrows, were sometimes re-used as warren mounds, as perhaps at Stratton Hall (TM251392). Indeed, some of the features shown on the 1690 map of Mildenhall may have been barrows, to judge from an earlier map of the warren, surveyed in 1580 (but surviving only as an eighteenth-century copy: NRO MC556/2).

If the East Anglian warrens lack many examples of mounds, those on Breckland in particular have left other important archaeological traces. The medieval lodges of Westwick Warren, north-west of Thetford, and at Mildenhall, have already been discussed (above, pp.82-3). Both are well-built tower houses (*52*). There are meagre remains of what is probably a similar building at Ickburgh, and Anne Mason has recently suggested that fragments survive, built into later structures, at a number of other places. At Methwold, for example, what appear to be the remains of an early stone building, incorporated into derelict eighteenth-century

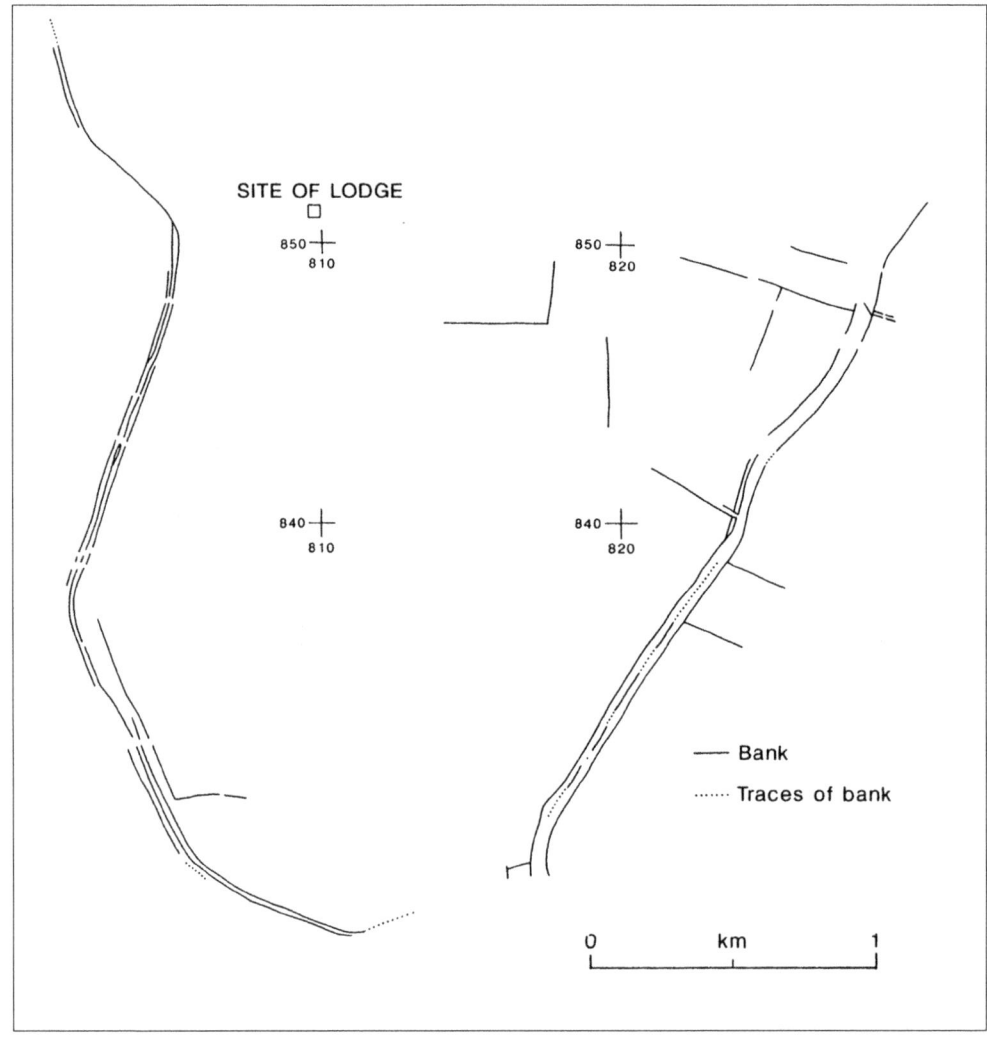

53 The boundary banks of the Breckland Warrens are still notable features of the landscape, although many have been destroyed by later agriculture and modern forestry. Those around Santon Downham High Lodge Warren, just outside Thetford in Norfolk, are particularly well preserved. The warren was bounded to the west by Brandon Warren and Wangford Warren, and to the east by Westwick Warren, which in part explains the multiple, complex character of its boundary banks

farm buildings, may be the lodge referred to in a document of 1413 (when it was roofed with 4200 tiles) (Sheail and Bailey 1996, 17); while at Santon parts of a medieval lodge have apparently been re-used as a field barn. At Lakenheath, the remains of an (early post-medieval?) lodge appear to be built into a nineteenth-century keeper's cottage and at Eriswell fragments of a probable sixteenth- or seventeenth-century lodge are again incorporated into later farm buildings.

All these appear, so far as it is possible to tell, to have been small tower-like structures, similar to the surviving lodges at Thetford and Mildenhall. Later post-medieval lodge, in contrast, in line with developments already outlined elsewhere in the country, are rather nondescript buildings, indistinguishable from other small farms in the area (Crompton 1972, 128; Sussams 1996, 119).

Boundary banks are the other main feature of the Breckland Warrens, and large stretches still survive in the district, most notably around Mildenhall Warren, and beneath the Forestry Commission plantations which now occupy the area of Santon Downham High Lodge and Brandon Warrens. Their layout is often complex (53): they have, to date, only been partially surveyed. It has been suggested that the medieval warrens in Breckland were generally unenclosed, and that it was only in the eighteenth and nineteenth centuries – as landowners began to undertake schemes of reclamation and improvement in the district, and as stocking densities on warrens increased – that they normally came to be bounded by banks (Sussams 1998). While there is much truth in this assertion, it is nevertheless clear that some examples were bounded, at least in part, from an early date. Lakenheath Warren had a *fosse* in the early fourteenth century (Bailey 1989, 131) while documents from a sixteenth-century court case refer to 'old banks' around Methwold Warren (TNA: PRO MPC 75). Nevertheless, the extent of enclosure clearly increased in the period after the mid-seventeenth century. A lease for Elveden Warren, dating to 1701, thus described how the tenant was:

> At his own cost to bank all along from Thetford warren side to the west end of the said borders so far in breadth from Downham warren as have been formerly meted parted and dooled out containing in breadth from said Downham warren to the intended new bank fifty rodds and no further and that if any of the conies shall break through or run over the said new bank to take their feed upon any of the sheepwalks or fields of Elden [Elveden] aforesaid that then it shall be lawful for any of the inhabitants of Elden to take and kill them … (WSRO E3/10/9,2)

At Mildenhall in 1730 a dispute between Thomas Hanmer, the owner of Mildenhall Warren, and Daniel Gwilt, a neighbouring landowner, was resolved by the construction of a bank to prevent the rabbits from straying, paid for jointly by the two landowners but with their respective tenants also contributing to the cost (WSRO HD/1720/19). As already described, the banks were usually around 1.5m in height and warrens were sometimes surrounded, in places, by a double line. Where – as was often the case, given their vast size – public roads crossed a warren, the banks were often turned in along the road side for several hundred metres, to provide additional security.

Internal subdivisions and enclosures, again defined by banks, are often shown on maps and sometimes survive as earthworks, like those on Mildenhall Warren examined by Taylor and Crompton (1972). Some were evidently used for growing fodder or managing systems of convertible husbandry; others may have been clapper enclosures. The extent of internal subdivision appears to have increased in the course of the eighteenth and nineteenth centuries. A plan of Downham High Lodge Warren made in 1752, for example, shows it as entirely open, but by 1792 there were islands of small enclosures within it, and these had grown still more extensive by 1824 (NRO NRS 2/391; WSRO M550/3; Barringer 1998). The area of Mildenhall Warren likewise contracted in stages through the later eighteenth and nineteenth centuries, as enclosed fields gradually came to occupy a larger and larger proportion of its area. In these cases, as in others, it is hard to distinguish an expansion of fodder cultivation – i.e., an intensification of rabbit farming – from a progressive reduction in the size of the warren, resulting from high grain prices and a growing enthusiasm for agricultural improvement, especially in the decades around 1800. The spirit of 'improvement' is certainly manifest in other ways in Breckland, an area which, by the end of the eighteenth century, was dominated by large landowners, their country houses and parks. The 1792 map of Downham High Lodge Warren shows that a number of tree clumps, presumably of a quasi-ornamental character, had also been established within the warren, and belts and clumps had appeared on many of the warrens in the area by the early years of the nineteenth century.

High grain prices and this same fashionable enthusiasm for reclamation saw the demise of several Breckland warrens during the late eighteenth and early nineteenth centuries. The great Methwold Warren, for example, was partially divided and enclosed by 1824 (Barringer 1998); White's Directory of 1844 described it as 'the previous warren ... all enclosed'. Nevertheless, some warrens continued to expand in this period, partly because on the very worst soils rabbit farming continued to make good use of the land, and in part because, as we have noted, the presence of rabbit warrens in an area tended to discourage or even preclude other forms of land use. In March 1784 William Smith, a tenant of the Merton estate, was given permission to 'add to his present warren in Sturston 48 acres of the arable lands belonging to the farm of the said Wm Smith adjoining to the north side of his warren bank and use the land as a warren during the continuation of his lease' (Wade Martins and Williamson 199, 42). The neighbouring Stanford Warren, also owned by the Merton estate, was still stocked with 7200 rabbits in the 1820s, and rabbits were also being systematically trapped on the adjoining arable and sheepwalks. Nearly 15,000 were taken between 17 August 1824 and 1 March 1825 (NRO WLS LXI/23 436 X 6).

The Sandlings warrens seem to have disappeared in the course of the nineteenth century but in Breckland a significant number continued to operate into the early twentieth when – with the severe agricultural depression of the decades around 1900 – some were further expanded in area. They were described in some detail by W.G. Clarke (1937, 108-117). Some were full-time enterprises, others formed part of arable and pasture farms: the largest examples of the former covered in excess of 1000 acres (405ha). Rabbits were normally taken with ferrets, nets and lurchers but type traps had been employed, since the mid-nineteenth century, on Thetford and Santon Downham Warrens (Clarke 1937, 116). Rabbits were also caught using 'trapping banks', although this term was here used in a rather different way from on the Wolds. Clarke thus described how:

> Some of the old boundary banks favoured by rabbits for their burrows are known to the warreners as 'trapping-banks'. In stiffer soil the burrows are fewer and rabbits in consequence more inclined to bolt (Clarke 1937, 111)

Nevertheless, trapping banks on the more familiar Wolds pattern were also probably employed here, to judge from the fact that, in places, the multiple banks around some of the warrens otherwise inexplicably converge, and from the wording on a map of Downham High Lodge Warren, surveyed in 1752 (NRO NRS 2/391).

The progressive afforestation of Breckland in the course of the 1920s and 30s led to the demise of almost all the remaining warrens, although that at Elveden appears to have continued to function, albeit on a reduced scale, into the 1950s, supplying skins to the hat factory at nearby Brandon.

THE DARTMOOR WARRENS

The rabbit warrens on Dartmoor are among the best known in England, and are particularly important for their large concentrations of substantial pillow mounds. They have been the subject of a number of important studies (Lineham 1966; Haynes 1970; Cook 1964; Gerrard 1997, 94-5). Many of the warrens were still operating in the early years of the twentieth century, when they were discussed by Crossing (1903, 56-63). The warrens – at least 17 in number – were mainly located towards the edges of the Moor, and some at least of their area usually lay on sheltered ground, within the valleys cutting through it. The largest concentration was in the south west, in the parishes of Shaugh Prior and Sheepstor, where the warrens of Hen Tor, Trowlesworthy, Willings Walls, Ditsworthy, and Legis Tor (the latter, also called New Warren, perhaps in origin an extension of Trowlseworthy) together covered an almost continuous area of over 8sq km on either side of the Plym valley, with Sheepstor adjoining Ditsworthy to the north, on slightly higher ground (54). The warrens at Redlake Tramway, Yalland, Zeal Burrows and Huntingdon were situated – some distance apart – towards the south eastern margins of the Moor; Headland and Vaghill lay near its eastern edge; Skaigh was

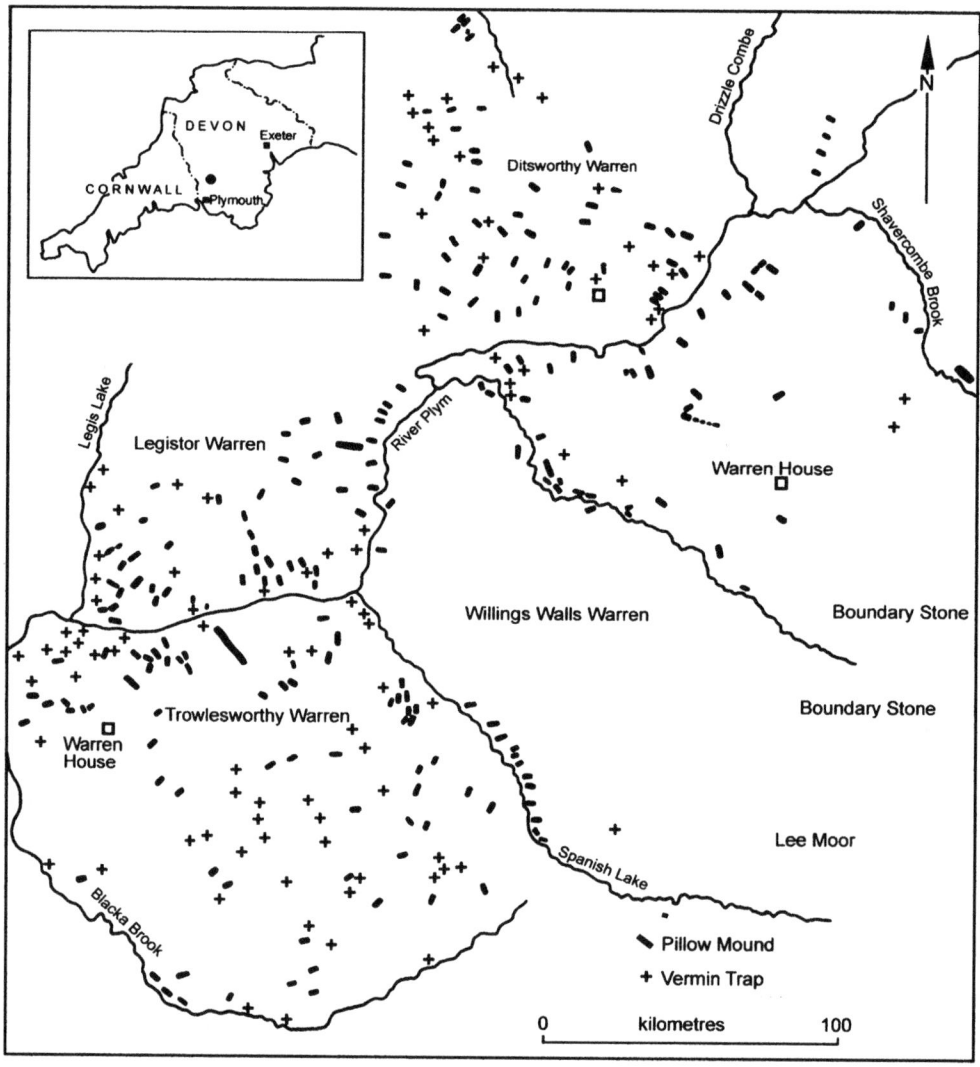

54 The remarkable concentration of warrens, replete with substantial pillow mounds and numerous vermin traps, in the upper Plym valley in south-western Dartmoor (after S. Gerrard)

located on the northern edge; while Beardown, Wistman's Wood, and Merrivale were all in valleys towards the centre (Lineham 1966, 114; Haynes 1970, 156-64).

Trowlesworthy Warren may have been established as early as 1292 and a medieval origin is also possible for Ditsworthy (Lineham 1960, 139; Hayes 1970, 147; Risdon 1811, 392; Beresford 1958, 72). But most of the Dartmoor warrens, and certainly their surviving remains, appear to be of post-medieval date. That at Vaghill, covering 520 acres (210ha), is mentioned in a lease of 1613; and a sixteenth- or seventeenth-century origin is likely for Willings Walls, Headland, Hentor, Legis Tor, and Sheepstor (Haynes 1970, 156-64). Huntingdon Warren, however, probably began life soon after 1808, when the area it occupies was enclosed from Dartmoor Forest; while Beardown seems to have been established around 1800, and certainly by 1808 (Probert 1989, 230). The warrens at Merrivale, Wistman's Wood, Skaigh, Yalland and New House are also probably of nineteenth-century date (Haynes 1970, 163-164). It is noteworthy that many of these later warrens are found towards the interior of the Moor.

On Dartmoor, in marked contrast to the situation on the chalklands of southern England, the Wolds, the Cotswolds and the Mendips, warrening was evidently considered a viable form of land use right through the agricultural revolution period. Indeed, no less an agricultural improver than William Marshall could recommend, as late as 1796, the establishment of rabbit warrens on the 'higher, weaker lands' of the West. He presumably had Dartmoor in mind as he went on to state that 'the markets of Plymouth and its Dock [Devonport], would not fail to take off the produce' (Marshall 1796, 271). Several of the Dartmoor warrens, as already noted, continued to operate into the twentieth century, when they were described by Crossing. At that time the Plym valley warrens sold most of their rabbits to Plymouth and Devonport:

> Though from Ditsworthy many are sent to Birmingham. Birmingham and Sheffield are also markets for those caught in the warrens on the east side of the moor, the rabbits being dispatched from Moretonhampstead (Crossing 1903, 63)

By this time, however, the profits from rabbit farming were falling. Crossing reported how the market for skins had declined, so that the rabbits were sold principally for their meat.

The Dartmoor pillow mounds are particularly impressive, being for the most part substantial high-backed types, although some lower examples can also be found. The largest stand nearly 2m above the base of their ditches (55). The mounds are also often picked out by marked differences in vegetation (they generally carry a mat of coarse bent-grass, while the surrounding land is covered with sheep's fescue and wavy hair-grass) (Sheail 1971, 40). They are, nevertheless, sometimes difficult to locate, owing to the height of the bracken which now infests much of the area. Mounds were particularly necessary in this area of high rainfall and waterlogged, peaty soils. Indeed, the largest concentrations of pillow mounds in England are to be found on the Moor, with over 180 in the five Plym valley warrens, 50 at Beardown and around 80 on Huntingdon Warren (Haynes 1970). Dartmoor mounds never exhibit signs of 'segmenting' but many were provided with artificial burrows, cut into the ground surface beneath them, to judge from Crossing's description of 1903 (Crossing 1903, 62: above, p.46).

55 Typical example of a high-backed Dartmoor pillow mound

In other cases the spaces between large stones at the base, visible in many mounds, may have provided the rabbits with ample opportunities for making burrows, although these may also have served to improve drainage. The mounds vary in length from around five metres to as much as 80m, although most are between 25 and 35m long. The more extended examples are generally found where earlier walls have been used as a base, although conjoined chains of mounds were also sometimes created in such circumstances. Circular mounds are rare, although three examples are known from Beardown Warren, and four from Vaghill.

It is a moot point whether the Dartmoor mounds housed all, or rather most, of the warren population. On some warrens, such as Beardown, the 50 mounds are tightly packed within the boundaries of the warren, which occupies in all a mere 4.2ha of land (56; Probert 1989, 232-3). But the majority of the warrens in the district were much larger, usually between 100 and 400ha in extent, and within them the mounds, while widely scattered, tend to occur in clusters, especially on lower slopes, and south-facing ones especially. Large areas of the warren are thus devoid of mounds: moreover, the largest groups tend to be close to the warren houses. The implication is that the warreners expected that the rabbits would colonise more widely, and that the mounds represent the initial pioneer

THE LANDSCAPES OF WARRENING

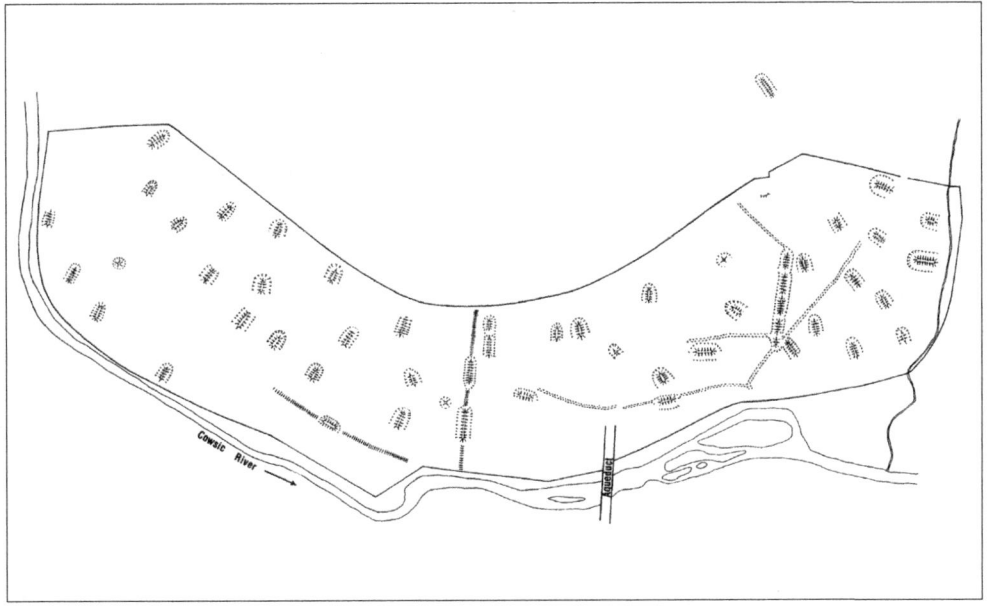

56 The warren at Beardown Warren, near Princetown, Dartmoor was established in the early nineteenth century. The pillow mounds are closely packed within the warren boundaries, which are in places defined by both watercourses and walls (after S. Probert/RCHME)

population, as well as clappers for the young and breeding does. In this context it is noteworthy that on some warrens, such as Huntingdon, deep drainage ditches have been cut across the surface of the moor, not only in the vicinity of the mounds but also more widely, again suggesting that it was anticipated that the rabbits might establish burrows in the natural ground surface, or at least in those parts where the soils were deep yet dry (57). On the other hand, drainage gripes could just as easily have been intended to improve the quality of the sward, and more generally make the environment an amenable one for the creatures. Certainly, surviving descriptions of the warrens in their last years imply that most of the rabbits lived in the mounds, and this is certainly fairly hostile territory for them. Populations could probably only be sustained by good maintenance of the buries, as well as by winter feeding and careful control of predators. Indeed, the absence of rabbits today from the Dartmoor mounds is striking. On a recent visit, examining a large number of mounds on the warrens of Trowlesworthy, Legis Tor, and Ditsworthy, only two mounds had rabbit holes in them – in each case, a single hole, and one of these appeared long-abandoned.

Most of the warrens were bounded for part of their length by dry-stone walls but, perhaps to a greater extent than elsewhere, warreners on Dartmoor used significant watercourses (such as the Plym or the Blackabrook) as boundaries.

57 Aerial view of Huntingdon Warren, Dartmoor. Like Beardown, this warren was established in the early nineteenth century, but it covers a far greater area of ground. Note the prominent drainage ditches and the wide variety of prehistoric remains

Some sections of warren boundaries, located towards the edges of the Moor and close to farmland, made use of both. The nineteenth-century warren at Beardown, for example, was enclosed along its long and north and south sides both by substantial walls and by the River Cowsic and the Devonport Leat respectively (*56*; Probert 1989, 230-31). Warrens in more remote locations, in contrast, often lacked any physical barrier in the direction of the open moor,

58 A typical Dartmoor pillow mound on Trowleworthy Warren, its form made clearer by modern improvement of the surrounding pasture. The walled enclosures beyond may have been fodder fields

although the notional bounds are marked in some cases by boundary stones. The warreners presumably counted on the fact that few rabbits would wish to escape onto the moor, away from familiar territory and regular supplies of food.

Most of the warren houses occupy relatively low-lying, sheltered positions so that the higher areas of the warren are sometimes invisible from them. The buildings vary in character but are all relatively simple structures, little different from the other farms in the district. A few are long houses of seventeenth- or early eighteenth-century date, generally now ruinous (as at Sheepstor, Willings Walls and Hentor), although the thatched example at Headland is still occupied. A number of others were built or rebuilt in the later eighteenth or nineteenth centuries, as at Huntingdon Warren (now demolished) and Trowlesworthy. Most have stone-walled fields attached, some of which were fodder enclosures although others represent later additions to the landscape, post-dating the demise of the warren in question (58). The former are sometimes bounded by dry stone walls slightly higher than is usual in the area, and some (as at Headland) lack gates. One of the fields at Trowlesworthy was used as a dog enclosure, with walls eight feet high.

59 Dog kennels built into the thickness of the yard wall beside Ditsworthy Warren House

The warren house at Ditsworthy is particularly interesting. It is a seventeenth- or eighteenth-century building, extensively rebuilt in the nineteenth century, constructed of stone with a slate roof. It is now abandoned and derelict. It has a number of associated fields, surrounded by walls in some places more than 1.7m high; a garden and yards, also enclosed by substantial walls; an enclosed dog yard to the east of the house, with high walls (and overhanging coping in places) and three kennels, megalithic structures, built into the thickness of the wall (59). There are three ruined outbuildings, some of which were presumably used for storing fodder.

The most striking features of the Dartmoor warrens are, perhaps, the vermin traps which survive in various states of ruination, and which have been discussed in much detail by Cook and Hayes (Cook 1964; Hayes 1970), and earlier in this book (above pp.78-80). Fewer seem to survive intact on the Moor than when Haynes carried out his survey work here in the 1960s, although the opposed chevrons of earth and stones which funnelled the prey towards them still remain in many places (60). They are often difficult to spot, however, partly because of the amount of bracken that now infests the Moor,

60 The characteristic opposed chevrons, defined by lines of stone, marking the site of a vermin trap on Trowlesworthy Warren, Dartmoor

especially on Legis Tor Warren, and partly because of the amount of stone lying around on the surface – either natural, or the remains of prehistoric stone walls and hut circles. Vermin traps were, however, clearly common features on the older warrens, with more than 80 being recorded from the Plym valley group, while even the early nineteenth-century Huntingdon Warren has four small examples. From the late eighteenth century vermin traps were supplemented with 'vermin houses', stone-built ambush points which could conceal the warrener, armed with a gun. These were located near to the tors and stony areas where the stoats and weasels bred. Most were simple screens of stones but some were small huts, with roofs and doors (Haynes 1970, 155). Tip traps were never used on the Dartmoor warrens, presumably because the ground was either waterlogged for much of the time, or too rocky to make the excavation of deep pits feasible.

All in all the Dartmoor warrens, and especially the group in the upper Plym valley, represent the most important and impressive archaeology of rabbit farming to be found in England, or indeed the world.

THE WARRENS OF THE WELSH MOORLANDS

The documentary evidence, discussed in some detail by Matheson (1941) and more recently by the RCAHM (1982), suggests strongly that in the early Middle Ages rabbit warrens in Wales were largely restricted to offshore islands like Skomer, and to areas close to the coast. Warrens are thus mentioned at Rhuddlan in 1282 and at Kenfig, near Margam in South Glamorgan, in 1316. In 1317 there is a reference to 'the rabbit warren of Pennard [near Penmaen, South Glamorgan] in the sand-burrows' (*cuniculario nostro de Pennarth in la Sanborghwys*) (RCAHM 1982, 323). Coastal sands continued to be important areas for warrens into the post-medieval period. In the 1590s there was a legal dispute between Griffith Williams, who leased the manor of Candleston (South Glamorgan), and Sir Edward Stradling, lord of Merthyr Mawr, concerning the former's establishment of a warren without permission in the sand dunes beside the mouth of the Ogmore river: he had 'erected there a little howse and made a warren of conies, no lesse for his profit than pleasure' (RCAHM 1982, 325). But by the fifteenth and sixteenth centuries warrens were becoming more widely dispersed, although still largely restricted to the coastal lowlands. Most were in parks or associated with high-status residences, such as that documented at Ewenny in Glamorganshire in 1578 (James 1983, 113). This late medieval and early post-medieval phase is reflected archaeologically by the single mounds, or small groups of mounds, scattered through South Glamorgan, like those at Penmaen (SS53338804) or Nash Point (SS91506850); at various places in Anglesey; and thinly along the narrow coastal lowlands of Dyfed and Gwynedd. The majority of Welsh pillow mounds, however, including all the largest groups, are located in the interior of the county, generally in areas of high moorland, and it is easy to assume that these are associated with the spread of rabbits, and warrens, into the inland parts of the principality in the decades after *c*.1800. As already noted, as late as 1813 Davies reported that while rabbits were numerous in coastal areas, there were 'but few in the interior' (Davies 1813, 347).

These inland warrens display much variety. Most are represented by small groups of pillow mounds, or even by single mounds, with no obvious associated archaeology (*61*). But some were evidently huge enterprises, like those at Ystradfellte and Cefn Cul in the Brecon Beacons, which were unquestionably established in the middle decades of the nineteenth century, following the enclosure and sale of this part of the Great Forest of Brecknockshire in 1820 (RCAHM 1982, 316; Spurgeon 1967, 1969). On Cefn Cul around 100 pillow mounds occupy an area of moorland lying at 300-500m OD and fall into two distinct groups, one centred on SN873202 near Cray and another near Traianglas at SN855184 (*62*). Both seem to have formed part of the same huge warren, covering more than 6sq km. The pillow mounds are well preserved and evidently recent features with sharp

61 A lone pillow mound on unimproved pasture below the hillfort on Carregwiber Bank near Llandrindod Wells, Powys. It is one of many single mounds, and small groups, scattered across the moorlands of central Wales. Most are of eighteenth- and nineteenth-century date, although a minority are probably earlier

profiles, some of which display signs of (usually transverse) segmenting. They vary considerably in length, from less than 30m to more than 60m, but are mostly less than 8m in width. Some, lying roughly parallel with the slope, are ditched only on their uphill side but have a well-constructed stone revetment on their lower side. Other remains include a number of stone-lined types, mostly set into the sides of small enclosures; other enclosures, some of which contain signs of ploughing and were presumably for cultivating fodder; at least one house platform, presumably the site of a (not very elaborate) warren house; and drainage channels. Some eight kilometres to the south east, the huge warren lying on the open moorland just to the north of the village of Ystradfellte is in many respects very similar, with 90 or more well-built pillow mounds scattered across an area of more than 1700 acres

62 The remains of the large nineteenth-century warren at Traianglas in the Brecon Beacons include numerous well-defined pillow mounds and a number of enclosures. Some of the latter contain slight plough ridges and were presumably used to cultivate fodder crops

(c.690ha) (63). Here, too, there are tip traps set in stone-walled enclosures and five walled, ungated fields. A substantial stone wall surrounds much of the area. The mounds are, once again, relatively narrow and high-sided, and vary in length from 20m-140m; some are slightly V-shaped. It is possible that both the Cefn Cul and the Ystradfellte warrens were created by the same person, for both areas seem to have been owned in the 1830s and 40s by one individual, Mr Thomas Claypon. But it is noteworthy that the pillow mounds on the two warrens display a number of differences in construction, with (for example) those at Ystradfellte lacking any

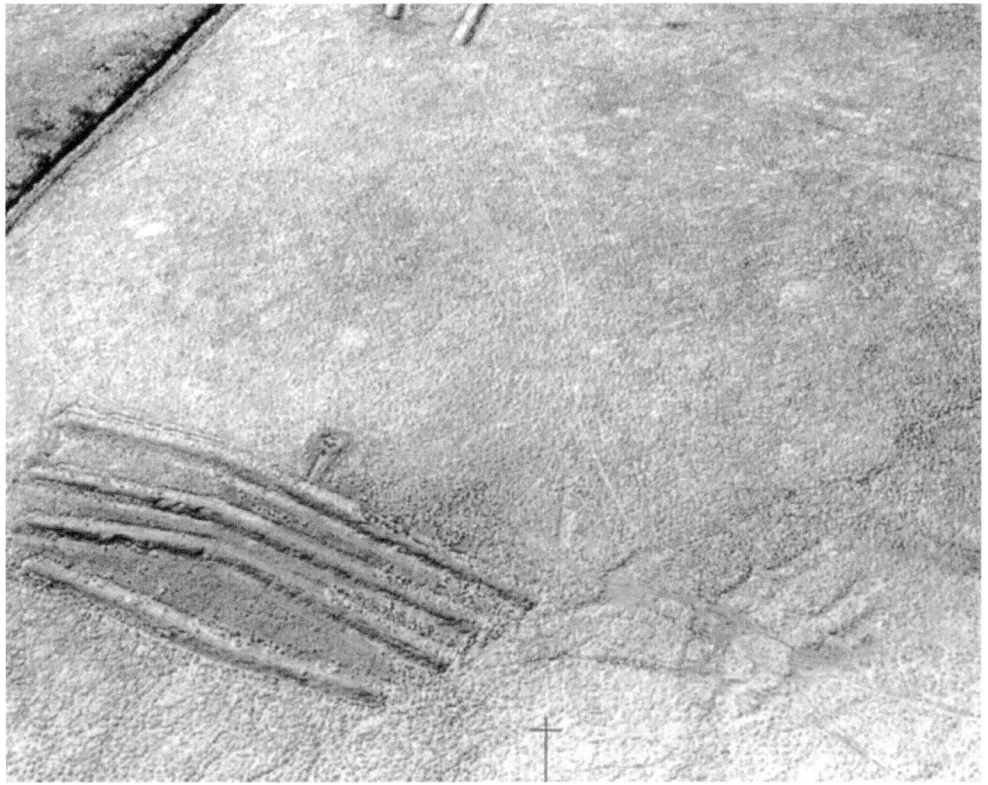

63 The warren at Ystradfellte in the Brecon Beacons is of early nineteenth-century date, postdating the enclosure of Brecknockshire Forest in 1819

signs of segmenting, and those on Cefn Cul displaying more evidence of stone reveting (RCAHM 1982, 314-5; Spurgeon 1967, 1969).

Other large and evidently late warrens are found further north, in the old county of Montgomeryshire (now Powys), most notably at Y Foel and Cwm Ednant. The former has been referred to on a number of occasions in the course of this volume because of the meticulous excavations carried out by Robert Silvester (Silvester 1995). The warren originally – before much destruction by quarrying and pasture improvement – comprised around 52 pillow mounds scattered across a high, narrow ridge some 5km west of Llanllugan (*64*). The mounds, all except one circular example being of narrow rectangular form, display no surface signs of segmenting but, on excavation, were found to cover artificial burrow systems dug into the old ground surface (above, pp.44-5). A nineteenth-century date for the warren had been proposed by the RCAHM on the not unreasonable grounds that the pillow mounds overlay an area of narrow rig of the type often created by the ploughing up of marginal land during the

Napoleonic Wars. However, a rather earlier origin, in the eighteenth century, was suggested by Silvester, in part on the basis of the name given to an adjacent property in a document of 1772 – Gwaun-y-maglau, 'the meadow of the snares' (Silvester 1991, 87). Either way, the warren was a short-lived affair for (in contrast to those at Cefn Cul and Ystradfellte on the Brecon Beacons) the nineteenth-century census records make no reference to a warrener in the area. The warren's physical remains – again in marked contrast to those on the Brecon Beacons – include only pillow mounds: there are no tip traps or fodder enclosures, possibly because it was established on an area of unenclosed common land. There is likewise no trace of a warren house, and the enterprise was presumably managed from one of the farms or cottages which lie to the south, outside the area of the warren. The large warren, represented by more than 60 mounds, on Cwm Ednant, Darrowen (Powys) is probably of similar age, for here too the mounds overlie 'narrow rig'. This warren again lacks fodder enclosures and trapping pits, and the mounds do not display any evidence of segmenting; but there is a house platform close to the valley bottom, with traces of foundations, which may well mark the site of the warren house. Almost all the mounds are visible from it (Silvester 1991).

It is possible that both Y Foel and Cwm Ednant were established some time before the start of the nineteenth century. But the most dramatic evidence that some warrens existed in the upland interior of Wales before *c*.1800 comes from David Austin's excavations at Llanfair Clydogau (centred on SN63825168). The pillow mounds here, 34 in all before destruction by land improvement, fell into two distinct groups (Austin 1988). To the west, one small round mound and nine small oval or rectangular mounds, varying in length from 9-17m, were associated with the earthworks of four buildings of the kind characteristic of medieval *hafods*, seasonally occupied farmsteads associated with summer grazing on upland moors (65). Charcoal found immediately beneath one of the mounds produced radiocarbon dates of AD 1315-1415 (Austin 1988, 151), suggesting that warrening had begun on the site in the fourteenth century. The central and eastern parts of the warren, in contrast, were occupied by very different pillow mounds. Twenty-two were rectangular and more uniform in appearance than those in the eastern group, and also much larger, varying in length from 19 to 31m; one was L-shaped, but otherwise of similar general character; and three were oval mounds, but set within circular ditches. The earthworks of three vermin traps were also found in this area, together with some areas of apparently contemporary ploughing. Austin suggested that the original, eastern group of mounds represented a warren which had developed in the later Middle Ages from a seasonally occupied *hafod*, 'from which one structure at least was subsequently selected to house a labourer or overseer for the rabbit warren' (Austin 1988, 151). The more extensive area of

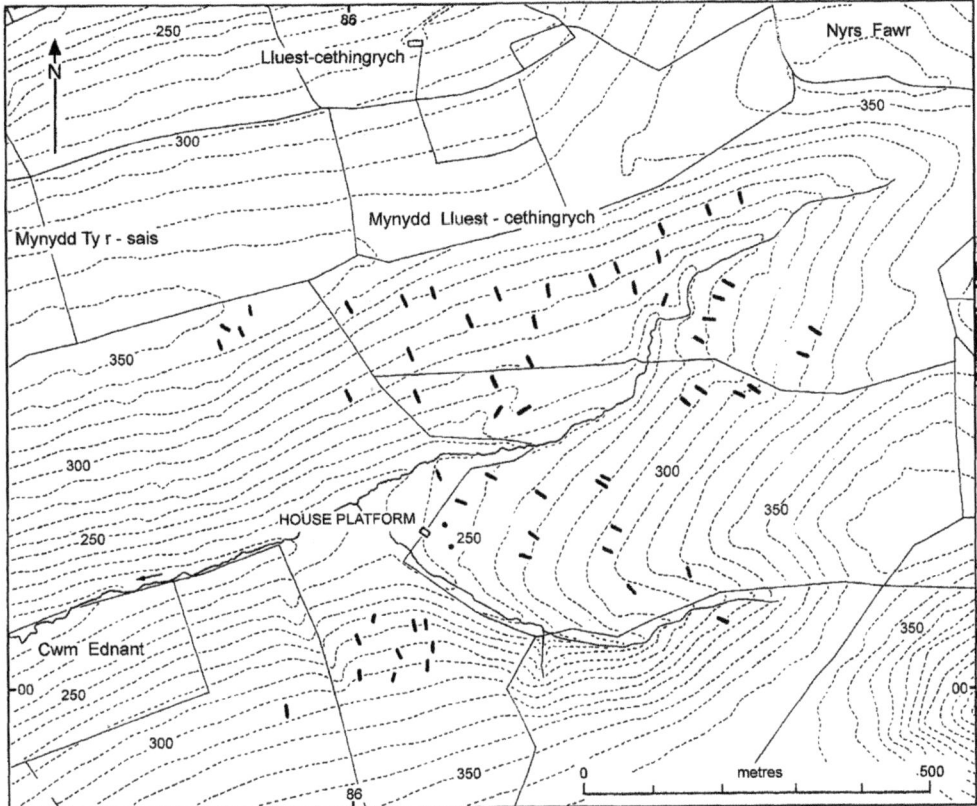

64 Plan of the extensive warren at Y Foel, neat Llanlugan in Powys (after R. Silvester)

regular mounds was clearly later, but almost certainly of eighteenth-century or earlier origin. Austin noted that one of the mounds was overlain by a wall of probable early nineteenth-century date. Of equal significance, however (and not commented on by Austin) are the vermin traps, more common on seventeenth- and eighteenth- than on nineteenth-century warrens.

Whether or not we accept the extremely early date for the first phase of warrening at Llanfair Clydogau, scattered documentary references suggest that rabbit warrens were becoming common in the upland moors well before 1800. In 1760, for example, the lessee of the Corwon lands at Maelienydd in Radnorshire (now Powys) ordered his agents to destroy a warren in the parish of Llanddewi Ystradenny, 'dug for keeping rabbits, without licence or authority' (NLW/Harpton/1785). It is probable, in fact, that the warrens in the uplands of the Welsh interior have a more complex, and rather longer, history than has sometimes been assumed, and a chronology not entirely dissimilar to that of the Dartmoor warrens, with possible medieval origins, an expansion through the

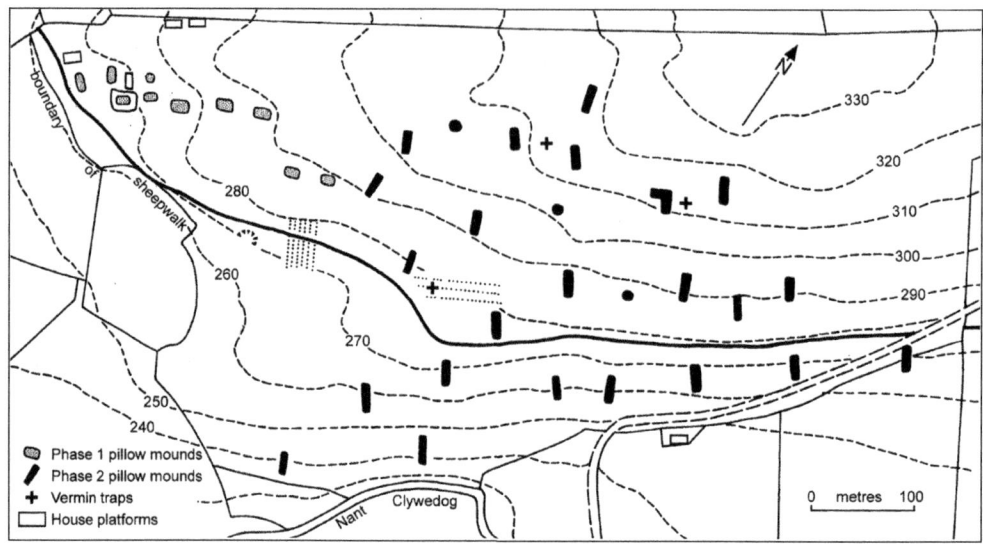

65 Plan of the warren at Llanfair Clydogau, Dyfed (after D. Austin)

seventeenth and eighteenth centuries, but continued vitality – encouraged by the growth of neighbouring industrial areas – into the nineteenth. Some of the smaller groups of mounds, and single mounds, scattered across the most remote areas of moorland may be of eighteenth- or possibly even seventeenth-century date, although the majority are perhaps nineteenth-century. They evidently represent widespread, small-scale enterprises, perhaps farm warrens run as an adjunct to normal hill farming. Some were perhaps established, like that at Llanddewi Ystradenny, without permission on areas of common land, rather than being enterprises financed by major landowners.

CONCLUSION

This brief examination of the documentary and archaeological evidence allows us to make a few general points about the chronology of, and regional variations in the character of, large-scale commercial warrens. There is no doubt that these had already appeared on a small scale in the period before the Black Death, mainly although not exclusively in areas of coastal and inland sand, especially in East Anglia. The period following the Black Death saw some expansion of the industry, as landowners attempted to diversify their incomes at a time of agricultural depression, but not to any real extent into new areas. This began to occur in the sixteenth and early seventeenth centuries, however, as commercial warrens appeared in some numbers in many lowland forest areas, on Dartmoor, in the Mendips and on the Cotswolds, as well as on the chalklands of Wessex and southern England. The period of agricultural depression in the later seventeenth and the first half of the eighteenth centuries saw the further growth of commercial rabbit farming and, in particular, expansion into a number of new districts, especially the Tabular Hills, the Yorkshire Wolds, the Lincolnshire Wolds, and the Welsh Moors. This chronology, it should be emphasised, may oversimplify a more complex reality, in the sense that some commercial warrens almost certainly existed in the areas in question before the main periods of expansion which I have highlighted.

The greater suitability of land for rabbit farming than for other kinds of agrarian enterprise, together with the presence of extensive commons (on which warrens could be created by manorial lords without formal enclosure), were the key factors determining the location of these concentrations of post-medieval rabbit farming activities. But in addition, the size and strength of local communities was perhaps of some importance. Warrens flourished best, and tended to occupy the greatest area of land, in districts in which population levels were low and the area of arable limited, for rabbits did great damage and evoked considerable hostility from local people. For the same reasons warrens tended to cluster in contiguous groups, for the establishment of a rabbit farm on one piece of land tended to limit the uses which could be made of another, lying next to it.

Understanding the decline of large commercial warrens is more straightforward. The chronology of disappearance was principally related to the ease with which, and the extent to which, the areas in which they were found could be reclaimed and improved using the new agricultural techniques of the seventeenth and eighteenth centuries, together (once again) with the strength of local farming communities. Large warrens thus declined first – during the later seventeenth and eighteenth centuries – on the chalklands of southern England. Those on the Cotswolds, the Mendips, and on the Wolds of Lincolnshire and Yorkshire, disappeared rather later, in the late eighteenth and nineteenth centuries. On heaths and the higher moors, in contrast, reclamation and improvement made much less headway and here even ardent agriculturalists like William Marshall could advocate rabbit farming as a rational form of land use. In these districts rabbit warrens often survived in some numbers well into the nineteenth and, in some cases, the twentieth century.

It will also be apparent from the foregoing discussion that the archaeology of large-scale commercial warrens displays much regional variation. This was in part a consequence of the period in which the industry flourished in particular districts, and in part the result of environmental circumstances. The latter influenced, for example, the extent to which stone walls or turf banks were used to demarcate warren boundaries. Environmental factors, as I have already suggested, also probably lie behind the extent to which pillow mounds were used on warrens. The great warrens of eastern England – on the Wolds, the Tabular Hills, and in East Anglia – never seem to have been provided with large numbers of mounds. In these districts they were used primarily to establish pioneer populations, or to shelter the young and the breeding does. In central and western areas, in contrast – where the climate was wetter and soils more likely to be thin or seasonally waterlogged – mounds were more numerous, and in some high moorland warrens they were used to accommodate most if not all of the population. It should be emphasised, however, that the distinction is not entirely straightforward, for some substantial concentrations of mounds can be found on the eastern warrens (at Hutton-le-Hole in Yorkshire, for example), and to some extent the idiosyncracies of particular owners or warreners must have been a factor in deciding the character of accommodation provided for the rabbits.

The extent to which tip traps were employed in different areas may also be a consequence, at least in part, of environmental circumstances. They were principally a feature of the warrens of north-east England – on the Yorkshire and Lincolnshire Wolds and the Tabular Hills – where a relatively dry climate, and generally porous soils, prevented them from filling with water. Their absence from the East Anglian warrens (with the exceptions already noted) is probably due to the difficulties of constructing and maintaining the pits, and keeping the rabbits within them, where soils were particularly loose and sandy. This said, at least three nineteenth-century warrens on the damp Brecon Beacons were provided with types, again presumably a reflection of the particular ideas of individual owners. Their apparent absence from the dry chalklands of Wessex is superficially curious, but can perhaps be explained by the fact that the warrens in this district were beginning to decline and disappear at precisely the point – the first half of the eighteenth century – when this form of trapping was coming into general use. But there may be another factor in all this. It is noteworthy that while tip traps can be found in some warrens which were equipped with pillow mounds, as on the Brecon Beacons, they were more characteristic of warrens which lacked them, such as those on the Tabular Hills. Pillow mounds, as I have argued, were probably constructed as much to aid trapping as to provide accommodation, and where they were employed warreners were perhaps reluctant to go the effort of digging tip traps as well.

5
WARRENS AND ARCHAEOLOGISTS

Pillow mounds, and other aspects of the archaeology of rabbit warrening, are of importance in their own right, as evidence for an important medieval and post-medieval industry. But in addition, pillow mounds in particular have caused considerable confusion to archaeologists over the years and several examples, including some excavated ones, continue to be misinterpreted and misunderstood in the literature – as burial mounds, buildings, or 'ritual features'. What follows is a brief account of the complex history of the relationship between archaeologists and the physical remains of rabbit warrens, from the late nineteenth century until the present day.

EARLY ENQUIRIES

Archaeologists, as explained in the introduction, have been aware of pillow mounds as a distinct class of monument since at least the late nineteenth century. Canon Greenwell noted them as an enigmatic feature of the landscape as early as 1877. He excavated several examples without meaningful results and suggested that some might have been 'cenotaphs' of uncertain date (Greenwell 1877, 201-2). Yet even as early as this some archaeologists were quite clear that the mounds were artificial warrens, of no great antiquity. In 1879, while Hilton Price was excavating an example just outside the hillfort on Herefordshire Beacon (Herefordshire), he was visited by the eminent archaeologist General Pitt Rivers:

> Whose opinion I at once solicited; he informed me that it would be only a waste of time to continue the digging, as he, in company with Canon Greenwell and Professor Rolleston, had opened precisely similar mounds in Oxfordshire, Surrey, and elsewhere with like results. But whilst on Dartmoor, some years back, he observed some of these raised mounds, and upon making enquiries, ascertained

that were thrown up as artificial rabbit burrows … . They are even made there at the present day (Price 1881, 321-22, 331)

Price ordered the trenches to be filled in at once but was not entirely convinced by the General's comments. The mound contained fragments of burnt brick, charcoal, a thin copper ring and fragments of rock not native to the immediate locality, and he speculated that it might have been raised as a *botontinus* – a terminal mark for a Roman estate:

At such limits the Agrimensores would deposit not only charcoal but broken pottery, pebbles, pieces of iron, coins … over such a deposit they would erect a mound. It is certainly a coincidence that we should have met such a deposit in the so-called barrow, and that it should be closely associated with the respective boundaries of "territoria", or, in other words, adjoining counties

Other people continued to puzzle over the mounds, and to excavate them. Some time around 1910, for example, the rector of Llanelwedd (Powys), the Rev. D. Edmondes-Owen, dug into a mound on Carneddau Hill, and found burnt bones and other features which suggested that it was a burial mound (RCAHM 1977, 318-9). What is noteworthy about this example is that warrens on the Brecon Beacons were well endowed with pillow mounds; Ystradfellte and Cefn Cul, little more than 40km away, had almost certainly still been operating within living memory. The RCAHM *Inventory of Ancient Monuments* for Radnorshire, published three years later, accepted Edmondes-Owen's interpretation, and classed the mounds as long barrows, although it also noted a local tradition that they were warrens (RCAHM 1913). Two years earlier the Commission's *Inventory* for Montgomeryshire had similarly speculated that the mounds called *Beddau Cewri* ('Soldiers' Graves') found at various places in the county were rabbit warrens, although local traditions for their sepulchral origin led to an uncertainty about their true character which was reflected in their eventual categorisation as 'unclassified' (RCAHM 1911, xiv-xv). Other field archaeologists in the period were similarly puzzled or confused by particular examples. Hadrian Allcroft, while failing to identify pillow mounds as a distinct class of earthwork in his seminal *Earthwork of England*, discussed in passing a number of examples, including those within the hillfort at Dolebury, apparently unaware that some earthworks of this type at least had been built as warrens (Allcroft 1908, 604).

As already noted, interest in the enigmatic mounds reached something of a peak in the 1920s. One example was excavated within the Iron Age hillfort on Bury Hill, just outside Bristol, by J.A. Davies and C.W. Philips in 1926 (Davies and Philips 1926). The various stone structures within the mound, as well as its location, provided

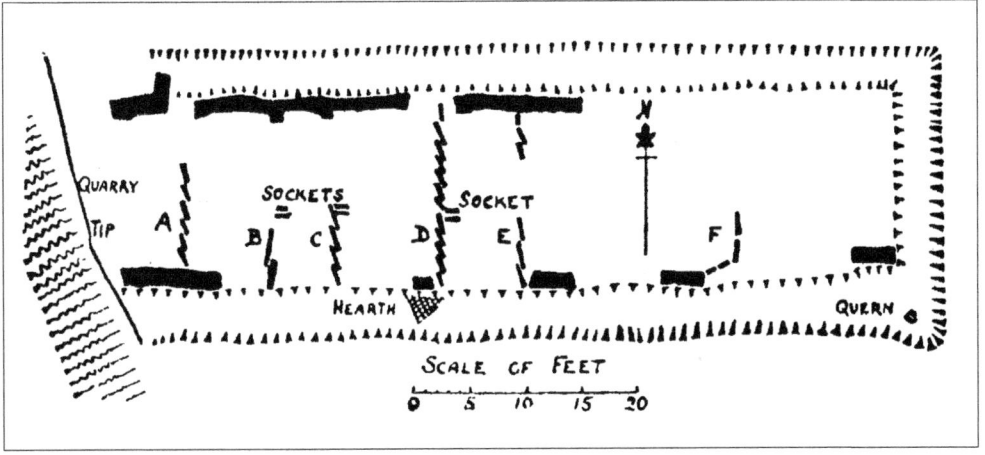

66 Diagram of features excavated within the pillow mound at Bury Hill Camp, Bristol, in 1926; from the excavation report by Davies and Phillips. The mound was interpreted as the remains of a Roman military building

fertile grounds for confusion (*66*). The perimeter retaining wall was interpreted as the remains of a 'foundation wall … along both sides of the mound', much of which had been robbed out at some stage in the past. The remains of stone-capped artificial burrows were particularly hard to explain: 'a number of slanting transverse rows of undressed Pennant flags … embedded about 9-ins in the earth, the flag against the south wall being embedded first, and the next overlapping it about 3-ins, and partly resting on it, and so on throughout the row, tilewise' (Davies and Philips 1926, 10). One row ran the full width of the mound, the others only part way across. Some seemed to be associated with 'leads or sockets … rather less than a foot deep.' The arrangement was interpreted by the excavators as 'a very crude system of tile drainage'. Sherds of both Iron Age and Romano-British pottery were recovered from the mound, which was duly interpreted as the site of a building with walls of turf raised on low stone foundations, and with a roof of brushwood, similar to early Roman buildings found 'in the forts of Gellygaer, Newstead, Great Chesters, Housteads, and elsewhere' (Davies and Philips 1926, 10-11).

In the same year the noted Essex archaeologist, the aptly named Hazeldine Warren, excavated four mounds in the group of 20 at High Beech in Epping Forest. His results, however, were very different from those obtained by Davies and Philips at Bury Hill Camp. Warren knew that some archaeologists, including 'so high an authority as Pitt-Rivers', believed that the mounds were artificial rabbit warrens. But he rejected this hypothesis, at least in the case of the High Beech mounds, on a number of grounds, the most important being that the whole area was composed of loose dry sand in which rabbits could and did burrow freely:

A good deal of labour would be entailed in throwing up these banks. The High Beach group would represent, I should think, some 4,000 to 5,000 cubic yards. Who would do that work for the benefit of rabbits, when they live in the natural hillside just as well without the banks? (Warren 1926, 222)

The mounds, moreover, overlay areas of 'baked sand', and contained fragments of Iron Age pottery (*67*). Warren, noting the more general association of pillow mounds and Iron Age hillforts, and the fact that Price's excavations on the Malvern Hills had likewise recovered evidence of burning, came to the tentative conclusion that the mounds represented the sites of Iron Age funeral pyres, and suggested that 'the absence of interment or the remains of bone (so far as we have observed) might be accounted for by the cremated ashes having been gathered up and ceremonial interment having taken place elsewhere' (Warren 1926, 223-25).

O.G.S. CRAWFORD AND ACCEPTANCE OF THE 'WARREN' HYPOTHESIS

The upsurge of interest in pillow mounds in the 1920s culminated in a series of contributions by the noted aerial archaeologist O.G.S. Crawford. The first was in an article on barrows published in the first edition of *Antiquity*, a journal which he himself edited, in 1927. In this, Crawford described:

> A class of mound that is sometimes called a barrow, but which seldom, if ever, yields an internment. It consists of a low, flat, rectangular mound rather like a pillow: there is often a longitudinal crease down the middle, and sometimes grooves and creases at right angles ... The mounds often occur near, and within hill-top camps, but they may be of more recent date. No satisfactory explanation for the purpose of the mounds has ever been put forward. It has been suggested that they are artificial rabbit warrens, but I have never seen a rabbit using one ... (Crawford 1927, 341)

Crawford provided a more extended treatment of the subject in his seminal work, written with Alexander Keiller and published the following year, *Wessex from the Air*. In this he discussed the surface morphology and location of the mounds, which he now called 'pillow mounds' for the first time. He described their main, defining features, including 'segmenting'; and discussed some of the more striking examples, including those at Minchinhampton Common (Gloucestershire) and Pilsdon Pen (Dorset), together with monuments of related form which he had observed on Steeple Langford Cowdown (Wiltshire) (*68*) (Crawford and Keiller 1928, 18-24). Crawford also drew on the results of the excavations already discussed, carried out by Price, Davies and Phillips, and Warren (the latter two were still at

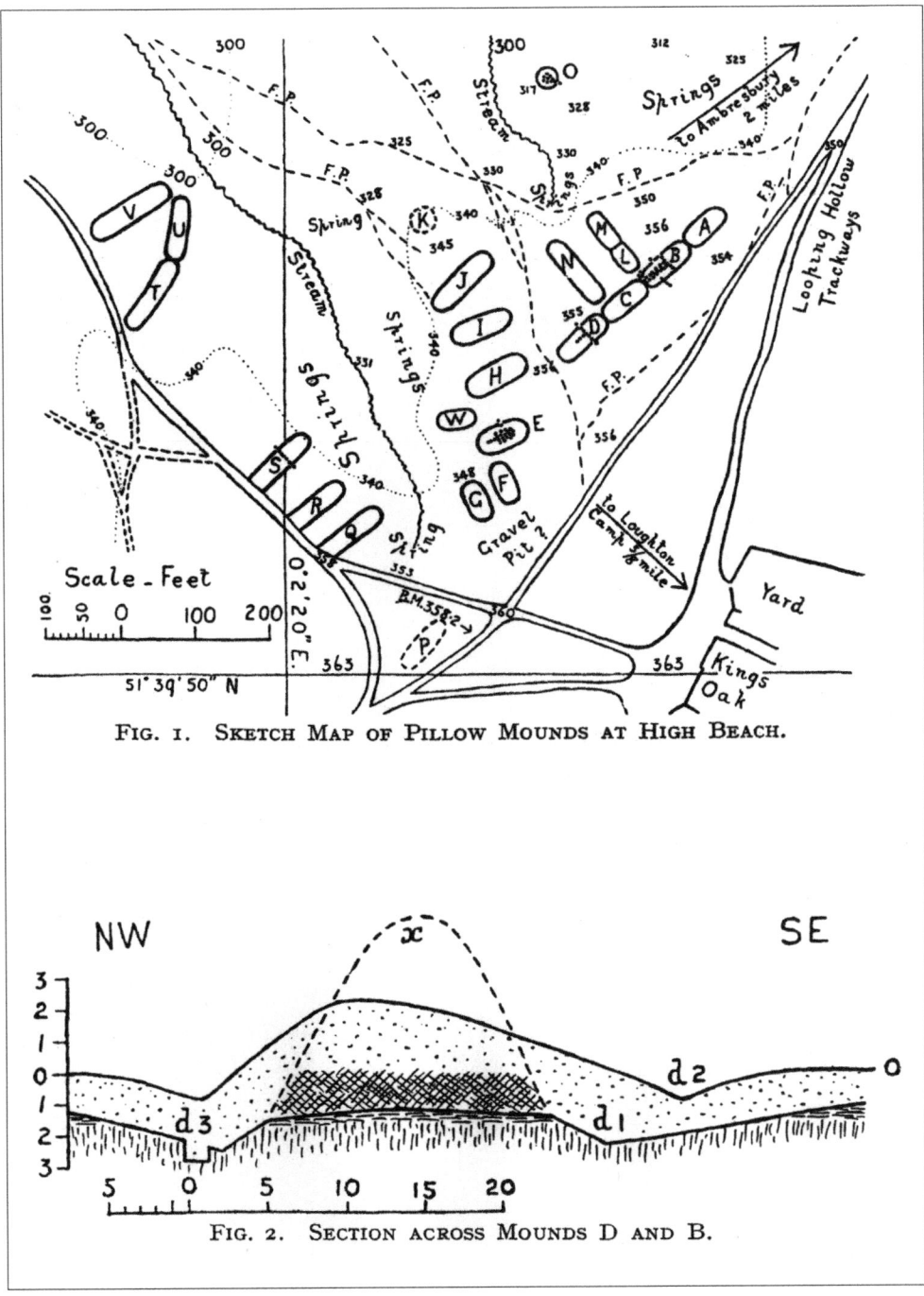

67 Illustrations from Hazeldine Warren's report of the excavations at High Beech, Epping, in 1926 – plan of the site, and cross-section through one of the mounds

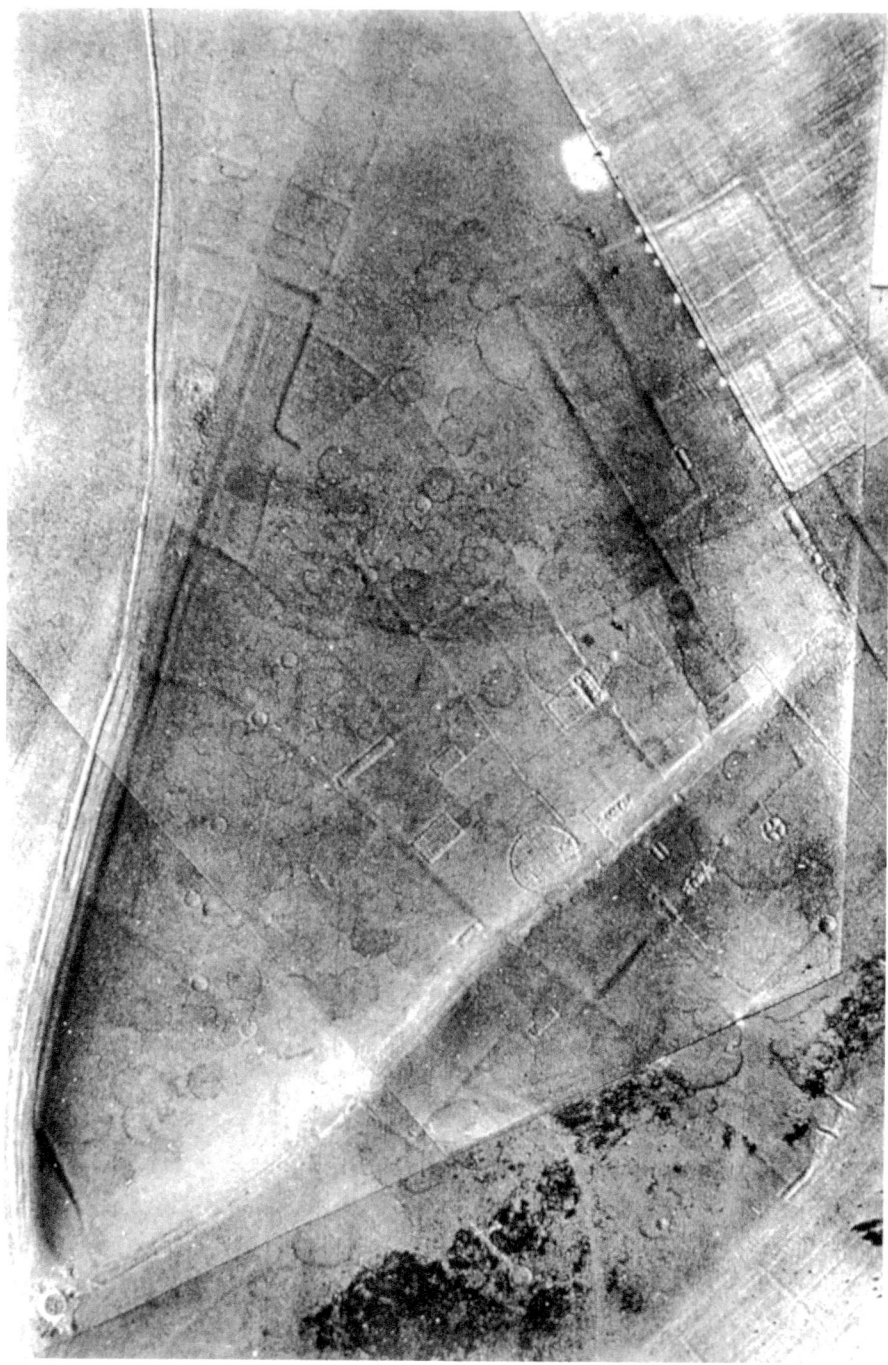

68 This curious group of mounds on Steeple Langford Cowdown, in Wiltshire, now destroyed, was photographed from the air by O.G.S. Crawford in the mid-1920s. It included pillow mounds of normal rectangular and circular form, but also some larger mounds. All displayed considerable evidence of 'segmenting'

the time of writing unpublished). He again emphasised the fact that the mounds were often found in areas of loose dry soil or beside early earthworks, places where rabbits would have had little difficulty in establishing themselves without the construction of artificial warrens, although he acknowledged that there were many 'supporters of the rabbit-warren theory' (Crawford and Keiller 1928, 24). The regular shape of the mounds, and the fact that many exhibited signs of 'segmenting', likewise seemed hard to square with the 'warren' explanation. Above all, Crawford drew attention to the fact that the mounds were frequently associated with Iron Age and Roman sites, which seemed to suggest that the mounds were themselves 'of prehistoric or Romano-British date'. He did, however, note the 'remarkable' fact that local tradition at both High Beech and Minchinhampton held that the mounds had been built as warrens (Crawford and Keiller 1928, 23).

In the same year *Antiquity* published a short note from R.C. Bosanquet, of the RCAHM in Wales, in which various groups of pillow mounds were briefly described and evidence for the 'rabbit warren' hypothesis put forward. He discussed the mounds at Llanelwedd (Powys) and reported that 'a belief is current among some of the residents that they were formed as breeding-shelters for rabbits on their first introduction into the country nearly a century ago'. Bosanquet also quoted an account in Osgood MacKenzie's recently published *A Hundred Years in the Highlands* (1921) which described how, at the end of the eighteenth century, mounds of earth had been constructed when rabbits were being introduced into the Scottish highlands (Bosanquet 1928). In a footnote to the article, Crawford drew attention to the discussion of the subject which had just appeared in *Wessex from the Air* and commented: 'The evidence is conflicting, but the rabbit theory seems to be supported by a number of witnesses.'

By 1930 Crawford's position had shifted further. In that year Stuart Piggot published an article, again in *Antiquity*, on the earthworks on Butser Hill in Hampshire. These included a pillow mound, and Piggot rejected the 'warren' explanation in this particular case on the by now familiar grounds that 'although the hill swarms with rabbits, which find ample accommodation in the loose clay soil, not one of them has selected this mound for its home' (Piggot 1930, 199). Crawford, however, again commented in a footnote: 'I am now convinced that some pillow mounds at any rate were certainly built to provide accommodation for rabbits', quoting the evidence from Dartmoor, and particularly from Ditsworthy Warren, where the mounds were still 'full of rabbits'.

Yet some archaeologists, especially amateurs or those whose work was otherwise confined to relatively limited areas of the country, continued to have doubts. Francis Villy, after a lengthy study of mounds in the north of England carried out in the first decades of the century, published a short article in 1929 in the *Antiquaries Journal* in which he firmly rejected the 'rabbit warren' explanation (Villey 1929). In part his arguments were based on aspects of the mounds' internal construction, as revealed by excavations which he had carried out at Sutton-in-Craven (North Yorkshire) and at Norton Tower, Rylstone (North Yorkshire) (Villy 1912, 1921). Some of the mounds appeared to have been 'carefully built in layers, which pass unbroken through the mounds and have not been burrowed into by rabbits' (Villy 1929). The mounds, moreover, often contained more material than could have been excavated from the surrounding ditch, and in some cases this had evidently been brought to the site from a distance (a problem which Crawford himself had previously highlighted). Even more curious, however, was the fact that at Sutton fragments of pottery appeared to have been placed in layers within the mounds. In addition, a group of mounds would often include a broader example, 'almost square as a rule, and surrounded by a fosse and vallum which are sometimes so close to the mound that the nature of the latter is not apparent, and the whole looks like a "camp"'. But once again it was the location, and associations, of the mounds which seemed the strongest argument against the 'warren' explanation:

> Associated with the groups are (i) most often long, vague, and slight entrenchments ... (ii) prehistoric remains, especially barrows, and (iii) occasionally medieval remains. In Craven, where the mounds can be counted with certainty, they are always in threes or nines, and they are roughly orientated a little west of north, or at right angles to that direction ... Whatever the use of the mounds, their builders may have been influenced by some superstition which would explain the selection of sites, the presence of pottery, the numbers in the groups and their orientation (Villy 1929)

Villy suggested that these features hinted at 'a connexion with the dark ages about A. D. 700'.

While Crawford's acceptance of the warren explanation was qualified, some archaeologists in the 1930s were more forthright in their conviction that pillow mounds were warrens. In 1935 the great Cyril Fox, in a brief note on examples in Glamorganshire, was able to accept without question that they were 'constructed as artificial warrens, to establish rabbits in new areas, as a source of food and fur'. He admitted that 'a curious feature' of the mounds was that 'all are situated in areas whereon Early Man might be expected', but rather than seeing this as an indication that the mounds themselves were prehistoric he interpreted it as a consequence of the fact that 'from such areas the tide of human life had by the Middle Ages receded, and they were suitable for "warrens"' (Fox 1935, 220-23).

THE SHORTNESS OF MEMORY

Nevertheless, some professional archaeologists remained circumspect. In 1936 no less a scholar than Mortimer Wheeler discussed what he described as a 'somewhat puzzling series of mounds' in one of the RCHME volumes for Westmorland, examples of which had been recorded at Waitby, Ravenstonedale, Brampton, Mallerstrang, and elsewhere (Wheeler 1936, xxxv). He noted that such features had been christened 'pillow mounds' elsewhere in the country, and agreed that in many cases they had 'undoubtedly' been built to accommodate rabbits. But the Westmorland examples posed problems. Not only were most examples found in close association with hut-circles of presumed Iron Age or Roman date, but in addition they were called 'giant's graves' by the local inhabitants. In Wheeler's words, such a name:

> Implies a degree of antiquity and oblivion: for it was current by the middle of the last century, when the Ordnance Survey collected the names from local correspondents, and indicates the original purpose of the mounds ... was then forgotten (Wheeler 1936, xxxvi)

The Westmorland mounds were not the only examples which had, by the later nineteenth or early twentieth century, attracted fanciful or mythical names. Others include the 'Giant's Graves' at Swanage (Dorset), Wye (Kent), Llangrillo (Powys), and Sutton-upon-Derwent (North Yorkshire): the 'Soldiers' Graves' at Chirbury (Shropshire) and at various places in Powys; the 'Celtic Grave' at Cellan (Dyfed). Two examples at Llandeilofawr (Dyfed) were known as *Beddau'r Derwyddon*, 'the Druid's Graves'; one in Meifod (Powys) was described as 'Gwyddfarch's Bed', after a local saint; while the group of mounds on Bucklebury Common (Berkshire) was known as 'The Civil War Graves'. Some mounds had acquired more than one name. That in the middle of Warbstow Bury hillfort in Cornwall, for example, was recorded by the Ordnance Survey as the 'Giant's Grave', but by Allcroft in 1908 as 'King Arthur's Grave' (Allcroft 1908, 533). It is also known locally as 'King Arthur's Tomb'. In one story, it is the resting place of a giant who was killed when the giant of Launceston Castle threw a tool at him. Of course, there were examples of mounds which were widely considered to be redundant rabbit warrens by local people in the first half of the twentieth century. But the way that the origins of many could have been so completely forgotten is striking.

For we should not assume that such mounds were necessarily early examples, related to medieval rather than to post-medieval warrens. Most if not all of the Welsh mounds with such fanciful names seem to be of eighteenth- or nineteenth-century date. The 'Giants' Graves' at Ravenstonedale in Westmorland

(Cumbria) are particularly noteworthy in this respect. The Ordnance Survey described them as 'Giant's Graves' in the mid-nineteenth century but they had certainly been a functioning warren half a century earlier, when Pringle, in his *General View of the Agriculture of the County of Westmoreland*, noted how 'A few rabbits are kept in the neighbourhood of Brough and Orton, and there is a small warren at Ravenstonedale, but it is rare to see them in other parts of Westmoreland' (Pringle 1794, 332) (the mounds at Brampton, it should also be noted, lie only *c*.10km from Brough).

These indications of 'antiquity and oblivion' were thus misleading. The rural memory was evidently short – unless nineteenth- and twentieth-century surveyors, and archaeologists, were simply misled by humorous local inhabitants, or imposed their own layer of mythical nomenclature upon the landscape. Certainly, the extent to which some researchers strove to ignore the more practical testimony of local residents regarding the origins of the mounds, while confidently expounding their own fanciful interpretations, could be remarkable. When Hazeldine Warren excavated the examples at High Beech in 1924 he went out of his way to ignore the evidence of the obvious, as he proposed his theory that they were 'ritual structures' of Iron Age date. He noted that the area had been 'enclosed and preserved as a rabbit warren up to the time that Epping Forest was taken over by the Corporation of London', and even went so far as to describe, in a memorable phrase, how 'Several old inhabitants of unimpeachable veracity are confident that the mounds were made within their own memory to serve the purpose of artificial rabbit warrens' (Warren 1926, 221). Other opponents of the 'warren' hypothesis in the pre-war period similarly ignored the evidence for the obvious. Francis Villy, as convinced as Warren that pillow mounds could never have been constructed as rabbit accommodation, published a plan in his article in the *Bradford Antiquary* showing the group of mounds at Rathmell lying within an area clearly labelled 'Coney Garth' (Villy 1912, 341). On the other hand, some evidence shows that by the early twentieth century even professional warreners could be puzzled by the function of pillow mounds, and other aspects of the archaeology of warrens. Hadrian Allcroft was shown the remains of funnel walls for vermin traps within the hillfort at Dolebury Warren by the warrener, features which he described as 'some small "dry dykes" arranged saltire-fashion in convenient hollows of the camp'. The warrener:

> Laughed at the perplexities of wiseacres who had mistaken these for ancient vestigia. ... It is all as obvious as can be; but when the box has vanished, and Nature has had a century or so in which to tumble the walls about ... then the obvious is not altogether so obvious (Allcroft 1908, 690-1)

And yet the warrener interpreted these not as the remains of vermin traps, but of *rabbit* traps; and he was presumably unable to enlighten Allcroft concerning the true character of the various pillow mounds within the fort, 'built with mathematical straightness', which had been interpreted by some as the remains of a Roman fort but which Allcroft simply found perplexing, although he noted with customary perspicacity: 'One is tempted to attribute them to a comparatively recent date' (Allcroft 1908, 693).

THE POST-WAR PERIOD: CONTINUING DOUBTS AND CONFUSION

By the middle decades of the twentieth century few archaeologists doubted that *most* earthworks of pillow mound form were constructed as warrens. But many continued to believe that *some* were not, arguing or implying that this class of earthwork included a range of monuments with very varying origins. In part this was because excavated mounds continued to exhibit features, such as internal stone lines or 'unburrowed' layers, which appeared incompatible with their function as rabbit accommodation. When in 1950 F. Willett and T. Seddon excavated the mounds on Everage Clough near Burnley they thus concluded:

> The excavations did not produce any evidence for the date of the mounds, but they are comparable with many other groups of pillow mounds, in that they are close to a medieval manor. ... In this position they are sometimes thought to be rabbit-warrens. If the Everage Clough mounds were built for this purpose they were never used for it. The intercalated layers of shale showed no signs of disturbance, as they could not have failed to do if rabbits had burrowed in them ... (Seddon and Willett 1953, 199)

The excavators considered that the mounds might have been constructed as the bases for bracken stacks (a suggestion which had already been made by archaeologists of the Ordnance Survey with reference to some examples in Westmorland (Wheeler 1936, xxxvi)), although they noted that this practice was unrecorded in the local area. More importantly, they drew attention to the wide variations in form, size and regularity exhibited by the features classed as pillow mounds and argued that:

> Before much progress is made a survey of this ragbag of field archaeology is necessary. The many types of pillow mounds need classifying according to their outward form, and the validity of the classification checked by excavation (Seddon and Willett 1953, 199)

Certainly, excavated mounds continued to display a bewildering variety of features, and to be interpreted in a wide range of ways. In 1955 the Axbridge Caving and Archaeological Society excavated one of a group of three mounds on Shute Shelve, to the north of Axbridge (Sylvester 1956). These had been identified by Leslie Grinsell, the leading expert on prehistoric barrows, as possible pillow mounds but the excavator nevertheless considered that they had 'barrow characteristics'. The discovery that the mounds were carefully built structures, with a 'well-laid retaining wall' and a capping of large stones, suggested that they had not simply been raised for rabbits to live in. Nor was it not only local amateurs who interpreted particular mounds as funerary monuments. Shortly before the First World War, as already noted, the rector of Llanelwedd, the Rev D. Edmondes-Owen, had excavated one of a group of pillow mounds on Carneddau Hill, Llanelwedd (Powys). His report on the excavations has not survived but the contents of the mound, which included burnt bones, convinced him that it was a prehistoric burial mound. In the 1960s the Royal Commission on Ancient and Historical Monuments in Wales was alerted to the fact that further pillow mounds on the hill were about to be destroyed by quarrying, and promptly excavated two of them. Both overlay the lines of stones already described (above, p.40), but one in addition contained over 100 sherds of Neolithic pottery. C.J. Spurgeon was well aware that other mounds in the region – on Cefn Cul and at Ystradfellte – were unquestionably warrens, and probably quite recent, nineteenth-century ones at that. But the unexpected discovery of the lines of stone, coupled with the fragments of Neolithic pottery and the reports of Edmondes-Owen's excavations, made him entertain for a short while the possibility that 'Though most pillow mounds must be artificial rabbit warrens ... some long low mounds indistinguishable from them are, in fact, a type of Neolithic burial mound' (Spurgeon 1969).

Field archaeologists, as well as excavators, continued to voice doubts over whether pillow mounds were, indeed, really all the same thing. The RCHME noted a number of examples which displayed features which did not appear to fit in with the rabbit warren explanation. Some, as at Croydon-cum-Clopton in Cambridgeshire, seemed to sit neatly within areas of ridge and furrow with which they appeared to be contemporary. Many mounds continued to be discovered in 'superfluous' locations, further fuelling doubts about their function. In 1974 even Christopher Taylor, in his masterly *Fieldwork in Medieval Archaeology*, while recognising that some long, low mounds (as on Dartmoor, or in Ashdown Forest) were warrens, could write of the generality of pillow mounds:

> These were first noted and described by O.G.S. Crawford in Wessex and subsequently they have been found all over the British Isles in every type of country and in every conceivable position. But even now, although we can be sure

that they are of medieval date, we have no clear idea of their purpose, and neither excavation nor documentary research have enlightened us so far (Taylor 1974, 28)

The following year the RCHM volume for Northamptonshire was able to state that 'their exact date and purpose remains enigmatic'. Popular accounts also continued to hold back from fully embracing the 'warren' interpretation. James Dyer's *Archaeological Guide to Southern Britain*, for example, defined pillow mounds as 'small oblong mounds of uncertain age or purpose: possibly constructed in medieval times as artificial rabbit-warrens' (Dyer 1973, xxxi). As late as 1998 Paul Ashbee, one of the leading experts on long barrows, would only go so far as to state that 'Pillow mounds were possibly artificial rabbit warrens' (Ashbee 1998, 2). It is not surprising then, that pillow mounds, and other aspects of the archaeology of warrens, continued to be misinterpreted by excavators and others throughout the second half of the twentieth century.

WARRENS AS BUILDINGS

Pilsdon Pen is a fine multivallate hillfort in Dorset occupying a commanding situation nearly 300m above sea level. Within the fort are a number of pillow mounds, four rather narrow examples of which, in the centre, are arranged in the form of a square. The site was excavated by Peter Gelling in the 1960s and a series of interim reports published in the *Proceeding of the Dorset Archaeological and Natural History Society*, with a final report appearing in the *Proceeding of the Prehistoric Society* in 1977 (Gelling 1965, 1966, 1967, 1968, 1969, 1970, 1971; Gelling 1977). As part of the excavations the area occupied by three of the four central mounds was stripped down to the 'natural'. Beneath them two kinds of features were found, cut into the natural clay: curvilinear gulleys with U-shaped profiles, similar to those already examined elsewhere in the hillfort, which were evidently the sites of Iron Age huts; and 'flat-bottomed straight-sided slots more or less neatly cut in the clay which are interpreted as sleeper trenches', that is, the slots in which the base timbers of a timber-framed building had been laid (Gelling 1977, 270). These were unquestionably superimposed on, and therefore later than, the circular huts.

The slots seemed to define some kind of rectilinear structure which ran underneath the three excavated mounds and also, presumably, beneath the fourth unexcavated one: 'the plan of this timber structure is followed very closely by the mounds which eventually marked the square, but it must be emphasised that the evidence suggests very strongly that the mound was a later feature, and never co-existed with the timbering as part of a single structure' (Gelling 1977, 276). The north-eastern side, which was at least 29m long, consisted of a single slot, from which lateral projections ran at intervals, normally not quite at right angles to it. On the north-western side, in contrast — which was around 55m long — there were two or in places three parallel slots, linked at intervals by transverse trenches, and again with lateral projections at intervals (*69*). The south-western side, 34m in length, had one and, in places, a second long slot, again with links and projections. The slots seemed to define a building ranged around at least two sides of a courtyard, with the third side defined by no more than a substantial fence. The character of the fourth side, beneath the unexcavated mound, remained uncertain (Gelling 1977, 276-81). Yet it was a curious building, especially the north-western range. In spite of its considerable length this was little more that a metre wide, and was divided at irregular intervals by transverse walls. In Gelling's somewhat puzzled words, 'The simplest solution would appear to be to regard it as a range of store rooms: it certainly does not seem to be suitable for any obvious kind of human activity' (Gelling 1977, 282). Indeed, the fact that after the building had been taken down — possibly still uncompleted — its position was marked by the low mounds hinted at some kind of 'ritual' significance. 'The mounds can never have been a serious obstacle, but only a token demarcation, which suggests that the area inside them was in some sense a *temenos*, an area set apart from secular usage, whose limits were respected without the need for an effective barrier' (Gelling 1977, 281).

The complex of 'beam slots' uncovered by Gelling is so similar to the artificial burrow systems excavated at Danebury, or at Y Foel, that there would be little doubt, even without the presence of the overlying mounds, that this is indeed the remains of a rabbit warren, presumably of post-medieval date. Gelling's dating of the 'rectilinear building' to the late Iron Age rested on the fact that the principal sleeper trench on its the south-western side coincided with two pits containing sling-stones in a way that suggested purposeful association. But he admitted that the chronological relationship between pits and trench was by no means clear: one was 'taken to be later than the sleeper trench, though not on conclusive grounds, and the chronological relationship between the trench and the other was quite uncertain' (Gelling 1977, 277). The overlying mounds were, in spite of initial reservations, eventually deemed to be late Iron Age on the grounds that 'in the region of the more southerly of the two pits containing sling stones ... a collection of nearly 1,000 slingstones lay on top of the mound immediately under the humus' (Gelling 1977, 281). An alternative explanation would be that the pits were earlier than both mound and trenches, and that the contents of the more southerly pit had, at some point in the past, been partially redeposited by the action of rabbits. Indeed, Gelling noted that in this precise area 'there had been a considerable amount of disturbance by rabbits', something which had also served to obscure the outline of some of the lateral projecting 'slots' (Gelling 1977, 276).

WARRENS AND ARCHAEOLOGISTS

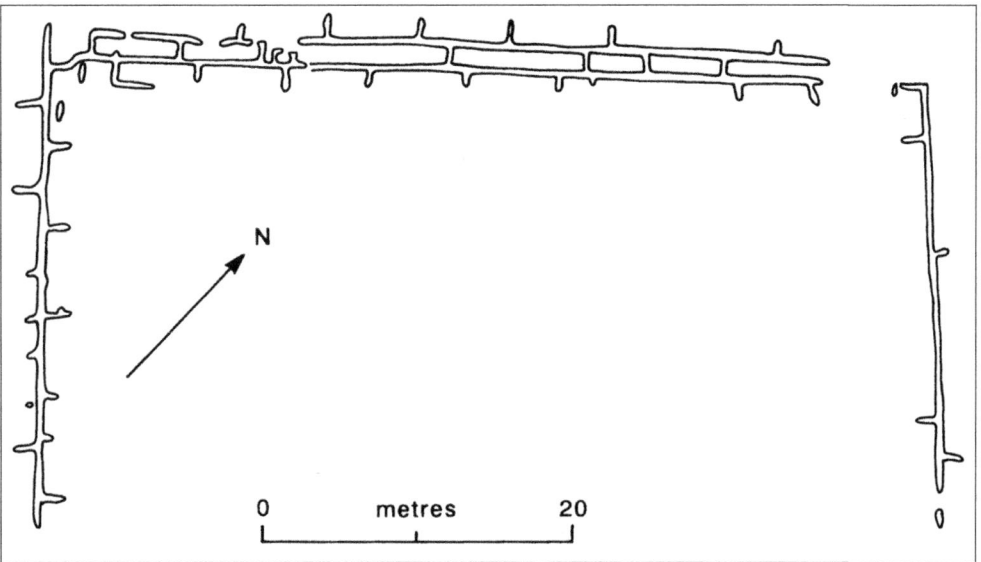

69 A complex of artificial burrows revealed when a group of conjoined pillow mounds within the hillfort at Pilsdon Pen in Dorset was excavated in the 1970s. The networks of slots were interpreted as the remains of an Iron Age 'ritual' building (after P. Gelling)

The rabbits, as at Y Foel (above, p.44), had evidently expanded their burrows beyond the original, man-made tunnels. It is perhaps surprising that this evidence for rabbit occupation, as well as the presence of what were unquestionably pillow mounds elsewhere in the hillfort, did not alert the excavator to the real significance of his discovery. But his confusion is, to a large extent, understandable given that this was an archaeological 'first'. It was the first occasion, that is, on which a more or less complete sub-mound warren complex was carefully excavated and planned, and the lack of *comparanda*, coupled with the location of the warren within an Iron Age hillfort, clearly explains the nature of the conclusions reached.

Gelling's discovery soon entered the wider archaeological literature. Barry Cunliffe, in his seminal *Iron Age Communities in Britain*, refers in passing to the 'pre-Roman sanctuary' at Pilsdon Pen (Cunliffe 1974, 259) while at a more popular level, Dyer's *Southern Britain: an archaeological guide*, published in 1973, discussed the 'rectilinear building' here. A more extended treatment appeared in an article published by Warwick Rodwell in 1978 concerning the character of later Iron Age buildings in lowland Britain (Rodwell 1978). In this, the Pilsdon Pen building is described as 'one of the most outstanding structures in later British prehistory':

The excavator saw this structure merely as a fenced 'tenemos' supported by buttresses and having a range of long narrow store rooms on the north west side. It is surely better identified as a large courtyard building, probably square in plan, and having aisled ranges which contained a large number of small rooms
(Rodwell 1978, 34)

Shallow, relatively narrow 'beam slots' excavated on archaeological sites, particularly within hillforts, should perhaps always be treated with some suspicion, especially where they are poorly dated, rectilinear, and appear to come late in the stratigraphical sequence. The remains of warrens can also, however, cause confusion when recorded from the air. At Mount Down in Hampshire aerial photographs revealed what appeared to be a group of Anglo-Saxon houses associated with a prehistoric field system (Hampton 1981). A subsequent geophysical survey, carried out in 1981-2, confirmed the outlines of the 'houses' as planned from the aerial photographs, but also detected a number of strong magnetic anomalies associated with the features. These were provisionally interpreted as masses of daub, burnt *in situ* when the buildings were abandoned (Clarke *et al.* 1983). However, 'The dearth of archaeological finds, the unusual compactness and disposition of the strongly magnetic signals, and the lack of magnetic enhancement of the soil in the area of a 'building' apparently associated with much burning, all combined to indicate that something was wrong' (Clarke *et al.* 1983, 123). A portion of the site was then excavated and the features were revealed to be part of a 'large, artificially created rabbit-warren complex'. The outlines of the buildings turned out to be rectangular ditched enclosures which the excavators believed had never contained overlying mounds but which, in terms of size and shape, were clearly closely related to pillow mounds. In addition, there was a 'system of chalk-cut drains which were covered over with chalk blocks and at the time of construction had been deliberately back-filled': evidently an artificial burrow complex of the kind excavated at Danebury or Pilsdon Pen. One of the magnetic anomalies was caused by 'a tangled and partly disintegrated mass of chicken wire', apparently used to block off one end of a 'drain' (Clarke *et al.* 1983, 124).

PILLOW MOUNDS AS 'RITUAL MOUNDS'

Some mounds excavated during the second half of the twentieth century were, as in earlier decades, interpreted as 'ritual features'. The hillfort of Croft Ambrey in Herefordshire is one striking example. Large parts of the enclosure were systematically excavated by Stan Stanford in the 1960s and a number of important discoveries made, including numerous rectangular wooden huts or granaries laid

WARRENS AND ARCHAEOLOGISTS

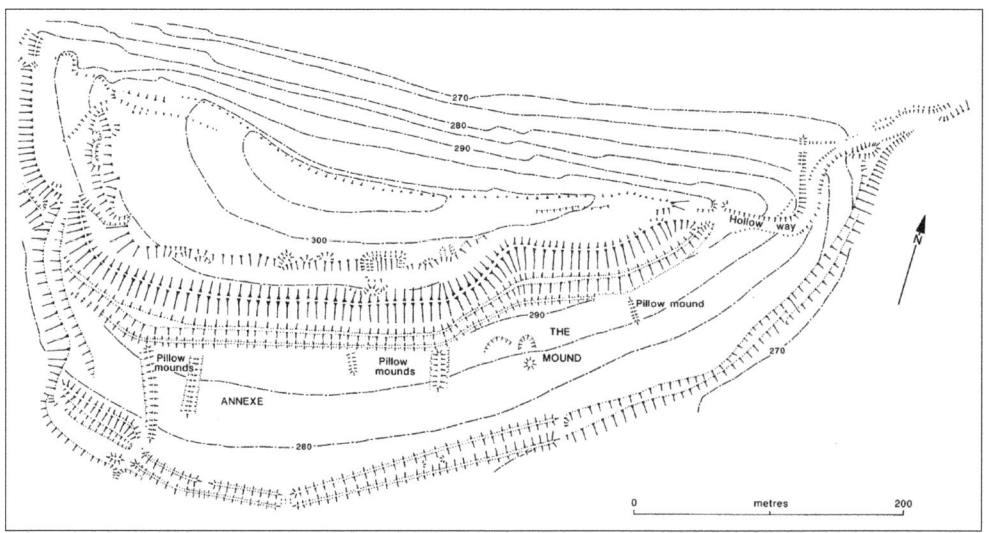

70 Plan of the hillfort at Croft Ambrey, showing the distribution of pillow mounds within the outer enclosure, and the location of the 'ritual mound'

out in orderly rows (Stanford 1974). In the later stages of the campaign Stanford turned his attention to the hillfort's outer annexe, which covers some 4.5ha. Here, below the main rampart, at least five pillow mounds were scattered. Their character was clearly appreciated by the excavator, for they are prominently labelled on the site plan included in the excavation report — indeed, they had been recognised as pillow mounds as early as 1934 by the Royal Commission (RCHM(E) 1934, 13). But among them was a low, circular mound which he (although not apparently the RCHM) considered to be different in character (*70*). This Stanford decided to excavate, in the hope that it 'might be the barrow of an early hill-fort prince in whose grave material might be found both to date the invasions thought to be responsible for the establishment of Croft Ambrey and to indicate the cultural associations of the newcomers' (Stanford 1974, 131). In the event the mound was found not to be a barrow, but — in the excavator's opinion — a ritual feature. It overlay a levelled terrace, on which fires had been lit and stakes erected, apparently as part of ceremonial activities. Large numbers of sherds from the immediately adjacent area indicated the ritual destruction of pottery, while quantities of burnt animal bones suggested that sacrifices had taken place (Stanford 1974, 133-6).

The mound was raised immediately above this terrace. It was circular, about 11.6m across and just over a metre high, and was bounded on its southern, downhill side by a rectilinear stone kerb. The mound had been dug into on a number of occasions and at one point contained two 'small, intersecting holes': similar features were found penetrating the terrace beneath (Stanford 1974, 138).

Stanford suggested that the mound must have replaced the terrace as a focus for ritual activities, but noted that 'there had also been some change in the nature of the ceremonies that took place here. They do not seem to have involved the same amount of fire lighting as before' or, indeed, the same amount of pot breaking. He believed that the activities on the terrace could be dated to the early Roman period and thus indicated the continued importance of the fort as a religious focus for local communities. The mound itself could not be dated with certainty but Stanford suggested that it was probably late Roman.

Whatever the meaning of the features and artefacts found beneath it, there is little doubt that the mound itself was constructed as rabbit accommodation. The fact that other pillow mounds occur within the outer annexe of the fort, and that the 'ritual' mound fits rather neatly into their distribution, is in itself suggestive. The dry-stone retaining kerb, the 'intersecting holes' and the fact that (to judge from the published cross-section) the mound was constructed of a number of distinct layers of material, are all noteworthy features. The pits dug into the mound may represent attempts to recover rabbits or ferrets. There is no reason to believe that the feature was ritual in character: there was no evidence that it was used in a similar way as the ground surface beneath, and in particular 'no sign of any occupation surface or features such as hearths or post holes was found in the course of the careful excavation of the top'. Nor is there any evidence that the mound was erected over the terrace while this was still in use, or indeed that it was Roman at all: 'quite a pronounced turf-line' had developed before the mound was erected (Stanford 1974, 138).

A perhaps more important example of a 'ritual mound' was excavated in the late 1970s and early 80s within another Iron Age hillfort, Crickley Hill in Gloucestershire. Its excavator, Philip Dixon, suggested that it was of Neolithic date. The feature remains only partially published, in interim reports and in the popular archaeological press, and is thus difficult to discuss in detail, but in essence it comprises a long, low mound surrounded by a shallow ditch, with large stones placed at intervals around its perimeter. It contains material brought to the site from elsewhere and overlies the beam slots of a number of 'timber fences' (Dixon 1981, 1985, 2005). The survival of such a slight earthwork within an area fairly intensively occupied in the Iron Age might itself be enough to raise doubts about the real antiquity of this 'ritual feature': but a more thorough discussion must await the final publication of the site.

PILLOW MOUNDS, BARROWS AND MORTUARY ENCLOSURES

The Crickley mound, if indeed it is a pillow mound, is by no means unique in being interpreted as a Neolithic ritual feature. On the face of it there should be only a very small possibility of confusing pillow mounds with long barrows, the most familiar form of Neolithic 'ritual' mound. Long barrows are generally more substantial and less markedly flat-topped than pillow mounds, and are often higher at one end (usually the eastern). Unlike pillow mounds, moreover, they normally have quarry ditches which run only along the sides of the mound, rather than all around it (Ashbee 1970). Confusion arises from two things. Firstly, while the majority of warren mounds are indeed relatively slight features, often less than a metre in height, there are some rather larger examples, on Dartmoor for example, and at places like Ascott in Buckinghamshire or Sutton Common in Suffolk. These can, on occasions, reach a height of around two metres, thus overlapping in dimensions with the more diminutive examples of long barrows. Secondly, research over the last three decades has demonstrated the existence of a range of Neolithic monuments related to, but significantly different from, classic long barrows. These include the rectangular ditched enclosures often referred to as 'mortuary enclosures' and, merging imperceptibly into these, low rectangular turf mounds ditched all around their periphery (Loveday and Petchey 1982; Kenward 1982).

A typical example was excavated by David Buckley and associates at Rivenhall (Essex) in 1986 (Buckley *et al.* 1988). It appeared as a crop-mark enclosure, 'very regular in plan, with parallel sides and rounded corners', enclosing an area some 49m in length and 16m in width (*71*) (Buckley *et al.* 1988, 77). As with a pillow mound, the ditch was continuous, with no sign of any entrance causeway. Four sections were cut through this and the character of the fill suggested that the central area had once carried a low mound or bank, which had eroded into the ditches. Finds of Neolithic pottery and flint were made from the lower fill, but these could not necessarily provide a firm date for the feature because fieldwalking revealed that such material was abundant in the surrounding ploughsoil. The rectangular enclosure is located on a terrace of sandy gravel overlain by brickearth and – typically for such monuments – close to cropmarks of other prehistoric features, circular enclosures and ploughed-out round barrows. But this kind of association, of course, is common with pillow mounds. Moreover, the enclosure's highly regular shape, and its size (slightly wide for a typical pillow mound, but within the known range); the fact that its ditches were, in most places, vertically sided and with a flat bottom, unlike the more U-shaped ditches usually associated with early monuments, dug without the aid of iron spades; as well as the fact that they had been re-cut on a number of occasions; might all be grounds for suspicion. This is especially true given the monument's location, on a river terrace a few hundred metres to the south of a place called Durwards Hall. Little is known of the land-use history of the immediate area but it is noteworthy that the field immediately to the north-east is still known as 'Durward's Common', that to the west as 'Durward's Park' – both names suggesting precisely the kinds of location

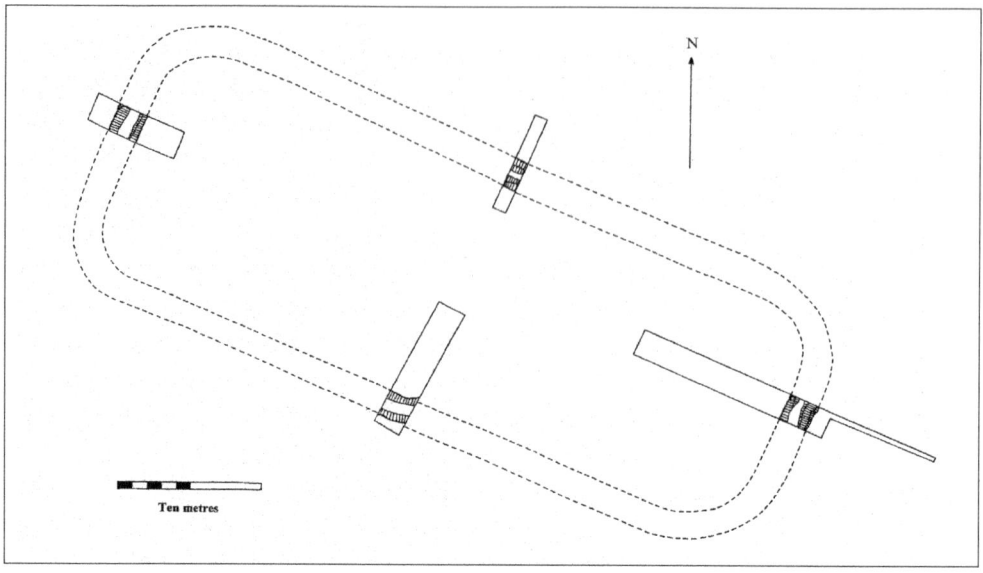

71 Plan of the Neolithic rectangular enclosure at Rivenhall, Essex, excavated by David Buckley and colleagues (after D. Buckley)

in which warrens were created. Moreover, in Essex – a county largely occupied by poorly draining clay soils – warrens were often placed on freely draining terraces overlooking rivers. The Knights Templars' warren at Cressing, for example, some eight kilometres to the north-west, occupied a situation almost identical to that of the Rivenhall 'enclosure' (Hunter 1999, 116). None of this proves that the latter was a pillow mound, and on balance it probably wasn't one. But it is curious that the possibility was not even considered in the excavation report.

Similar cropmarks have been recorded, and in some cases excavated, at a number of places in England, including Lawford, Birch, and Feering in Essex; Roughton in Norfolk; Stratford in Suffolk; and Charlecote in Warwickshire (*72*). Examples have been noted as far west as mid-Devon (Buckley *et al.* 1988; Loveday and Petchey 1982; Griffith 1985). Most clearly are of early prehistoric date, but it is not impossible that some represent ploughed-out pillow mounds from which, indeed, they can be indistinguishable on morphological and locational grounds. But it is not only with ploughed-out mounds and cropmarks that confusion can arise. Some low, relatively narrow mounds which remain as upstanding features, and which are currently dated to the Neolithic, could well be pillow mounds. One example is the unexcavated 'bank barrow' on Penn Hill near Wells in Somerset. This lies a short distance (*c.*50m) from, and *appears* to be aligned on, the more substantial Penn Hill Long Barrow (Grinsell 1971, 86). But its flat top, relatively narrow width (*c.*9m) and sharp profile (its ditches are still clearly visible,

WARRENS AND ARCHAEOLOGISTS

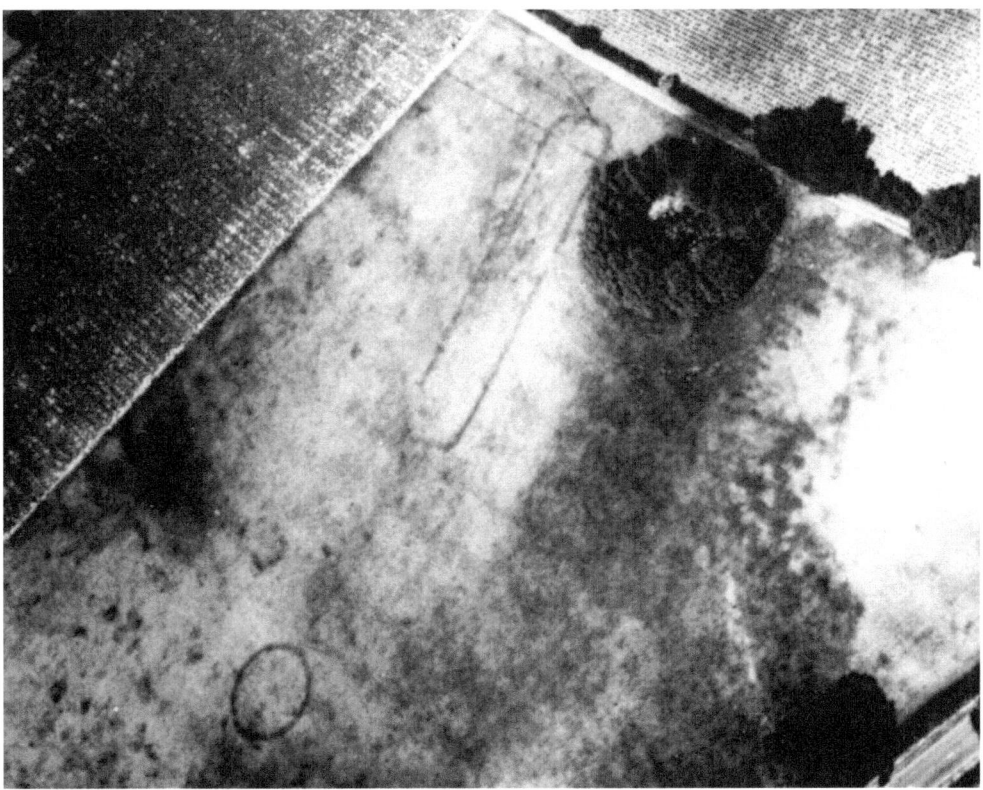

72 A rectangular mortuary enclosure of Neolithic date at Charlecote in Warwickshire, with associated ring ditch

in sharp contrast to those of the – supposedly roughly contemporary – long barrow) strongly suggest that it is, in fact, a rather elongated warren mound. It is, at 200m, long for a pillow mound: but similarly elongated examples do occur, in south-east England and sporadically elsewhere.

Further potential confusion arises from the way that warreners sometimes added pillow mounds to existing barrows. The long barrow called Adam's Grave in Alton Barnes (Wiltshire) thus has two possible pillow mounds built into its sides, while a short distance away another pillow mound runs between, and links, two round barrows (73). The difficulty here is that some barrows and cairns of Neolithic or Bronze Age date had 'tails' or terraces added to them relatively soon after their construction, part of the evolving ceremonial use of these sites. Examples include the excavated chambered cairns at Bryn yr Hen Bobl (Anglesey), Tullach an t'Sionnach (Caithness), Great Ayton Moor (North Yorkshire), and Long Low (Derbyshire): in all cases except the last the extensions were relatively flat topped, less than 1m in height, and 6-9m in width (Williamson and Loveday 1988, 306-9;

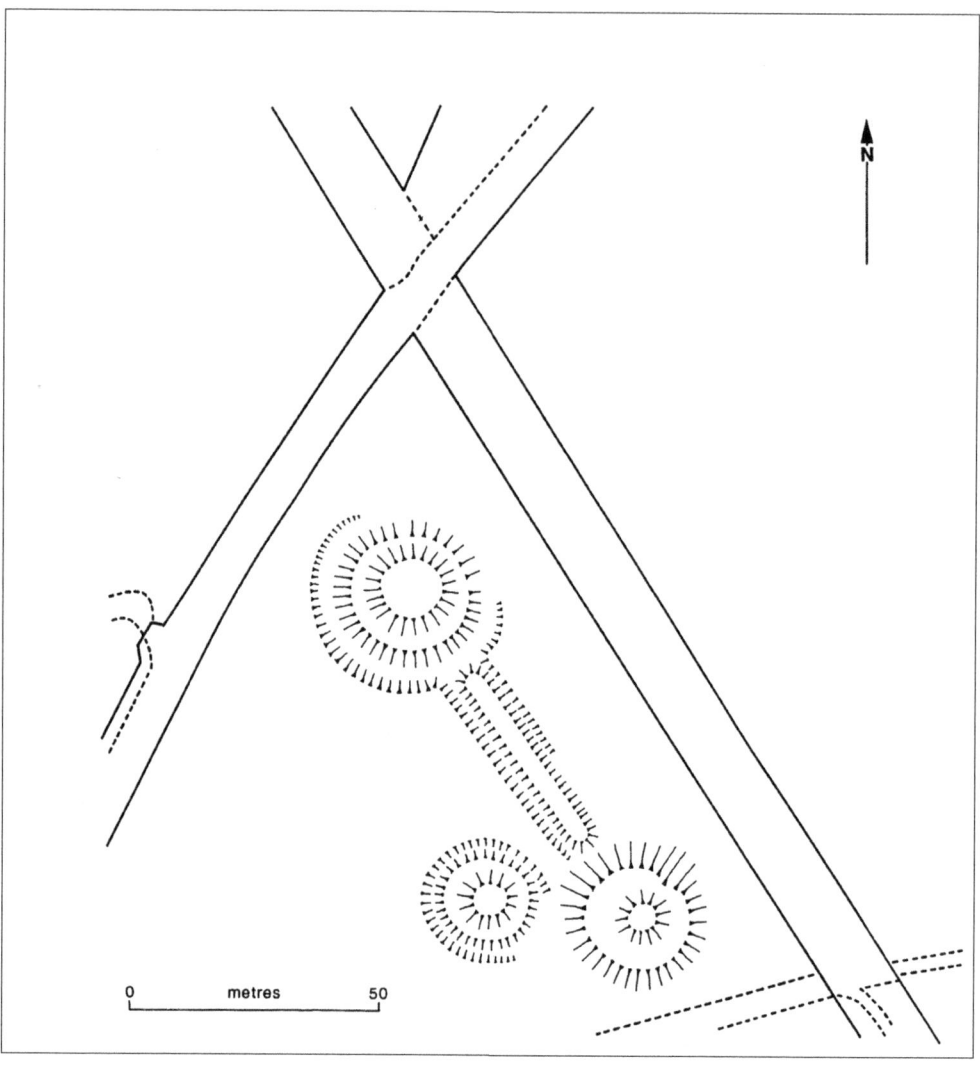

73 A pillow mound, closely associated with a small group of Bronze Age round barrows, at Alton Barnes, Wiltshire

Hayes 1967; Hemp 1935). 'Tails' of less certain character are known from round barrows in south-east England, including the two examples associated with the Combe Hill causewayed enclosure, Willingdon, East Sussex. Again, it is by no means impossible that some 'extensions' of this type represent additions made by warreners. When the Capo long barrow in Aberdeenshire was recently surveyed attention was drawn to the low, slightly disturbed mound which formed a thinner 'extension' to the barrow's eastern end. Resistivity and topographic survey were unable to throw any light on its origins and purpose, but its dimensions – 45m in length, 15m across and *c.*1.5m high – are suggestive; so too the fact that both barrow, and mound, are surrounded by a series of rectilinear ditches and banks 'which form a trapezoidal enclosure', earthworks which are clearly of post-medieval date. Both mound and barrow were much disturbed by rabbit burrows (Collier and Bruce 2003).

There is thus some potential for confusing pillow mounds with low Neolithic mounds and mortuary enclosures. On the face of it, warren mounds should not be confused so easily with long barrows of more normal form, for the reasons already outlined. But there are some examples. The rectangular mound within Warbstow Bury hillfort (Cornwall), for example, was for a long time considered to be a possible long barrow, in part because of its archaic folk name (above, p.135), but is now accepted as a pillow mound. In 1982 John Barrett and Philip Reader reported the discovery of a large, long mound buried in woodland on the Yorkshire Wolds. It was around 2m high, reaching nearly 3m at the downslope end (Barrett and Reader 1982). But, in typical warren mound form, at its widest it was only 15m across, narrowing to 10m towards the centre; it was ranged roughly at right angles to the contours; and it lay within an area called Melton Warren. Barrett and Reader argued that the feature 'does not resemble a warren', and it is true that it does not resemble a typical pillow mound. Yet in height and width it is comparable to warren mounds like that on Sutton Heath (east Suffolk) (above, p.104) and, without excavation, its true character must remain uncertain. Even some long-accepted, apparently certain examples of long barrows, might be worth another look. On Nine Barrows Hill near Corfe (Dorset) there is a group of 17 round barrows and a single long mound strung out along the ridge. The mound is interpreted as a long barrow but its size (34.1m long, a mere 12.2m wide and only 0.9m high) suggests that it may be a pillow mound, a number of examples of which are known from the immediate locality (Dyer 1973, 97; RCHM 1970, 443). Another good example is the scheduled long barrow in the area called the Querns, immediately to the west of the Roman amphitheatre in Cirencester. This is 55m long, 15m wide but nowhere more than a metre in height. The survival of a genuine long barrow in such a situation – 'within an area of Roman quarrying, adjacent to a Roman road, and on the edge of a known Roman cemetery' – would be remarkable, and in a recent assessment of the monument Tim Darvill concluded that it is, indeed, a pillow mound (Darvill and Holbrook 1994, 40; Gerrard 1994, 118).

OTHER CONFUSIONS

In a host of other ways pillow mounds, and other relics of rabbit farming, have caused confusion to archaeologists. Where pillow mounds, especially those of abnormally large dimensions, occur in hilly terrain they have sometimes been mistaken for defensive earthworks. The most important example is at Streatley in Bedfordshire, where two lengths of bank separated by c.36m – one 33m long, and 6-8m wide, the other 58m long and 10-13m wide – appear to be the remains of a rampart which served to cut the promontory called (significantly) Sharpenhoe Clapper off from the main mass of the Chilterns Hills to the south. The site was identified as a 'British Camp' as long ago as 1874 (Dix 1983, 65) although the banks are fairly low features, ranging in height from 0.7-c.1.8m. The site continued to be recognised as a hillfort throughout the twentieth century, Dyer in 1973 for example describing it as a small promontory fort commanding:

> Superb views of central Bedfordshire. A wide, flat ditch and damaged (possibly unfinished) rampart cut off the tree-covered fort spur from the main hill mass to the south. The steep hill-slopes on three sides must have provided sufficient protection to require no obvious fortifications (Dyer 1973, 4)

The 'rampart' was excavated in 1979 by Brian Dix (Dix 1983). It was found to be composed of alternate layers of soil and chalk rubble, the excavator suggesting that this material had been stripped from the areas either side of the bank, leaving the bare chalk bedrock exposed. Beneath the mound were two 'trenches', cut into the chalk and backfilled before the mound had been constructed. Dix interpreted them as 'drains' and the larger one may have been, although the narrower one to the south seems to have been an artificial burrow. The mound contained sherds of prehistoric and Roman, but also of medieval pottery, showing 'unarguably that at the point where it was sectioned, the bank is of medieval or later date' (Dix 1983, 72). 'Clapper' is first recorded as a name for the promontory in 1575 and Dyer concluded, surely correctly, that the earthworks had originally been constructed 'to encourage rabbits to inhabit the place and breed there'.

Equally striking is the monument known as Cockmoor Dykes on the Tabular Hills of North Yorkshire. This comprises 20 closely spaced parallel banks and ditches which run along the Troutsdale escarpment, part of an extensive system of late prehistoric boundary earthworks which delineate large territories in the limestone uplands. It has been suggested that only the six largest dykes are actually prehistoric: the other 14 seem to have been added later, perhaps in the eighteenth century when the area became a large warren, to provide accommodation for rabbits (Harris and Spratt 1991,193; Spratt 1989, 47-8). Perhaps more bizarrely, the impressive series of conjoined pillow mounds at Quarrendon, on the skyline above Aylesbury (below, p.169) was interpreted by Allcroft in 1908 as a Civil War gun emplacement (74):

> A line of entrenchments running chevron-wise along the crest of the high ground – a considerable vallum rising 4-5 feet, with gaps at intervals of 20 yards or so,

74 Quarrendon in Buckinghamshire. In the bottom-right corner is the edge of the earthworks marking the site of Quarrendon Hall and its gardens. The earthworks in the middle distance represent the site of a deserted medieval settlement. On the hill beyond are a number of pillow mounds. Those forming a long, conjoined line have been interpreted as the remains of a Civil War gun emplacement, facing the town of Aylesbury

marking the embrasures of a full dozen guns. A peculiar feature of these fieldworks is that the soil for the vallum was obtained from both sides, the trenches in front and in rear being equally deep (Allcroft 1908, 604)

Like many archaeological misinterpretations, this one, once established, was to run and run. Successive Ordnance Survey maps described the mounds as 'Civil War earthworks', and the interpretation was even repeated (albeit cautiously) by no less an authority than Maurice Beresford in an otherwise exemplary discussion of the important earthworks in the immediate area (Beresford 1958, 123).

Cross-shaped pillow mounds have, perhaps not surprisingly, caused their own particular brand of confusion. That at Banwell near Cheddar in Somerset, set within an earthwork enclosure, was described in some detail by Allcroft in 1908:

> A rectangular enclosure contained within a slight outer fosse and small vallum, measuring 55 yards by 45 yards, with a single entrance at the eastern end. The floor of the enclosure is quartered by a raised bank of earth about 2 feet in height and 10 to 12 feet in breadth, in the shape of a cross, the arms reaching almost to the surrounding vallum (Allcroft 1908, 555)

The monument had been discussed as early as 1810 by Richard Colt Hoare, who considered that 'its form proclaims it to be Roman', although he had no idea what its function might have been (Hoare 1810, 43). Others suggested that it was an 'agrimensorial cross', associated with Roman land surveying. The feature was for a time scheduled by English Heritage as a Roman camp. More recently, the historian Harry Jelley has argued – in an article published in *British Archaeology* – that the village of Banwell can be identified with *Bannaventa*, the birthplace of St Patrick, and that the cross was constructed 'by missionary Irish monks a few centuries after Patrick's lifetime' as a memorial to the saint (Jelley 1998). Local tradition offers another explanation. The people of Banwell tried to raise a cross on the hill, but the Devil repeatedly blew it down by raising great storms each night: eventually they came up with the solution of building one lying down on the ground (Tongue 1965). In reality, of course, there is little if any doubt (as the Somerset HER has long recognised) that the cross bank is a warren, and the surrounding enclosure almost certainly contemporary with it.

CONCLUSION

No apologies are offered for this somewhat extended treatment of the many and varied ways in which rabbit warrens have confused archaeologists over the years. The various reasons for this should by now be obvious. The most important is the simple fact that warreners made frequent use of existing earthworks as sites for warrens, thus ensuring that pillow mounds, artificial burrows and the rest were often brought into close association with a range of archaeological sites, especially hillforts, and frequently contain artefacts which provide archaeologists with misleadingly early dating evidence. Secondly, pillow mounds do have a broad resemblance to certain kinds of early prehistoric ritual or ceremonial site, especially the range of Neolithic monuments related to long barrows. Added to this is the fact that archaeologists have shown little real interest in pillow mounds, in spite of their prominence in the historic landscape, and thus still sometimes remain ignorant of the often complex character of their construction, and in particular of such things as retaining walls, stone capping, and artificial burrow systems. The mythical names and stories which have become associated with the mounds, in large measure due to their resemblance to barrows or graves, has contributed further confusion – a salutary reminder of the caution with which we should treat this kind of evidence as an indication of antiquity. But lastly, in a number of cases excavators in particular seem to have misled themselves, ignoring the obvious evidence for the modernity of particular mounds, reluctant perhaps to recognise that they have wasted time and money investigating recent and rather mundane features of the landscape. This is itself, of course, a manifestation of the lack of interest that many archaeologists share in the physical traces of practical and agrarian activities left by our comparatively recent ancestors.

6

THE SYMBOLISM OF THE WARREN

'INTERMEDIATE EXPLOITATION'

So far rabbit warrens have been discussed entirely in practical, economic terms. But, like other features in the landscape, they also had a symbolic significance – an iconography. The distinctive collection of features they contained – boundary banks, traps, mounds, lodges and the rest – were not only once familiar, but also *meant* something to contemporaries. Lodges stood removed and often remote from other settlements, prominent and striking features – especially on the more open warrens, located on heaths and moors. Not surprisingly they became an image of solitary isolation. In Shakespeare's *Much Ado About Nothing* Claudio is described as being 'as lonely as a lodge in a warren'. But rabbit warrens had other, more complex meanings and associations which we can now only recover with an effort.

It is difficult to consider the social and symbolic significance of rabbits separately from the wider exploitation of wild and semi-domesticated animals, such as deer or pigeons, in the historic period. In most agricultural societies, as a number of archaeologists have observed, the exploitation of wild resources is unnecessary for survival and hunting is therefore essentially a social action, restricted to an elite and thus expressive of status (Sykes 2004, 82-3; Kent 1989; Hamilakis 2003). This was certainly true in medieval and post-medieval England (Cummins 1988). But archaeologists and historians, it can be argued, have sometimes posited too sharp and simple a dichotomy between hunting and farming, and more generally between man and nature, the domesticated and the natural – Hodder's *domus* and *agrios* (Hodder 1990). In reality, throughout the Middle Ages, and well into the post-medieval period, much investment was poured into what we might call 'intermediate exploitation', that is, forms of livestock management which lay somewhere between the hunting of truly wild animals and the farming of fully domesticated ones (Williamson 1997). Such activities were, as much as true hunting, closely associated with, and largely if not entirely restricted to, the landed elite, and were likewise important symbols of status.

Medieval deer parks have received much attention from historians, geographers, and to a lesser extent archaeologists (Rackham 1986, 122-9; Stamper 1988; Birrell 1993). Like warrens, parks were enclosed areas, often on relatively marginal land, which usually contained a specialised building called a lodge, which served as a base for the park keeper. Their principal denizens, fallow deer, were – like the rabbit – a Norman introduction, and while some parks evidently existed in Anglo-Saxon England the majority were established, like warrens, from the twelfth century (Liddiard 2003). Beyond this, it might be thought that there was little resemblance between the two forms of land use. Most parks were well-wooded, while warrens had an open aspect; parks were high-status landscapes, not least because they were used for recreational hunting. But as we have seen some warrens – especially those associated with high-status residences – were well-treed wood-pastures; recent research has tended to emphasise the role of parks as venison farms, rather than just as hunting grounds (Birrell 1993); while, conversely, some warrens were used on occasions for recreational hunting. The two kinds of landscape thus had much in common.

From the twelfth and thirteenth century some deer parks formed part of the 'landscape of lordship' laid out around the greatest residences, especially castles and palaces (Liddiard 2000). But the majority lay in remote places, some way away from the homes of their owners, because they had been enclosed from the residual areas of woodland surviving towards the edges of the cleared and cultivated land. Surrounded by a substantial earthwork bank and fence, they were powerful symbols of lordly appropriation of the remaining areas of wild land. From the later fourteenth century, moreover, parks began to be more closely associated with manorial residences, and by the later seventeenth century most were to be found next to, or even surrounding, mansions. This change of location was associated with a change in appearance. These later parks were more open landscapes, and more carefully designed for visual effect, than their early medieval predecessors. By the start of the seventeenth century the well-wooded, isolated hunting grounds and venison farms of medieval times had largely disappeared (Williamson 1995, 22-4). Nevertheless, in the new and more ornamental parks deer continued to be exploited, managed and on occasions hunted.

Fish ponds were another form of elite food production, and again an important marker of status in medieval England (Dyer 1988). Purpose-built fish ponds may have existed from the early Middle Ages but they unquestionably increased in both numbers, and sophistication, from the later thirteenth century, when carp – yet another foreign import – became the principal fish kept within them (Currie 1991).

Fish ponds took a variety of forms but there was a broad distinction between the large ponds or *vivararia*, which were substantial affairs, often with massive retaining dams; and the smaller, usually rectangular *servatoria*, or holding ponds (Aston 1988). The latter were located close to manor houses and castles; the former often lay at a distance, frequently (like rabbit warrens) within deer parks, where they could be more effectively protected from poachers. Fish ponds continued to be maintained in both locations in the sixteenth and seventeenth centuries, those close to the mansion now often doubling as ornamental 'basons' or 'canals' within formal, geometric gardens (Currie 1990).

Lastly, medieval and early post-medieval landowners usually kept dovecotes or *columbaria*, a privilege reserved by law to manorial lords: 'to erect a dove house or dovecote is the right onely & badge of a lordship or signorye', as one Norfolk landowner explained in the 1640s (NRO LeStrange ND 22.34). Given that pigeons gorged indiscriminately on the fields of landowner and tenants alike, this legal restriction is hardly surprising. Dovecotes provided a good source of year-round protein, for each pigeon produced two chicks between eight and ten times a year for six or seven years (Grant 1988, 186-7; McCann 1998). They also afforded a good supply of rich fertiliser, and for this reason dovecotes were often located within easy reach of gardens. But their symbolic significance was also considerable, and they were usually placed prominently in the vicinity of the manor house, a clear statement of manorial status and prestige.

Parks, fish ponds and dovecotes are often thought of as essentially medieval and early post-medieval phenomena but they continued to flourish, and may even have increased in economic and social importance, following the Restoration of 1660. Indeed, in many ways the period between 1660 and 1750 represents the heyday of 'intermediate exploitation'. The number of parks being created seems to have increased significantly in the late seventeenth century, and both dovecotes and fish ponds were regarded with renewed interest (Barley 1985, 647; Thirsk 1985, 575-6). The most comprehensive treatise on the latter subject, Roger North's *A Discourse on Fish and Fish Ponds*, was published as late as 1713 (North 1713), and many new ponds were constructed in the late seventeenth and early eighteenth century, archaeologically indistinguishable from those of medieval date. There was, moreover, a new form of 'intermediate exploitation', introduced from Holland at the start of the seventeenth century. 'Decoys' consisted of a number of curving 'pipes' – tapering channels covered by netting, supported on a framework of hoops made of wood or (later) iron – leading off from an area of open water. Each pipe terminated in a long bow-net which could be detached from the rest of the apparatus. Along one side of the pipe was a series of overlapping screens, usually made of wood and reeds, behind which the decoy man would conceal himself (Payne Galwey 1886; Wentworth Day 1954; Heaton 2001).

Wildfowl were lured into the net by using a combination of tame decoy ducks and a dog called a 'piper'. The former were trained to enter the pipe when commanded to do so by a low whistle from the decoy man; at the same time the dog would run around the screens, jumping over the low boards or 'dog jumps' placed between them. The wildfowl gathered near the mouth of the pipe were attracted towards what – to them – must have looked like an appearing and disappearing fox. Encouraged by the behaviour of the decoy ducks, they swam towards it. When they had proceeded some way, however, the decoy man would appear, waving his arms or a handkerchief and driving the birds in flight down the tapering pipe, and into the bow-net at the end. The earliest known decoy in England was at Waxham on the north-east coast of Norfolk where, as early as 1620, Sir William Wodehouse had constructed 'a device for catching DUCKS, known by the foreign name of a koye' (Payne Galwey 1886, 2). That at Purdis Farm, to the east of Ipswich, must be almost as old for it is mentioned in a lease of 1646 (ESRO HA 93/3/48). By the early eighteenth century decoys were widespread throughout the East Anglian Fens, in the Norfolk Broads, and in the coastal marshes of Suffolk and Essex. They also appeared in some numbers in the wetlands of western England, and at many coastal locations. Most were commercial ventures, leased to professional decoymen, but some were intended to supply the needs of great households, and were in some cases perhaps created more for polite recreation than for anything else.

The reasons for this post-Restoration resurgence of interest in the various forms of 'intermediate exploitation' were in part economic. This was a period of low population growth and thus low grain prices and, as Joan Thirsk has argued, in a period of depression it made sense to diversify production. Deer, rabbits, and the rest formed a useful alternative source of income for hard-pressed landowners (Thirsk 1985, 574-6). But there may also have been a political and ideological dimension (Williamson 1997). The Restoration of 1660 came after a long period of internal uncertainty and unrest – the Civil War and Interregnum – during which traditional rights and privileges had been threatened, and at times wider social revolution had seemed a real possibility. The various forms of 'intermediate exploitation' long monopolised by the aristocracy and gentry featured prominently in the struggles of the day. The deer parks of leading royalists, and those of the king himself, were sequestered by the revolutionary government, their timber felled and their deer destroyed. Ponds and dovecotes were casually trashed by parliamentary troops. Those stationed at Leamington, busy vandalising the dovecote belonging to Baron Trevor, told their commanding officer that:

> Pigeons were fowls of the air given to the sons of men, and all men had a common right in them that could get them, and they were as much theirs as the barons, and

therefore they would kill them ... and not part from their right: upon which the captain was so convinced by their arguments he could not answer them, and so came away, letting them do as they would (quoted in Thomas 1983, 49)

In the 1640s Parliament actually debated whether the manorial monopoly on keeping pigeons should be rescinded, although the move was opposed, one MP going as far as to argue that it would be a:

Blemish of government that the enferiour sort of people should assume that power and libertye wch in reason and policye of state ought to belonge to great estates and persons of qualitye and commission (NRO Le Strange ND 22.34)

Given all this, it is hardly surprising that the return of political stability at the Restoration of 1660, in the form of a modified version of the old order, saw a renewed interest in the exploitation, and ostentatious display, of these traditional symbols of status. Moreover, country houses in the sixteenth and seventeenth centuries continued, like their medieval predecessors, to be surrounded not only by enclosed geometric gardens but also by farm yards, nut grounds, orchards and kitchen gardens; features which, like dovecotes and fish ponds, vividly demonstrated to tenants and neighbours their owner's superior resources of production. The late seventeenth century was a period in which landowners prided themselves on maintaining their place in 'their country', closely involved in the productive life of their estates. In 1681, when John Evelyn visited Mr Denzil Onslow at Pyrford in Surrey, he was agreeably surprised by:

An extraordinary feast ... there was not any thing, save what his estate about it did afford, as Venison, Rabbits, Hairs, Pheasants, Partridges, Pigeons, Quale, Poultrie, all sorts of fowle in season (from his own decoy nere his house) ... all sorts of fresh fish. After dinner we went to see sport at the decoy (De Beer 1955, 255)

The period after $c.1750$, in contrast, saw a marked decline in elite interest in deer, rabbits, pigeons, fish and wildfowl, both as a form of domestic production and elite display, and as a way of making money. Meat was now becoming cheaper and more abundant, especially in winter, as a result of improvements in both the breeding and the feeding of domestic livestock. Sheep and cattle were now more likely to be fattened in the summer on improved pastures than on rough commons or fallows, and in the winter to be kept on turnips or clover hay. As a result, the appetite and the market for pigeons, carp and rabbits tended to decline. The gentry's loss of interest in such matters may also, however, have been fuelled by important social changes. Landowners were increasingly interested both in agricultural improvement, *and* in the organised hunting of wild animals like pheasants and foxes. The old forms of semi-domestication occupied an uncomfortable position between recreational hunting and scientific farming, and also (in the case of warrens in particular) often took up large areas of land which, with the new agrarian technologies now available, could be 'improved' and turned over to agriculture. Moreover, while many landowners thus embraced a fashionable interest in modern agriculture they no longer wished to associate their residences directly with farming and food production. Important changes in social organisation – the emergence, in particular, of a more horizontally stratified rather than vertically integrated society – ensured that they were keen to express the fact that their lifestyle was very different from that of the local farming community. By the middle of the century signs of direct involvement in agricultural production were being ostentatiously rejected (Williamson 1995). As the landscape parks of Lancelot 'Capability' Brown and his followers became the accepted setting for great houses not only were walled gardens thus swept away, but also fish ponds, nut grounds, orchards, dovecotes – and warrens. By the end of the eighteenth century the homes of the elite stood, 'solitary and disconnected' in an expansive, irregular, 'naturalistic' landscape of grass and scattered trees.

THE SYMBOLISM OF THE WARREN: THE WIDER COUNTRYSIDE

Rabbits were thus only one of several kinds of semi-domesticated animals the exploitation of which was the sole prerogative of the landed elite in medieval and early post-medieval England. But, so far as the evidence goes, while all of these were widely resented for the damage they did, and for the exclusivity and privilege they proclaimed, rabbits and warrens were regarded with particular hatred. This was mainly because warrens were often established on common land: rabbits were one of the relatively few ways in which lords could maximise their income from their manorial wastes without enclosing them. As explained in the opening chapter of this book, where a manorial lord possessed a right of free warren – a royal grant, conveying the exclusive right to hunt a range of wild animals across a particular tract of countryside – it was generally held that he was permitted to establish a rabbit warren on the manorial commons, even though the rabbits would there compete with the livestock of the commoners for the grass and other herbage. The legal situation was neatly explained by Harting in 1898: 'The lord of a manor with a grant of free warren generally may place his coneys wherever he pleases, either within the manor, or elsewhere, and not even a commoner may interfere with him' (Harting 1898, 37).

Such was the impact of the warren that the commoners might be obliged to agree to its enclosure: might, on occasions, even be expected to pay for it (Sheail 1971, 45). But the banks or walls intended to keep the rabbits in also served to exclude their own stock, so that some portion of the common grazing was lost to them. Moreover, few such barriers were very effective and before long the rabbits would be invading the common again, as well as causing damage to standing crops on a scale much greater than anything inflicted by deer or pigeons. Lastly, and to add insult to injury, local inhabitants were forbidden to kill the escapees, even those which had taken up residence in the surrounding countryside.

Rabbits were already causing difficulties in the fourteenth and fifteenth centuries. In 1388 at Wilton in Norfolk, for example, a survey noted that 60 acres of arable were 'worth nothing by the year because of destruction of the coneys of the duke of Lancaster's warren there' (Cal. IPM 16, 235). But, so far as the evidence goes, the problem grew worse during the late medieval period and by the sixteenth century disputes over warrens were frequent and bitter, as both their number, and the number of rabbits they contained, increased; and as the human population grew and pressed more heavily on resources. Typical was the dispute which occurred during Elizabeth's reign at Cawston in Norfolk (Whyte 2005, 178-80; TNA: PRO E134/43&44Eliz/Mich7). This was a complex legal case, one part of which involved accusations that a warren, originally contained within the bounds of the adjacent Jerbridge Park, was expanding across the common heath, partly because the boundary between the two areas had not been adequately maintained. New 'burrowes' or pillow mounds had been erected on the heath itself 'where there were never any before'; and numerous 'falls' or traps had been dug, as well as holes to extract rabbits and ferrets. Some of the local inhabitants were accused of killing rabbits on the heath, something they claimed they had every right to do. More importantly, the commoners complained of the damage being done to the grazing on the common, as well as to the adjacent arable land, by the increase in rabbit numbers.

The warreners responded that the area of the warren had always included the heath, and claimed that they had always had the right of entering the enclosed grounds adjacent to it, in order to catch rabbits 'with ther hayes and netts'. They insisted that the owners of these fields had always been prevented from hunting rabbits within them, and that the warreners had the right to take away their nets and confiscate their ferrets. The warreners also asserted that there were no more rabbits on the heath than there had ever been, and that there had always been ten 'old and ancient' pillow mounds there. While it was true that one additional mound had lately appeared – equipped with five or six 'eyes', presumably the artificial burrows which were a feature of so many pillow mounds – no rabbits were actually living in it. They alleged that the inhabitants of Cawston were exaggerating the effects of the rabbits, and that they had 'a sufficient comon for the feede of ther great cattell in the said great heath of Cawston notwthstandinge the nomber of conyes there as the same ten[a]ntes in former tyme have had'. The poor condition of the heath, they asserted, was in reality due to the activities of the Cawston people themselves, and especially to their habit of allowing the poor to cut turfs as fuel for their fires. Whatever the truth of the various claims, the common heath was evidently in a mess. One witness described how:

> Sand and gravell is cast upp in such great heapes uppon the playne grownd by reason of the digging therof that ther will noe grasse growe upon the said grownde in a verie long tyme and ... the digging now lately used is a great hindrance to the inhabitants of Cawston as well in the fede of the cattell as in dangering ther said cattell (PRO E134/43&44Eliz/Mich7)

While local communities often complained of the impact of rabbits on arable crops, their main concern was usually, as here, with the effect they had on the common grazing. In 1660 the commoners in the Mendip Hills submitted a petition to the Lord Chancellor claiming that there were now so many warrens in the district that there was insufficient grazing for their livestock, 'which will be to the utter ruin of them and theire poore families' (Aston and Bettey 1998, 134-5). In 1578 it was asserted in a court case that while in the past the inhabitants of Hockwold and Wilton in Norfolk had kept their livestock on the neighbouring heaths, grazing had been discontinued, due to the destruction caused by the rabbits (TNA: PRO DL4/104/1658/5). Indeed, at times there was little vegetation to sustain even the rabbits: it was alleged that during severe weather the warreners allowed them to stray into the adjacent arable open fields, and it was estimated that in the course of two winters they had consumed 300 acres (*c.*120ha) of corn (TNA: PRO DL4/20/7). The great heath had apparently supported two flocks of 1700 sheep at the turn of the sixteenth century, yet by 1578 this had been reduced to 800 (Whyte 2005, 179; TNA: PRO DL4/104/1658/5). But warrens did not only cause disputes between lords and their commoners. Neighbouring landowners were also brought into conflict. During a court case held in 1592 concerning the rights belonging to Castle Rising Chase in Norfolk it was alleged that the West Heath of Congham had become 'almost wholly burrowed w[i]th conies' during the previous decades. The sheep flock belonging to a neighbouring landowner, Sir Henry Spelman, had to be reduced:

> By reason of the great increasinge of coneys ther have been so small feede lefte for the feede of the sheepe as they could not tarry ther so yt by the space of this xxxi yeares the said Henry...hathe not kept annie sheepe ther but onelely for the p[re]servinge of the right and interest in the same (PRO E134/348 35 Eliz/Mich7)

It is not surprising, then, that throughout the Middle Ages and into post-medieval times warrens were a regular target for rebels and rioters. Many of the incidents that legal documents present as attacks by armed poachers were probably, in reality, acts of social protest — as in 1306, when a large group of people broke into the warrens of the Earl of Surrey at Methwold, Thetford, Castle Acre and Sculthorpe, and carried away rabbits (Cal. Pat. Rolls 1301-1307, 476). In this case the attack may have been inspired by the very direct effects that the rabbits were having on local grazing resources, but elsewhere warren breaking was a more symbolic act — a sign of generalised opposition to inequality and authority, rather than a protest against warrens *per se*. During the Peasants' Revolt of 1381 the rebels in St Albans placed one of the Abbot's rabbits, liberated from one of his many warrens, in the town pillory (Oman 1903, 65). Often perhaps motives were mixed: active social protest shaded easily into a simple desire to enjoy the privileges of the powerful. In 1548 a rumour spread that the extensive common called Northaw Great Waste in Hertfordshire was about to be enclosed by Sir William Cavendish, lord of the manor. A crowd of 500 armed rioters, drawn from Northaw, Cheshunt, North Mimms and other local villages which shared the common, laid siege to Cavendish's house. Ordered to disperse, they proceeded to Cavendish's rabbit warren, killed 1000 rabbits, and blew up the 'burrows' with gunpowder, in an expression of their 'great hate and dedlye dyspleasure' (TNA: PRO SWAC/1/49). Having enjoyed the unaccustomed feast of rabbit meat, 60 people returned the following day and helped themselves to more. Either way, rabbits and warrens were a key arena for social conflict: the gentry's passion for creating warrens was one of the complaints of Kett's rebels during the 'commotion time', the rising of 1549. The destruction of crops and the stripping of the common pastures ensured, they claimed, that the common people 'are not able to lyve & mayntene those wyfes & children but rather lyke to be Famyshed' (TNA: PRO E163/16/14).

The period after *c*.1660 seems, for the reasons already explained, to have witnessed a significant increase in the number of rabbit warrens. In the words of the historian E.P. Thompson, warrens 'became a craze in the early eighteenth century with lords of the manor anxious to improve, not their pastures, but their incomes' (Thompson 1975, 105). Not surprisingly, warrens continued to be a particular target for rioters. In 1749, for example, there was a major riot in Charnwood Forest in Leicestershire, when commoners — including miners from Cole Orton — attacked the warrens. One rioter was killed, many were arrested and tried. Here, too, the key issue was the impact that the rabbits had on the vegetation, reducing the feed available to the commoners' sheep and cattle, as a contemporary ballad described:

> The Turf is short bitten by Rabbits, And now
> No milk can be stroak'd from ye Old Woman's Cow
> Tom Thresher's poor Children look sadly, And say
> They must eat Waterporridge, three times a day

The 'buries' were an obvious target for the rioters, both symbolic and practical:

> See! How they troop from ev'ry Town
> To pull these Upstart Warrens down,
> All praying for the Church and Crown
> And for their Common Right (Thompson 1975, 105)

Disputes over rabbit warrens seem to have become less serious from the second half of the eighteenth century, as warrens themselves declined in numbers and importance. True, there was something of an upsurge in conflicts over rabbits in the nineteenth century, as they became a fashionable prey for game shooters. But, with some exceptions, rabbits were now seldom kept on warrens and, while the protected woods and scrub in which they found refuge might be regarded with hostility by the helpless estate tenants whose crops they regularly decimated, warrens themselves had ceased to have an iconic significance.

THE SYMBOLISM OF THE WARREN: DESIGNED LANDSCAPES

Warrens, especially those placed on common wastes, were thus widely detested as symbols of lordly privilege: and, as symbols of lordly privilege, warrens were also proudly displayed in the immediate vicinity of great mansions. Indeed, from the fifteenth century they were steadily brought into closer spatial association with elite residences. This was because, while some had existed since the twelfth century close to castles, monasteries and manor houses, rather more had been located within deer parks; and these, in the period before the Black Death, had usually been found at some remove from such lordly residences. As parks and mansions became ever more closely associated in the course of the fifteenth, sixteenth and seventeenth centuries, so the numbers of warrens in proximity to great houses correspondingly increased. But documents and maps, as well as archaeological evidence, make it clear that warrens were not simply one of the elements of status which were proudly displayed beside the mansion. In some cases they formed the principal view from the house, and were integral elements in extensive schemes of landscape design.

In part this importance reflects the fact that warrens, as well as being symbols of status and providing food (and usually a profit) for their owner, also afforded some recreational hunting. As we have noted (above, p. 16) rabbits were not highly esteemed quarry, yet nor were they entirely neglected, especially in districts where grander game was in short supply. Some medieval warren lodges, such as that at Thetford (Norfolk), almost certainly provided bases for lordly hunting, and places to which great landowners could retreat in a more general sense from the formality of household life. Deer park lodges were certainly used in this way, and it is perhaps worth noting again that the same term was used for both type of building, and that both usually took the same, tower-like form. That the importance of the warren for hunting continued into the sixteenth century is suggested by places like West Stow in Suffolk, where the upper floor of the great gatehouse – built in the 1520s or 30s, and which may conceivably have overlooked a rabbit warren to the east of the hall – has a first-floor room decorated in part with a painting of a hunting scene, featuring gigantic rabbits (Martin 1998).

But the close association of rabbit warrens and important medieval and post-medieval residences may, in some cases, have had a special and rather deeper significance, beyond mere status display and the love of the chase. In the words of David and Margarita Stocker:

> A small number of the many man-made earthwork rabbit burrows of the later medieval and early post-medieval periods in England, sites which usually appear in the archaeological literature as 'pillow mounds', may, in addition to being indicators of the high status of their owners, have been intended to have a very specific symbolic meaning when viewed in their wider setting, a meaning rooted in medieval theology (Stocker and Stocker 1996, 265)

This was part of a wider phenomenon in the medieval landscape, which has been discussed by Paul Everson: the use of practical and everyday features, including animals and birds, in schemes of religious and philosophical symbolism (Everson and Williamson 1998, 143-5). Rabbits may now be best known for their breeding qualities but in medieval Christian iconography they carried other connotations. Small, defenceless, and under the protection of the warrener, emerging from underground darkness into the light – in a deeply symbolic world rabbits came to signify mankind, and his salvation through Christ and the Church, especially through the sacrament of the Mass. The Stockers have noted how warrens were prominently displayed in the precincts of a number of medieval monasteries. At Sawtry Abbey in Cambridgeshire, for example, a pillow mound lies immediately inside the entrance to the precinct, on a slope facing the gatehouse (Stocker and Stocker 1996, 269). At Bruton in Somerset another pillow mound – 70m long, and 15m wide – lies within the outer precinct, some 325m to the south of the church, the only building which survives from the abbey complex.

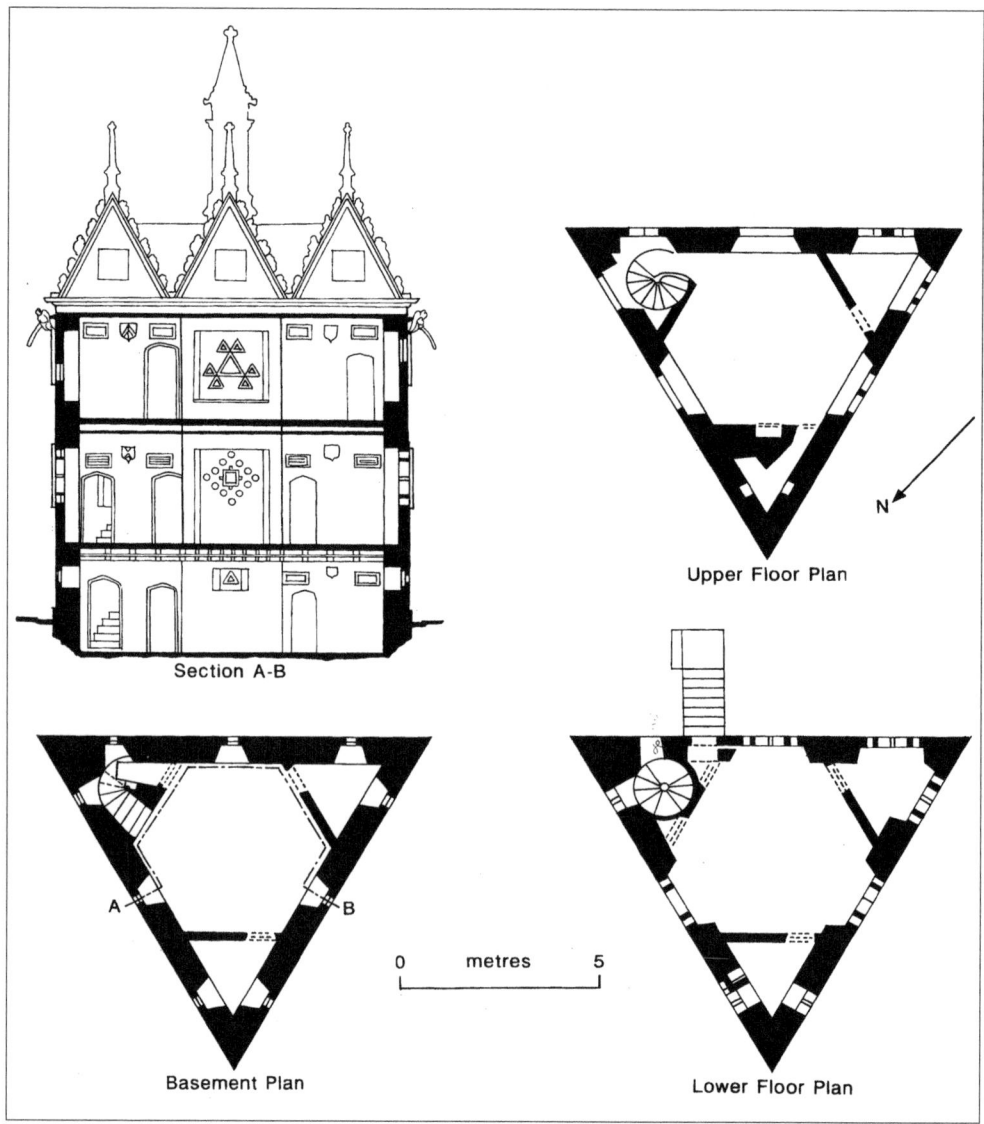

75 Plan and elevation of the Triangular Lodge at Rushton in Northamptonshire (after RCHME)

Such displays, according to the Stockers, might be seen as 'a symbolic introduction to the monastery itself, encouraging visitors to see the monks as symbolic warreners of the lay population'.

Such associations continued, the Stockers have suggested, into the new post-Reformation world of the sixteenth century. The design of the complex triangular lodge built within the rabbit warren a short distance from Rushton Hall in Northamptonshire by the Catholic recusant Thomas Tresham in the

1590s provided both a pun on Tresham's name and a statement of his belief in the tridentine mass, and thus represented a badge of allegiance to the old Catholic faith. As already noted, the building has three sides, each 33ft long and with three gables; three storeys; and a three-sided chimney; and boasted numerous similar numerical references and allusions in its structure and ornamentation (75) (Isham 1970). The Lodge was one of several symbolic structures erected by Tresham, including the 'New Bield' at Lyveden, some 15 miles away (Isham 1988), and it evidently functioned as a place of meditation and retreat, and as a destination for 'elaborate excursions from the main house by the owner and his house guests' (Stocker and Stocker 1996, 267). Yet the building nevertheless evidently served for much of the time as a working warren house (above, p.84).

The meaning of Tresham's building, the Stockers suggest, needs to be understood in association with the pillow mound that remains beside it:

although Tresham's architectural conceit is clearly playing with the illustrations of the Trinity and the Mass, the building is intended to be seen in a broader setting against the pillow mound, creating a tableau vivant which alludes to and enhances the main theological point: the illustration of the theme of human salvation through the Roman Mass (Stocker and Stocker 1996, 268)

The symbolic meaning of Tresham's lodge, and warren, seem clear enough. But how far such symbolism was more widely shared and employed within medieval and early modern culture is less certain. It is true that rabbits, and sometimes their homes, feature prominently in a number of medieval illuminated manuscripts, most notably the *Gorleston Psalter*, although in this case the ubiquity of the animal may also be a reference to the name of its probable patron – the Earl of Warrenne – and to his leading role as a creator of warrens in East Anglia and Sussex (Nishimura 2005). But it is hard to demonstrate that the prominent placing of warrens within medieval monastic precincts was generally dictated by the kinds of symbolic considerations suggested by the Stockers, and they themselves make little attempt to do so: 'No census has been done to establish where pillow mounds are usually located within monastic precincts, but it may be that any such census would show a preference for symbolically meaningful locations' (Stocker and Stocker 1996, 269). Certainly, their suggestion that a general symbolic meaning for pillow mounds is also demonstrated by the fact that a significant proportion are aligned east–west, like churches or graves, is not borne out by the evidence, which suggests that these earthworks in fact display no such preferential orientation and are largely aligned against the contours, for drainage reasons.

The Stockers' arguments are interesting and original, and to an extent may be correct. But we must always be wary of over-interpreting past landscapes

76 Aerial photograph of the site of Ascott House near Wing in Buckinghamshire. The site of the house is to the left, associated with the substantial banks of the terraced garden. To the right, partly superimposed on earlier ridge and furrow, is the warren, with a number of pillow mounds. This was clearly supposed to form a major element in the view from the gardens

and artefacts, of reading meanings when none were there. It is very difficult to distinguish religious motivation in the prominent placing of warrens from the simple desire of monks and others to use pillow mounds (and other features associated with rabbit farming) to display wealth and status, in precisely the same way as they used fish ponds and dovecotes. Moreover, if this iconography was still widely shared in the post-Reformation world, one might have thought that such public displays would have been considered an open invitation to persecution, or at least to a loss of favour or the imposition of financial penalties. At Ascott House near Wing in Buckinghamshire extensive earthworks survive of the late sixteenth-century house built by the Dormer family, including a series of huge terraces and a viewing mound. Immediately to the west, on sloping ground in full view of the terraces, are the remains of a contemporary warren, featuring a number of pillow mounds which appear to have been placed in such a way as to maximise their visibility from the house (*76*). The Dormer family did indeed have strong Catholic sympathies, and the house was built on the site of an earlier monastery, destroyed at the Dissolution (Everson and Williamson 1998, 147-9). But the warren was clearly visible, not only from the house, but also from nearby roads and footpaths: it would have been a remarkably public statement of the Dormer family's allegiance to the old faith.

Moreover, warrens were certainly used as major elements in designed landscapes by individuals or families who do not seem to have had strong Catholic sympathies, men like Sir Henry Lee who in the 1590s laid out an even more elaborate garden, again featuring a prominent warren, at Quarrendon a few miles from Ascott. Here, too, the house has been demolished but the garden earthworks remain, including a huge terrace walk running around four sides of a rectangle, within an external 'moat'. Some 350m to the east of the site of the house lies a substantial group of pillow mounds, of varied and complex form, marking the location of a warren which extended for some 300m along the crest and slope of a low ridge. What is particularly interesting is that several of the mounds were not only deliberately placed on the false crest of the hill, but were also raised higher than the others – higher, at nearly 2m, than most pillow mounds (*77*). In the words of Paul Everson, who wrote the report on the site:

> The most striking aspect about the warren is its prominent location on the skyline, when viewed from the lower land to the west. Like some prehistoric funerary monument or medieval castle it nailed or badged the landscape in an evidently deliberate way. This location makes it strikingly visible from the site of the 16th-century house within the moat, but also from the raised garden terraces ... and even across the fields from away to the west once the visitor turned off the main road and turned east facing towards the house (Everson 1999, 50)

What is also striking, although given less emphasis by Everson, is the way that another group of mounds runs in a long, conjoined line along the 'false crest' of the hill when viewed from the other side, from the direction of the town of Aylesbury (see *74*). Sir Henry Lee was evidently keen to advertise his presence and status to the local townspeople. The warren here was clearly being used as a symbol of status, not as a half-secret badge of religious allegiance.

Warrens featured prominently in the grounds of many other sixteenth- and seventeenth-century mansions. Chatsworth in Derbyshire was a substantial

77 Some of the pillow mounds at Quarrendon were specially heightened, and carefully placed on the false crest of the hill, so that they were clearly visible on the skyline when viewed from the house and gardens

courtyard house erected by Elizabeth ('Bess') of Hardwick and her husbands in the 1570s. It was surrounded by elaborate gardens and possessed an extensive deer park but this, unlike the later landscape park at Chatsworth, lay largely out of sight of the mansion, along the steep escarpment to north and south, and on the high plateau above it, to the east. The main approach to the house was from the west, and passed an extensive rabbit warren, traces of which still survive in the park in the form of eight rather denuded pillow mounds (Barnatt and Williamson 2005, 32-4, 44; Senior 1617) (*78* & *79*). This, together with an elaborate complex of fish ponds, also formed the principal view from the windows of the house. At Shrubland Park in Suffolk, similarly, the warren – shown on a map of 1668 as an area densely planted with trees, probably the sweet chestnuts which still grow here – occupied the falling ground immediately in front of the house and gardens. The small deer park occupied the area to the north, but seems to have formed a subsidiary element in the view (Shrubland Hall archives) (*80*).

At some high-status residences, as at Quarrendon, there was no deer park and the warren seems to have served almost as an alternative, providing an irregular and 'naturalistic' area which contrasted with the order and formality of the gardens.

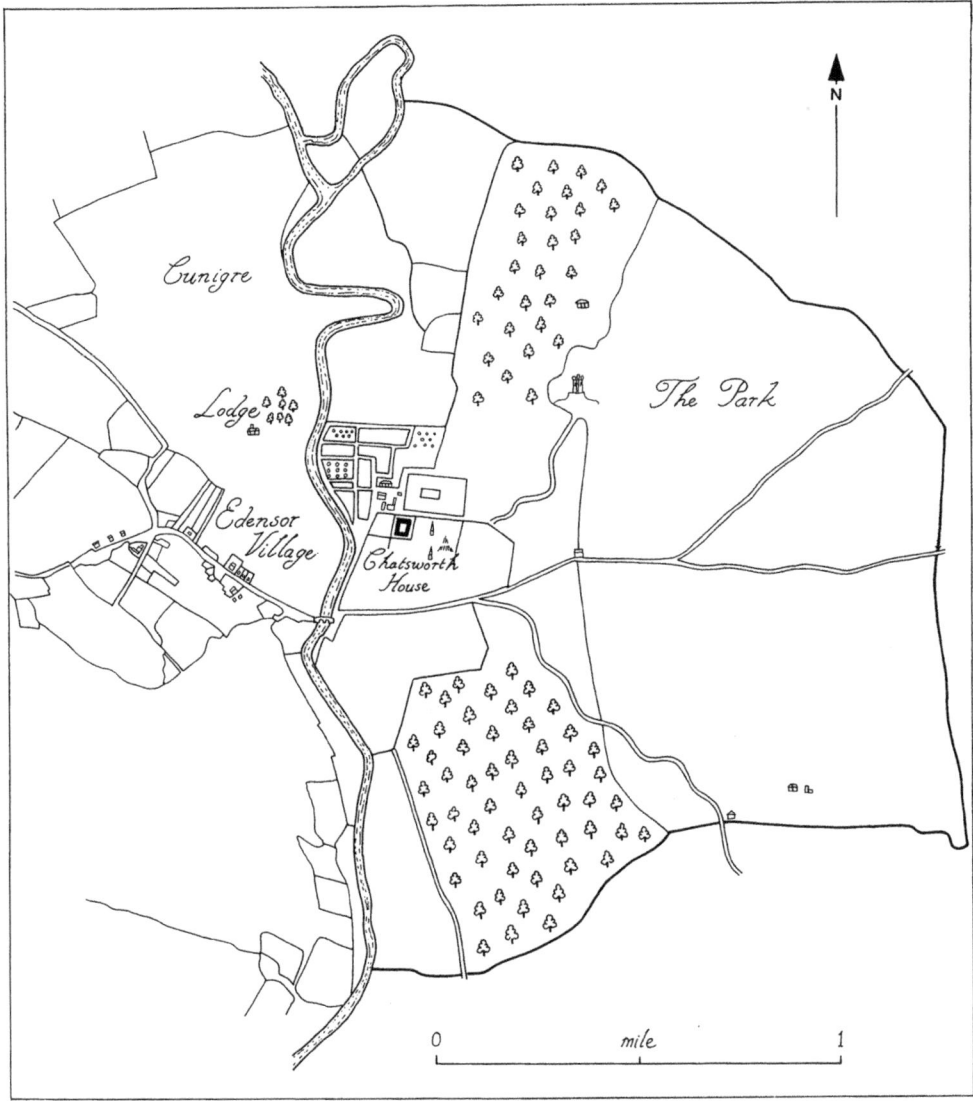

78 This redrawing of two maps made by William Senior in 1617 shows clearly how the rabbit warren formed the main element in the view from Chatsworth House. Although the house and gardens underwent extensive subsequent modifications, the warren remained in this prominent position until the 1750s

The gardens clustered around the house and the warren lay beyond. In other places, as at Sopwell House near St Albans in Hertfordshire in the mid-seventeenth century, the house looked out directly across the warren, and the formal gardens lay to one side (HALS XIII.30) (*81*). Of course, we have to be a

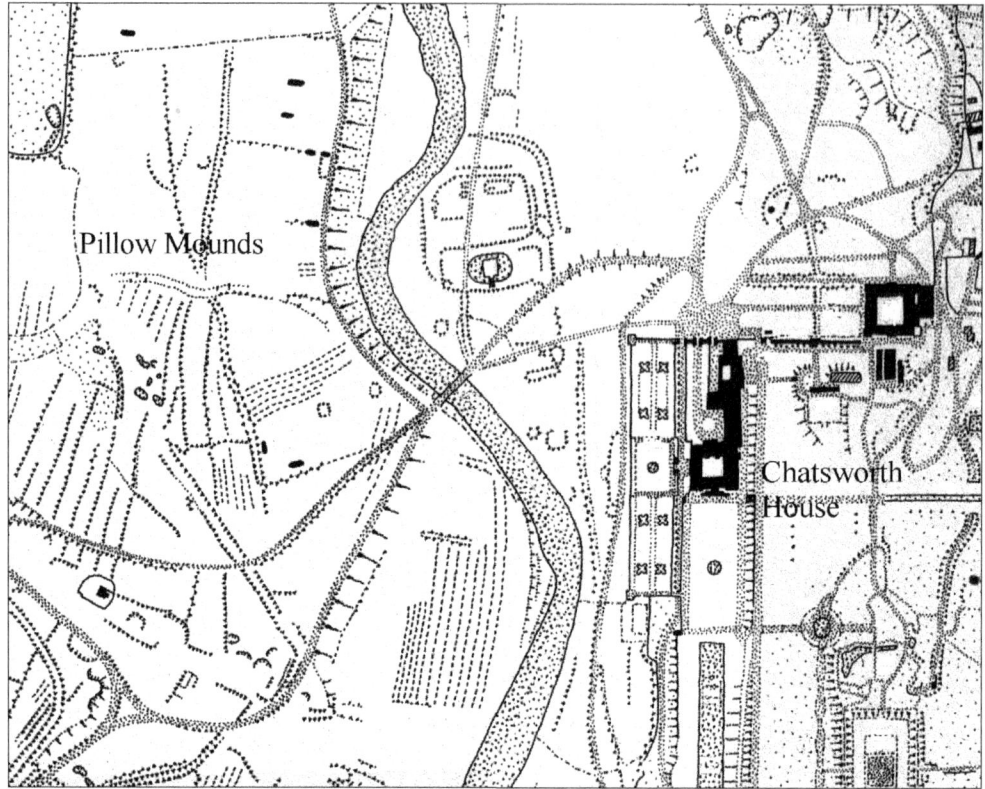

79 Earthwork survey of Chatsworth Park by John Barnatt. The prominent placing of the warren in relation to the house itself is very clear

little careful with cartographic evidence of this kind, for the term 'warren' could be used at this time to mean an enclosed piece of ground containing a variety of wild and semi-domesticated animals. But here at least, as the map makes clear, rabbits were the principal denizens. The warren lodge is also clearly shown, its size and shape typical for the period and its location – facing the mansion across the warren – strongly suggesting some recreational or at least ornamental role.

Warrens continued to serve as acceptable alternatives to deer parks, on occasions, well into the seventeenth century and even beyond. Balls Park, also in Hertfordshire, is a substantial and innovative house in the 'Artisan Mannerist' style which was built just outside Hertford shortly before the Civil War by John Harrison MP. In spite of the scale and importance of the house, there was no park here until after 1750. The county historian Henry Chauncy, writing in 1700, described how Sir William Lytton built:

THE SYMBOLISM OF THE WARREN

80 Ancient sweet chestnuts, survivors from the seventeenth-century planting within the warren at Shrubland Park

> A fair, stately fabric of brick in the middle of a warren … . It stands towering upon a Hill, from whence is seen a most pleasant and delicious prospect …
> (Chauncy 1700, 520-1)

We should not exaggerate the importance of warrens as elements in medieval and post-medieval designed landscapes: and places like these, where the warren was used, in effect, as a substitute for the park, were certainly rare. Moreover, it is likely that warrens were considered more aesthetically pleasing in areas like the champion Midlands, where rabbits remained relatively rare into the eighteenth century, than in those like the light soil districts of East Anglia, where they were already numerous, and causing considerable nuisance, by the sixteenth. Nevertheless, the rabbit warren – with its banks, lodge and pillow mounds – could clearly be seen as a very appealing element in the grounds of the country house in the early modern period.

173

81 An undated early seventeenth-century map of Sopwell House, near St Albans in Hertfordshire, shows that the rabbit warren formed the principal view from the house

THE SYMBOLISM OF THE WARREN

In the course of the eighteenth century new aesthetic sensibilities, and new fashions in landscape design, put an end to this. From the 1720s the greatest landowners began to remove all signs of useful production from the immediate vicinity of their homes, and by the 1750s and 60s the local gentry were following suit (Williamson 1995, 31-5, 117-8). Under the influence of designers like Lancelot 'Capability' Brown it became fashionable for country houses to stand 'free of walls', in open parkland. The manicured, casual simplicity of the landscape park was now what fashion demanded, a landscape symbolising, among other things, a disdain for all the old-fashioned aspects of domestic production. By the middle decades of the eighteenth century there was no place for rabbit warrens in the landscapes of gentility.

At Chatsworth, for example, the warren survived the rebuilding of the mansion in grand Baroque style by the First Duke in the decades either side of 1700, and the laying out of elaborate new gardens in its vicinity; and while the old complex of fish ponds was extensively remodelled into a series of formal 'canals' these were still stocked with fish, and the house continued to have yards, kitchen gardens and even a barn in its immediate vicinity (Barnatt and Williamson 2005, 101-2). But, with the accession of the Fourth Duke in 1755, this old-fashioned mess was transformed. In 1758 Capability Brown himself was called in to create a landscape park to the west of the river, and to remove all the productive clutter from view. Significantly, the warren was the first feature to be targeted. Its lodge was demolished and its area was incorporated within the new park. A note in the estate accounts records that 'The Warren was destroyed 1758, sold all the rabbits': the following year there are references to 'Pareing, burning and ploughing ye Warren', actions which presumably explain the poorly preserved character of the pillow mounds in the park (Chatsworth archives, AS/1062 and 1063). At many other country houses the middle decades of the eighteenth century saw the levelling of warrens and their earthworks, and their incorporation into the sweeping, 'naturalistic' landscape of the park: as at Offley in Hertfordshire, where an indenture of 1752 (HALS D/Elg T22) mentions 'all that Park formerly a Warren'. A few rabbits continued to be kept in some parks, as interesting ornaments (Sheail 1971, 107-9); but properly organised warrens had entirely disappeared from elite landscapes by the end of the eighteenth century.

CONCLUSION

As the last chapter will have made clear, the rabbit warren loomed large in the mental and social, as well as in the economic and agrarian, worlds of the medieval and early post-medieval periods. Its symbolic significance was not, it is true, as great as that of its grander cousin, the deer park. But rabbits, and warrens, were unquestionably far more important in this respect than is usually assumed, and in general played a greater role in the lives of our ancestors than we might expect, given the general academic neglect into which they have fallen.

Indeed, it is the speed with which the importance of the warren – together with the role of the distinctive features employed in rabbit farming – passed from the wider social memory which is perhaps the most striking aspect of this study. Within centuries, even decades, the physical traces of a major agrarian industry had been rendered mysterious, and not only to most archaeologists. In large measure this collective amnesia was a simple consequence of the success of the rabbit itself, developing from a semi-domesticated, vulnerable and valuable creature to the rampant and ubiquitous nuisance which it had become by the time that archaeologists first came to engage with the physical remains of warrening. In a landscape heaving with rabbits, it was hard for many to believe that special structures had ever been needed to sustain and protect them: 'such temptations to burrow seem rather superfluous'. Yet archaeologists arguably contributed to this act of social forgetfulness by their more general failure to find much to interest them in the more mundane and practical aspects of the past, or at least in those of the relatively recent past. This led to the kinds of confusion described at some length in Chapter 5: confusion which was, of course, further fuelled by the unfortunate tendency for early warreners to undertake their activities in precisely the kinds of places in which most archaeologists, interested primarily in the prehistoric and Roman periods, also undertake theirs – the earthworks remains left by yet earlier societies.

And, in a more general sense, the rabbit warren provides a particularly powerful example of why theoretical archaeologists – those interested in the symbolic and iconographic dimensions of past societies – need also to address their practical and agrarian aspects. For systems of symbolism and iconography only derive in part from the religious beliefs, philosophical ideas, or visual and literary cultures shared by social elites. They were, and indeed are, also firmly rooted in the routine, mundane and everyday structures of life – in ownership, production, and the control of natural resources. If we fail to address the basic agricultural world of our ancestors, much of their symbolic world will remain mysterious. Rabbits and warrens, as I have argued, once *meant* something.

For these and other reasons rabbits and rabbit farming should be matters of concern to archaeologists, and not only those whose main interests lie in the medieval or post-medieval periods. I hope this small book will have helped to fill an important gap in the archaeological literature, as well as providing me with a further opportunity to indulge in a life-long obsession.

BIBLIOGRAPHY

Aitken, G.A. (ed.) 1894. *Richard Steele's The Best Plays of the Old Dramatists*, London.
Alcock, L. 1960. 'Castell Odo: an embanked settlement on Mynydd Ystum, near Aberdaron, Caernarvonshire', *Archaeologia Cambrensis* **109**, 78-135.
Allcroft, H. 1908. *Earthwork of England*, Macmillan, London.
Almond, R. 2003. *Medieval Hunting*, Sutton, Stroud.
Ashbee, P. 1970. *The Earthen Long Barrow in Britain*, Dent, London.
Ashbee, P. 1998. 'Barrows, cairns and a few imposters', *British Archaeology* 32 (March 1998), 1-5.
Aston, M. (ed.) 1988. *Medieval Fish, Fisheries and Fish Ponds in England*, British Archaeological Reports British Series 182, Oxford.
Aston, M. and Bettey, J. 1998. 'The post-medieval rural landscape, c. 1540-1700: the drive for profit and the desire for status', in P. Everson and T. Williamson (eds) *The Archaeology of Landscape: studies presented to Christopher Taylor*, Manchester University Press, 117-38.
Austin, D. 1988. 'Excavations and survey at Bryn Cysegrfan, Llanfair Clydogau, Dyfed 1979', *Medieval Archaeology* **23**, 130-65.
Bailey, M. 1988. 'The rabbit and the medieval East Anglian economy', *Agricultural History Review* **36**, 1, 1-20.
Bailey, M. 1989. *A Marginal Economy? East Anglian Breckland in the later Middle Ages*, Cambridge University Press.
Barley, M. 1985. 'Rural buildings in England', in J. Thirsk (ed.) *The Agrarian History of England and Wales. Volume 2.1: 1640-1750*, Cambridge University Press, Cambridge, 590-685.
Barnatt, J. and Williamon, T. 2005. *Chatsworth: a landscape history*, Windgather Press, Macclesfield.
Barrett, J. and Reader, P. 1982. 'A probable long barrow, High Melton, south Yorkshire', *Proceedings of the Prehistoric Society* **48**, 487-9.
Barringer, C. 1998 *Bryant's Map of Suffolk, 1824*, Lark's Press, Norwich.
Beastall, T.W. 1978. *The Agricultural Revolution in Lincolnshire*, Society of Lincolnshire History and Archaeology, Lincoln.
Beer, E.S. De (ed.) 1955. *The Diary of John Evelyn*, Vol 4., Oxford University Press.
Beresford, M. 1958. *Medieval England: an aerial survey*, Cambridge University Press, Cambridge.
Bettey, J. 2004. 'Origins of the Wiltshire rabbit industry', *Antiquaries Journal* **84**, 381-93.
Birrell, J. 1993. 'Deer and deer farming in medieval England', *Agricultural History Review* **40**, 112-26.
Blomefield, F. 1805. *An Essay Towards a Topographical History of the County of Norfolk*, London.
Bosanquet, R.C. 1928. 'Pillow mounds', *Antiquity* **2**, 205-6.
Brown, A.E. and Taylor, C.C. 1974. 'The earthworks of Rockingham and its neighbourhood', *Northamptonshire Archaeology* **9**, 68-9

Buckley, D.G., Brown, N., Holgate, R., Turner, C. and Walker, H. 1988. 'Excavation of a possible Neolithic long barrow or mortuary enclosure at Rivenhall, Essex, 1986', *Proceedings of the Prehistoric Society* **54**, 77-91.

Chauncy, H. 1700. *The Historical Antiquities of Hertfordshire*, London.

Clarke, A.J., Hampton, J.N. and Hughes, M.F. 1983. 'Mount Down, Hampshire: the reappraisal of evidence', *Antiquaries Journal* **63**, 122-4.

Clarke, W.G. 1925. *In Breckland Wilds,* Heffer and Son, Cambridge.

Clarke, W.G. 1937. *In Breckland Wilds* (Second ed., revised and rewritten by R.R. Clarke), Heffer and Son, Cambridge.

Collier, L. and Hobbs, B. 2003. *Resistivity Imaging Survey of Capo Long Barrow, Aberdeenshire*, Scottish Archaeological Internet Report 6 (www.sair.org.uk/sair6).

Collis, J. 1983. *Wigber Low, Derbyshire: a Bronze Age and Anglian burial site in the White Peak*, Department of Prehistory and Archaeology, University of Sheffield, Sheffield.

Cook, R.M.L. 1964. 'Vermin traps on south-west Dartmoor', *Transactions of the Devon Association* **96**, 190-201.

Crawford, O.G.S. 1927. 'Barrows', *Antiquity* **1**, 419-34.

Crawford, O.G.S. and Keiller, A. 1928. *Wessex from the Air*, Oxford University Press, Oxford.

Crompton, G. and Sheail, J. 1975. 'The historical ecology of Lakenheath Warren in Suffolk, England: a case study', *Biological Conservation* **8**, 299-313.

Crompton, G. and Taylor, C. 1972. 'Earthwork enclosures on Lakenheath Warren, West Suffolk', *Proceedings of the Suffolk Institute of Archaeology* **32**, 113-20.

Crossing, W. 1903. *The Dartmoor Worker* (ed. B. Le Mesurier, Newton Abbot 1966).

Cummins, J. 1988. *The Hound and the Hawk: the art of medieval hunting*, Weidenfield and Nicholson, London.

Cunliffe, B. 1974. *Iron Age Communities in Britain*, Routledge, London.

Cunliffe, B. 1983. *Danebury: anatomy of a hillfort*, Batsford, London.

Cunliffe, B. 1984. *Danebury: an Iron Age Hill-fort in Hampshire*, Vol. 1, Council for British Archaeology, Research Report 52, London.

Cunliffe, B. 1991. *Danebury: an Iron Age Hill-fort in Hampshire*, Vol. 4, Council for British Archaeology, Research Report 73, London.

Currie, C. 1990. 'Fish ponds as garden features', *Garden History* **18**, 22-33.

Currie, C. 1991. 'The early history of carp and its economic significance in England', *Agricultural History Review* **39**, 97-107.

Daniel, W.B. 1801. *Rural Sports*, London.

Darvill, T. and Holbrook, N. 1994. 'The Cirencester area in the prehistoric and early Roman periods', in T. Darvill and C. Gerard (eds) *Cirencester: town and landscape*, Cotswold Archaeological Trust, 47-56.

Davies, J.A. and Philips, C.W. 1926. 'The Perecy Sladen Memorial Excavations at Bury Hill Camp, Winterbourne Down, Gloucestershire', *Proceedings of the Bristol University Speleological Society* **3**, i, 8-24.

Davies, W. 1813. *General View of the Agriculture and Domestic Economy of North Wales*, London.

Dennison, E. 2004. 'Wood Hall rabbit warren, Carperby', in R.F. White and P.R. Wilson (eds) *Archaeology and Historic Landscapes of the Yorkshire Dales*, Yorkshire Archaeological Society Occasional Paper 2, Leeds.

Dix, B. 1983. 'An excavation at Sharpenhoe Clappers, Streatley, Bedfordshire', *Bedfordshire Archaeological Journal* **16**, 65-74.

Dixon, P. 1981. 'Crickley Hill', *Current Archaeology* **7**, 145-7.

Dixon, P. 1988. 'Crickley Hill 1969-1987', *Current Archaeology* **10**, 73-8.

Doughty, P.S. 1965. 'The rabbit in Lincolnshire: a short history', *Journal of Scunthorpe Museum Society* **2**, 15-23.

Dyer, C. 1988. 'The consumption of fish in medieval England', in M. Aston (ed.) *Medieval Fish, Fisheries and Fish Ponds in England*, British Archaeological Reports British Series **182**, Oxford.

Dyer, J. 1973. *Southern England: an archaeological guide*, Faber and Faber, London.

East, R. 1891. *Extracts from the Portsmouth Records*, Portsmouth Corporation, Portsmouth.

Eastmead, W. 1824. *Historia Rievallensis : containing the history of Kirkby Moorside, and an account of the most important places in its vicinity; together with brief notices of the more remote or less important ones*, London.

Ettlinger, V. 2000. 'The warren of the manor of Dorking', *The Journal of the Dorking Local History Group*, 1-10.

Everson, P. 1999. 'Quarrendon, Aylesbury Vale, Buckinghamshire'. Unpublished report for English Heritage, Swindon.

Everson, P. and Williamson, T. 1998. 'Gardens and designed landscapes', in P. Everson and T. Williamson (eds) *The Archaeology of Landscape: studies presented to Christopher Taylor*, Manchester University Press, Manchester, 139-65.

Faull, M.L. and Morhouse, S. (eds) 1981. *West Yorkshire: an archaeological survey to AD 1500*, Vol. 3, West Yorkshire Metropolitan County Council, Wakefield.

Fox, C. 1935. 'Pillow mounds in Glamorgan', *Bulletin of the Board of Celtic Studies* **8**, 220-3.

Gelling, P. 1965. 'Excavations at Pilsdon Pen, 1965', *Proceedings of the Dorset Natural History and Archaeological Society* **87**, 90.

Gelling, P. 1966. 'Excavations at Pilsdon Pen, 1966', *Proceedings of the Dorset Natural History and Archaeological Society* **88**, 106-7.

Gelling, P. 1967. 'Excavations at Pilsdon Pen, 1967', *Proceedings of the Dorset Natural History and Archaeological Society* **89**, 123-5.

Gelling, P. 1968. 'Excavations at Pilsdon Pen, 1968', *Proceedings of the Dorset Natural History and Archaeological Society* **90**, 166-7.

Gelling, P. 1969. 'Excavations at Pilsdon Pen, 1969', *Proceedings of the Dorset Natural History and Archaeological Society* **91**, 177-8.

Gelling, P. 1970. 'Excavations at Pilsdon Pen, 1970', *Proceedings of the Dorset Natural History and Archaeological Society* **92**, 126-7.

Gelling, P. 1971. 'Excavations at Pilsdon Pen, 1971', *Proceedings of the Dorset Natural History and Archaeological Society* **93**, 133-4.

Gelling, P. 1977. 'Excavations at Pilsdon Pen 1964-1971', *Proceedings of the Prehistoric Society* **43**, 263-86.

Gerrard, C. 1994. '*Cirencester*: a medium-sized market town in the medieval period', in T. Darvill and C. Gerard (eds) *Cirencester: town and landscape*, Cotswold Archaeological Trust, Gloucester, 98-118.

Gerrard, S. 1997. *Dartmoor*, English Heritage, London.

Gilbert, J.M. 1979. *Hunting and Hunting Reserves in Medieval Scotland*, John Donald, Edinburgh.

Grant, A. 1988. 'Animal resources', in G. Astill and A. Grant (eds) *The Countryside of Medieval England*, Basil Blackwell, Oxford, 149-87.

Greenwell, W. 1877. *British Barrows*, Clarendon Press, London.

Griffin, F.M. 1985. 'Some newly discovered ritual monuments in mid Devon', *Proceedings of the Prehistoric Society* **51**, 310-15.

Grinsell, L.V. 1971. 'Somerset barrows, Part.2: north and east', *Somerset Archaeology and Natural History* **113**, 137-44.

Guilbert, G. 2004. 'Borough Hill, Walton-Upon-Trent – if not a hillfort, then what?', *The Derbyshire Archaeological Journal* **124**, 242-57.

Hamilakis, Y. 2003. 'The sacred geography of hunting: wild animals, social power and gender in early farming societies', in E. Kotjabopoulou, Y. Hamilakis, P. Halstead, C. Gamble, and V. Elefanti (eds) *Zooarchaeology in Greece: recent advances*, British School at Athens, London, 239-47.

Hampton, J.N. 1981. 'The evidence of aerial photography: elementary comparative studies applied to sites at Mount Down, Hampshire and Near Malmesbury, Wiltshire', *Antiquaries Journal* **41**, 316-9.

Harris, A. 1967-70. 'The rabbit warrens of east Yorkshire in the eighteenth and nineteenth centuries', *Yorkshire Archaeological Journal* **42**, 429-41.

Harris, A. and Spratt, D.A. 1991. 'The rabbit warrens of the Tabular Hills, North Yorkshire', *Yorkshire Archaeological Journal* **63**, 177-98.

Harris, D., Pearce, S., Miles, H. and Irwin, M. 1977. 'Bodwen, Lanlivery: a multi-period occupation site', *Cornish Archaeology* **16**, 43-59.

Harting, J.E. 1898. *The Rabbit*, Longmans, London.

Hayes, R.H. 1983. *Levisham Moor Archaeological Investigations 1957-1978*, North York Moors National Park Committee and the Scarborough Archaeological and Historical Society, Helmsley.

Haynes, R.G. 1970. 'Vermin traps and rabbit warrens on Dartmoor', *Post-Medieval Archaeology* **4**, 147-64.

Haynes, R.H. 1967. 'The chambered cairn and adjacent monuments on Great Ayton Moor', *Scarborough and District Archaeological Society Research Report* **7**, Scarborough.

Heaton, A. 2001. *Duck Decoys*, Shire, Princes Risborough.

Hemp, W.J. 1935. 'The chambered cairn known as Bryn yr Hen Bobl, near Plas Newydd, Anglesey, *Archaeologia* **85**, 253-92.

Henderson, A. 1997. 'From coney to rabbit: the story of a managed coloniser', *The Naturalist* **12**, 101-21.

Hoare, Sir R. Colt 1810. *The History of Ancient Wiltshire*, Vol. 1, London.

Hodder, I. 1990. *The Domestication of Europe*, Basil Blackwell, Oxford.

Hughes, I.T. 1924. 'Report on the excavations conducted on Midsummer Hill Camp', *Transactions of the Woolhope Club* **22**, 18-27.

Hunter, J. 1999. *The Essex Landscape: a study of its form and history*, Essex County Council, Chelmsford.

Hyslop, C.W., Campbell and Cobbold, E.S. (eds) 1904. *Church Stretton: some results of local scientific research*, L. Wilding, Shrewsbury.

Isham, G. 1970. *Rushton Triangular Lodge*, HMSO, London.

Isham, G. 1988. *Lyveden New Bield*, National Trust, London.

James, B.Ll. (ed.) 1983. *Morganiae Archaiographia: a book of the antiquities of Glamorganshire by Rice Merrick*, South Wales Record Society, Barry Island.

James, H. 1980. 'Topographical notes on the early medieval borough of Kidwelly', *The Carmarthenshire Antiquary* **16**, 6-17.

Jelley, H. 1998. 'Locating the birthplace of St Patrick', *British Archaeology* **36**, 10-12.

Kent, S. 1989. *Farmers as Hunters: the implications of sedentism*, Cambridge University Press, Cambridge.

Kenward, R. 1982. 'A Neolithic burial enclosure at New Wintles Farm, Eynsham', in H.J. Case and A.W.R. Whittle (eds) *Settlement Patterns in the Oxford Region: excavations at the Abingdon causewayed enclosure and other sites*, Council for British Archaeology Report **44**, 51-4.

Kerridge, E. 1967. *The Agricultural Revolution*, George Allen and Unwin, London.

Knox, R. (1855). *Descriptions Geological, Topographical and Antiquarian in East Yorkshire Between the Humber and the Tees*, London.

Liddiard, R. 2000. *Landscapes of Lordship: Norman castles and the countryside in medieval Norfolk, 1066-1200*, British Archaeological Reports **39**, Oxford.

Liddiard, R. 2003. 'The deer parks of Domesday Book', *Landscapes* **4,1**, 2-23.

Lineham, C.D. 1966. 'Deserted sites and rabbit-warrens on Dartmoor, Devon', *Medieval Archaeology* **10**, 113-39.

Lockley, R.M. 1964. *The Private Life of the Rabbit*, A. Deutsch, London.

Loveday, R.E. and Petchey, M. 1982. 'Oblong ditches: a discussion and some new evidence', *Aerial Archaeology* **8**, 17-24.
Lucas, J. (ed. and trans.) 1892. *Kalm's Account of his Visit to England, on his way to America in 1748*, London.
McCann, J. 1998. *The Dovecotes of Suffolk*, Suffolk Institute of Archaeology and History, Ipswich.
Marshall, W. 1788. *The Rural Economy of Yorkshire*, London.
Marshall, W. 1796. *Rural Economy of the West of England*, London.
Martin, E. 1998. 'West Stow Hall', *Proceedings of the Suffolk Institute of Archaeology and History* **39**, **2**, 403-9.
Matheson, C. 1941. 'The rabbit and hare in Wales', *Antiquity* **15**, 372-81.
Mingay, G.E. 1984. 'The East Midlands', in J. Thirsk (ed.) *The Agrarian History of England and Wales, Vol. V.1*, Cambridge University Press, Cambridge, 89-128.
Moore-Colyer, R. 1997. 'Land and people in Northmptonshire: Great Oakley, c.1750-1850', *Agricultural History Review* **42**, **2**, 149-64.
Morris, W.S. 1842. *The History and Topography of Wye*, Canterbury.
Munsche, P.B. 1981. *Gentlemen and Poachers: the English Game Laws*, Cambridge University Press, Cambridge.
Nishimura, M. and Nishimura, D. 2005. 'Rabbits, warrens and Warenne: the patronage of the Gorleston Psalter', *Cronaca* **30** (Web site).
North, R. 1713. *The Discourse of Fish and Fish Ponds*, London.
Oman, C. 1906. *The Great Revolt of 1381*, Clarendon Press, Oxford.
O'Neill, J. 1948. 'Excavations at Iron Acton', *Proceedings of the Cotteswold Natural History and Field Club* **30**, 34-8.
Orgill, C.L. 1936. 'The introduction of the rabbit into England', *Antiquity* **10**, 462-3.
Parry, J. 2003. *Heathland*, National Trust, London.
Payne Galwey, R. 1886. *The Book of Duck Decoys*, London.
Piggot, S. 1930. 'Butser Hill', *Antiquity* **4**, 187-200.
Price, F.G. Hilton 1881. 'Camps on the Malvern Hills', *Journal of the Royal Anthropological Institute* **10**, 319-31.
Pringle, A. 1794. *General View of the Agriculture of the County of Westmoreland*, London.
Probert, S. 1989. 'Beardown Warren, Princetown, Dartmoor', in M. Bowden, D. Mackay, and P. Topping (eds) *From Cornwall to Caithness: some aspects of British field archaeology*, British Archaeological Reports British Series **209**, Oxford, 229-34.
Rackham, O. 1986. *The History of the Countryside*, Dent, London.
Rackham, O. 1989. *The Last Forest: the story of Hatfield Forest*, Dent, London.
Risdon, T. 1811. *The Chorographical Description or Survey of the County of Devon: printed from a genuine copy of the original manuscript, with considerable additions*, London.
Roberts, E. 1998. 'The Bishop of Winchester's deer parks in Hampshire, 1200-1400', *Proceedings of the Hampshire Field Club and Archaeological Society*, **44**, 67-86.
Robinson, E. and Powell, D. 1984. *The Oxford Authors: John Clare*, Oxford University Press, Oxford.
Rodwell, W. 1978. 'Buildings and settlements in south east Britain in the later Iron Age', in B. Cunliffe and T. Rowley (eds) *Lowland Iron Age Communities in Europe*, British Archaeological Reports **5**, Oxford, 25-42.
Royal Commission on Ancient and Historical Monuments in Wales 1911. *An Inventory of the Ancient Monuments in Wales and Monmouthshire, Vol. 1: County of Montgomery*, HMSO, Cardiff.
Royal Commission on Ancient and Historical Monuments in Wales 1913. *An Inventory of the Ancient Monuments in Wales and Monmouthshire, Vol. 3: County of Montgomery*, HMSO, Cardiff.
Royal Commission on Ancient and Historical Monuments in Wales 1982. *An Inventory of the Ancient Monuments of Glamorgan Volume 3: Medieval Secular Monuments, Part II: non-defensive*, HMSO, Cardiff.

Royal Commission on Historical Monuments, England. 1934. *An Inventory of the Historical Monuments in Herefordshire,* HMSO, London.

Royal Commission on Historical Monuments, England. 1936. *An Inventory of the Historical Monuments in Westmoreland, Vol. 1.,* HMSO, London.

Royal Commission on Historical Monuments, England. 1970. *An Inventory of the Historical Monuments in the County of Dorset, Vol. 3,* HMSO, London.

Royal Commission on Historical Monuments, England. 1979. *An Inventory of the Historical Monuments in the County of Northamptonshire, Vol. 2: Archaeological Sites in Central Northamptonshire,* HMSO, London.

Royal Commission on Historical Monuments, England. 1981. *An Inventory of the Historical Monuments in the County of Northamptonshire, Vol. 3: Archaeological Sites in North-West Northamptonshire,* HMSO, London.

Royal Commission on Historical Monuments, England. 1982. *An Inventory of the Historical Monuments in the County of Northamptonshire, Vol. 4: Archaeological Sites in South-West Northamptonshire,* HMSO, London.

Rutledge, P. 1980. 'A rabbit warren at Swainsthorpe', *Norfolk Research Committee Annual Bulletin* **23**, 7.

Seddon, T. and Willet, F. 1953. 'Excavations at Everage Clough, Burnley', *Transactions of the Lancashire and Cheshire Antiquarian Society* **53**, 194-200.

Senior, W. 1617. *Lees* and *Edensor,* maps in bound volume of early seventeenth-century surveys, Chatsworth Archives, Chatsworth House, Derbyshire.

Sheail, J. 1971. *Rabbits and their History,* David and Charles, Newton Abbot, 1971.

Sheail, J. 1978. 'Rabbits and agriculture in post-medieval England', *Journal of Historical Geography* **4**, 343-55.

Sheail, J. 1984. 'The rabbit', *Biologist* **31**, 135-9.

Sheail, J. and Bailey, M. 1996. 'The history of the rabbit in Breckland', in P. Ratcliffe and J. Claridge (eds) *Thetford Forest Park: the ecology of a pine forest,* Forestry Commission Technical Papers **13**, Edinburgh.

Short, B. 1984. 'The South-East: Kent, Surrey and Sussex', in J. Thirsk (ed.) *The Agrarian History of England and Wales,* Volume V.1, Cambridge University Press, Cambridge, 270-317.

Silvester, R.J. 1995. 'Pillow mounds at Y Foel, Llanllugan', *Montgomeryshire Collections* **83**, 75-90.

Spratt, D.A. 1989. *Linear Earthworks of the Tabular Hills, North-East Yorkshire,* Department of Prehistory and Archaeology, University of Sheffield, Sheffield.

Spurgeon, C.J. 1966. in *Archaeology in Wales,* no. 23.

Spurgeon, C.J. 1967. in *Archaeology in Wales,* nos. 18, 41, 45, 46.

Spurgeon, C.J. 1968. in *Archaeology in Wales,* no. 34.

Spurgeon, C.J. 1969. in *Archaeology in Wales,* nos. 34 and 75.

Spurgeon, C.J. 1970. in *Archaeology in Wales,* no. 35.

Stamper, P. 1988. 'Woods and parks', in G. Astill and A. Grant (eds) *The Countryside of Medieval England,* Basil Blackwell, Oxford, 128-48.

Stanford, C. 1974. *Croft Ambrey,* Adams, Hereford.

Stocker, D. and Stocker, M. 1998. 'Sacred profanity: the theology of rabbit breeding and the symbolic landscape of the warren', *World Archaeology* **28**, 2, 265-72.

Strickland, H.E. 1812. *A General View of the Agriculture of the East Riding of Yorkshire,* York.

Sussams, K. 1996. *The Breckland Archaeological Survey,* Suffolk County Council, Ipswich.

Sykes, N.J. 2004. 'The dynamics of status symbols: wildfowl exploitation in England AD 410-1550', *Archaeological Journal* **161**, 82-105.

Sylverton, H. 1956. 'Preliminary report on the Shute Shelve excavations', *Proceedings of the Axbridge Caving and Archaeological Society,* 5-7.

Taylor, C. 1967. 'Late Roman pastoral farming in Wessex', *Antiquity* **41**, 304-6.

Taylor, C. 1974. *Fieldwork in Medieval Archaeology,* Batsford, London.

Tebbut, F.C. 1968. 'Rabbit warrens in Ashdown Forest', *Sussex Notes and Queries* **17**, 52-7.
Thirsk, J. 1985. 'Agricultural innovations and their diffusion', in J. Thirsk (ed.) *The Agricultural History of England and Wales. Volume 2.1, 1640-1750*, Cambridge University Press, Cambridge, 533-89.
Thomas, K. 1983. *Man and the Natural World*, Allen Lane, London.
Thompson, E.P. 1975. *Whigs and Hunters: the origin of the Black Act*, Allen Lane, London.
Thompson, H.V. and Warden, A.N. 1956. *The Rabbit*, Collins New Naturalist Series, London.
Thompson, H.V. and King, C. (eds) 1994. *The European Rabbit: the history and biology of a successful coloniser*, Oxford University Press, Oxford.
Tongue, R. 1965. *Somerset Folklore*, Folklore Society, London.
Topsell, E. (trans.) 1607. *C. Gesner's Historia Annimalia*, London.
Tusser, T. 1580. *Five Hundred Pointes of Good Husbandrie*, London.
Veale, E.M. 1957. 'The rabbit in England', *Agricultural History Review*, **5**, 85-90.
Villy, F. 1912. 'A preliminary note on certain earthworks at Sutton, near Keighley', *The Bradford Antiquarian* **3**, 325-47.
Villy, F. 1921. 'The site of Norton Tower, Rylstone', *The Bradford Antiquarian* **4**, 179-89.
Villy, F. 1929. 'Pillow mounds in Yorkshire and Lancashire', *Antiquaries Journal* **9**, 159.
Vyner, B.E. 1982. 'Archaeology and the M4 Bridgend Northern Bypass, II; a group of pillow mounds on Cefn Hirgoed, Bridgend, Glamorgan, *Bulletin of the Board of Celtic Studies* **29**, **4**, 85-58.
Wade Martins, S. and Williamson, T. 1999. *Roots of Change: farming and the landscape in East Anglia, c.1700-1870*, British Agricultural History Society, Exeter.
Walker, E.C. 1961. 'Cobham: manorial history', *Surrey Archaeological Collections* **58**, 41-9.
Warren, H. 1926. 'Excavations of pillow mounds at High Beech, Epping', *Essex Naturalist* **14**, 214-26.
Wentworth Day, J. 1954. *A History of the Fens*, Harrap, London.
Wheeler, Sir M. 1936. 'Prehistoric and Roman Westmoreland', in Royal Commission on Historical Monuments, *An Inventory of the Historical Monuments in Westmoreland, Vol. 1*, HMSO, London.
White, N. 2002. 'Minchinhampton Common: an archaeological survey of the earthwork remains'. Unpublished report for English Heritage, Swindon.
Whyte, N. 2005. 'Perceptions of the Norfolk landscape, c.1500-1700', unpublished PhD Thesis, University of East Anglia.
Williams, M. 1971. 'The enclosure and reclamation of the Mendip Hills, 1770-1830', *Agricultural History Review* **19**, 65-81.
Williamson, H. and Haggard, L. Rider. 1943. *Norfolk Life*, Faber and Faber, London.
Williamson, T. 1995. *Polite Landscapes: gardens and society in eighteenth-century England*, Sutton, Stroud.
Williamson, T. 1997. 'Fish, fur and feather: man and nature in the post-medieval landscape' in K. Barker and T. Darvill (eds) *Making English Landscapes*. Bournemouth University School of Conservation Sciences Occasional Paper 3, Bournemouth, 92-117.
Williamson, T. 1998. *The Archaeology of the Landscape Park: garden design in Norfolk, England, c.1680-1840*, British Archaeology Reports **268**, Oxford.
Williamson, T. 2002. *The Transformation of Rural England: farming and the landscape 1700-1870*, Exeter University Press, Exeter.
Williamson, T. 2005. *Sandlands: the Suffolk coast and heaths*, Windgather Press, Macclesfield.
Williamson, T. and Loveday, R. 1988. 'Rabbits or ritual? Artificial warrens and the Neolithic long mound tradition', *Archaeological Journal* **141**, 290-313.
Wright, T. 1668. 'A curious and exact relation of a sandfloud', *Philosophical Transactions* **37**, 722-5.

INDEX

afforestation 109
agricultural revolution 18, 29, 111
agricultural writers 50, 51, 53, 77, 98, 111, 125, 136
agriculture 28-30, 34, 48-9, 71-2, 91, 93, 98, 155, 159, 160, 178
  improvement of 12, 18, 95, 97, 107-8, 122, 125, 160
  depression in 17, 30, 89, 98, 103, 108, 125, 158
Alton Barnes, Wiltshire 36, 147, *148*
Anglo-Saxon period, the 142, 156
Ascott House, Wing, Buckinghamshire 145, *168*, 169
Ashdown Forest, Sussex 95, 138
Austin, D. 42, 48, 80, 86, 122-3

Banwell, Somerset 59, 152
Bettey, J. 90-1
Black Death, the 17, 103, 124
Box Warren, Ashridge, Hertfordshire 64-5, 67
Brecon Beacons 71, 77, 126, 128
Bronze Age, the 36, 147
  barrows 36, 62, 73, 105, 147
Bury Hill Camp, Bristol 39, 41-2, *125*, 128-9

Castle Odo, Gwynedd 39, 41, 42, 46, 54
Castle Rising, Norfolk 63, 162
castles 14, 37-8, 62, 156-7, 164
Chatsworth, Derbyshire 49, 53, 71, 169-70, *171-2*, 175
Chilterns 42, 65, 150
clappers 56-7, 59, 73, *74*, 96, 103, 108, 112, 150
common fields *see* open fields

common land 17, 19, 30, 36, 52, 89, 93, 94, 96, 125, 160-3, 164
coney *see* rabbits
Cotswolds, the 17, 18, 34, 68, 89, 93, 111, 125
country houses *see* high-status residences
Crawford, O.G.S. 31-2, 46, 55, 60, 130-4
Cray, Powys 51, 71, 77, 118
Crickley Hill, Gloucestershire 144
Croft Ambrey, Herefordshire 36, 39, 142-4
Croydon-cum-Clopton, Cambridgeshire 37-8, 48, 138
Cwm Ednant, Powys 49, 121-2

Danebury, Herefordshire 36, 39, 42, 49, 64, 87, 93, 142
Dartmoor 9, 17-19, 31, 34, 45, 48-9, 51, 53-4, 65, 70, 71, 78, 80, 87, 88, 109-17, 124-5, 133, 138, 145
decoys 157-8
deer 15-17, 94, 155, 156, 158, 159
deer parks 15, 156-8, 170, 172-3, 177
  lodges 83, 86, 156, 165
deserted settlements 37, 49, 63
Ditsworthy Warren, Dartmoor 49-50, *87*, 88, 109, 110-11, 113, *116*, 133
dogs 16, 23, 57, 74, 88, 109, 116, 158
Dolebury, Somerset 36, 49, 80, 93, 128, 136
dovecotes 157-9, 168
downlands 18, 25, 34, 47, 56, 68-9, 91, 125
Dunstable Downs, Bedfordshire *27*, 33

East Anglian Breckland 14, 18-19, 23, 30, 34, 57-8, 68, 71, 77, 82-3, 86, 89, 91, 100-9, 126

187

enclosure 18, 28-9, 97, 98, 125, 160, *see also* parliamentary enclosure
Everage Clough, Burnley, Lancashire 39, *40*, 48, 137
Everson, P. 165, 169

farm warrens 20, 76, 99, 124
ferrets 16, 23, 57, 74, 77, 109, 144, 161
fish ponds 14-15, 156-7, 158-9, 168, 170, 175
fodder, feeding 20-1, 25-6, 34, 54, 68, 71, 75, 88, 99, 107, 108, 113, 115, 122
forest law 19, 94
Forestry Commission 76-7, 99, 107
forests 17-18, 51, 93-5, 125, 138
Fox, C. 49, 134
free warren 17, 160

game birds 17, 29-30, 160
game keeping 29, 80
Game Laws 30
gardens 10

hares 11, 16, 17, 28, 30
Hartfield, Sussex 32, 49, 94
Hatfield Forest, Essex 36, 49, 85, *87*, 95
hat-making 18-19, 88, 99, 109
heathland 19-20, 25-6, 30, 34, 47, 56, 66, 68-9, 125, 155, 161-2
Herefordshire Beacon, Herefordshire 36, 38, 127-8
Hertingfordbury, Hertfordshire 23, 25, 78
High Beech, Essex 33-4, 39, 40, 47-8, 52, 57, 95, 129-30, 133, 136
high-status residences 10, 14, 20, 28, 52-3, 89, 93, 108, 118, 156-7, 159, 160, 164-5, 168-70, 172
hunting 16, 26, 82, 85, 155-6, 160, 165

Ireland 12, 20
Iron Age, the 36, 47, 129-30, 133, 135-6, 139, 140-1, 144
   hillforts 36, 42, 58, 62, 64, 91, 93, 128, 130, 139-43, 144, 149, 150

Knebworth, Hertfordshire 15, 21, 24

Lakenheath Warren, Suffolk 26, 67, 71, *72*, 86, 103, 106, 107
Llanelwedd, Powys, 39, 40, *41*, 128, 133, 138
Llanfair Clydogau, Dyfed 39, 40, *41*, 42, 48, 59, 72-3, *74*, 80, 86-7, 122-3, *124*
long barrows 32, 63, 144-9, 153

manorial courts 49, 77
manor houses *see* high-status residences
marginal land 12, 17, 18-20, 25, 30, 36, 52, 56, 89, 94, 98, 121, 156
Mason, A. 101, 105
medieval period, the 9, 11-12, 14, 15-18, 23, 28, 34, 37, 48, 49-50, 52, 59, 66-7, 71, 82, 85, 86-9, 98, 103, 105, 107, 110, 118, 122-4, 127, 135, 150, 155-7, 159, 160-1, 163-5, 167, 173, 177
Mendip Hills 17-18, 34, 68-9, 89, 93, 111, 125, 162
Methwold Warren, Norfolk *22*, 68, 83, 103, 105, 107, 108, 163
Mildenhall Warren, Suffolk, 54, 83, 103, *105*, 106-8
Minchinhampton Common, Gloucestershire 32, *63*, 80, 85, *92*, 93, 130, 133
modern period, the 12, 18-19, 28-9, 34, 48, 51-3, 63, 77, 88, 95, 97-100, 107-9, 110-11, 114-15, 117-18, 124-5, 127-8, 135-6, 164
monasteries 14, 37, 52, 164, 165-7
moorland 19-20, 25, 34, 47, 51, 66, 71, 89, 98, 109, 114, 118-19, 123-6, 155
myxamotosis 19, 30

narrow rig 48-9, *51*, 121-2
Neolithic period, the 32, 63, 138, 144-9, 153
nets 16, 23, 57, 74, 77

open fields 28-9, 91, 97

palaces 14, 156
parliamentary enclosure 28-9, 36
pillow mounds 14, 26-7, 31-58, 62, 72-5, 83, 85, 87, 89, 91, 93-6, 99, 103, *104*, 109, 111, *112*, *115*, 118-22, 126-7, 130, 139, 140, 142, 144-9, 152-3, 161, 163-5, 167-9, 170, 175, *see also* rabbit farming, physical remains of
   age of 46-53
   artificial burrows in 40-6, *47*, 57, 60, 62-3, 66, 72-3, 111, 121, 129, 140, 142, 150, 153, 161
   as 'pioneer' accommodation 45, 57-8, 62, 112, 126
   conjoined 32-3, 112, 150, 169
   construction of 39-46, 53, 74, 119-20, 138, 144
   destruction of 34, 52
   drainage 53, *54*, 112-13
   excavation of 38-9, 42, 46, 48, 122, 127-30, 134, 137-44

finds within 47-8
functions of 53-8
geographical distribution of 34, *35*, 36, 55-6, 89-90
grouped 34, 49, 51, 55-6, 95, 112, 118
maintenance of 53-5, 57, 113
misinterpretation of 10, 31, 38-9, 41, 47, 52, 127-30, 133-44, 149-53, 177
modification of earlier earthworks for 27, 36, 105, 152-3
morphology of 32, 39, 55, *56*, 111, 122, 146
names of 135-6
relationship with other earthworks 31, 36-8, 47-9, 58, 91, 95, 121, 133, 134-5, 147-8
segmenting 32, 46, 60, 63, 111, 119-22, 130, 133
size of 32, 57, 112, 122
variant forms 27, 59-60, *61*, *64*, 112, 121, 143, 151-2
Pilsdon Pen, Dorset 33, 36, 39, 42, 130, 139-42
place names 52-3, 62, 121-2, 145
poaching, poachers 14-15, 20, 26, 30, 66, 86
post-medieval period, the 9, 12, 17-22, 24, 27-9, 32, 34, 48-53, 59, 62, 68, 71, 77, 80, 82, 84-5, 87-9, 90-1, 93, 94-6, 98, 100, 103, 105-7, 108, 110, 115, 117-18, 121-5, 127, 135, 140, 149, 155-60, 162-6, 168-9, 172-3, 175, 177
predators 12-14, 20, 22, 26, 29-30, 42, 62, 65, 73, 80, 86, 113
prehistoric period, the 47, 142, 145-6, 150, 153, 177
earthworks 36-7, 62, 64, 138, 147, 150, 153

Quarrendon, Buckinghamshire 150, *151*, 169-70

rabbit farming 9-10, 31, 34, 36, 52, 94-5, 97-8, 108, 111, 117, 125, 168, 177, 178
commercial 17-19, 27, 53, 89, 90-1, 94-6, 99, 101, 118, 124-5
domestic 20, 53, 58-9
physical remains of 9-10, 95, see also pillow mounds, warrens
rabbits
accommodation for 59-60, 62, *66*, *67*, see also pillow mounds
black 20, 66, 95, 103
breeding 13, 21, 56-7, 71, 73, 103, 112, 126, 150, 165
catching of *14*, 16, 22-3, 57, 74, 161

Christian iconography of 165-9
culling of 30
destruction of crops by 21, 26, 28, 30, 65, 89, 91, 97, 125, 161-4
impact on commons 17, 28, 160-2, 163-4
in the wild 28-30
introduction to Britain 11-12
natural history of 12-13
silver 20, 66, 95-6, 103
status of 18, 88
use for fur 11-12, 18, 20, 88, 96
use for meat 11-12, 18, 20, 88, 96, 111, 159, 164
value of 83, 111
ridge and furrow 38, 49, *50*, 52, 71, 138
Rivenhall, Essex 145-6
Rockford Common, Ellingham, Hampshire 38-9, 48, 95
Rockingham Forest, Northamptonshire 17, 49, 95
Roman period, the 11, 41, 47-8, 73, 129, 133, 135, 144, 149, 150, 152, 177
Rylstone, Yorkshire 39, 53, 83, 134

Scotland 12, 133
'segmenting' 32, 46, 63, 111, 118, 120-1, 130, 133
semi-domesticated species 155-60
Sharpenhoe Clapper, Bedfordshire 42, 59, 150
shooting 29-30, 164
Shrubland Hall, Suffolk 25, 170, *173*
Shute Shelve, Axbridge, Somerset 39, 42, 93, 138
Silvester, R. 44-5, 62, 122
Stocker, D. and M. 165-7
Sutton Common, Suffolk 59, 103, *104*, 145
Suffolk coast 14, 19, 26, 34, 36, 100-1, 103, 108

Tabular Hills, Yorkshire 10, 17-19, 25, 34, 36, 64, 69-70, 76-7, 91, 97-100, 125-6
Taylor, C. 62, 73, 138-9
Thetford Warren, Norfolk 21, 68, 77, 103, 109, 163
tip-traps see traps
traps 22, 26, 34, 75-7, *78*, 96, 99, 108, 117, 119, 122, 126, 161
Traianlas, Powys 77, 118, *120*
Trowlesworthy Warren, Dartmoor 49-50, 88, 109-11, *115*, *117*
types, see traps

uplands 28, 56, 73, 123-4

vermin 20, 29, 78, 80, 117
    traps 26, 34, 62, 78-80, *81*, *94*, *100*, 116-17, 122-3, 136-7

Wales 17-19, 28, 34, 40-1, 51, 56, 63, 89, 118-25, 135
warreners 19-23, 26, 53, 57, 63, 65-6, 68, 82-3, 86, 96, 99, 112, 115, 122, 126, 136, 147, 152, 161-2, 165
warren lodges 26, 82-8, 91, 93-4, 105-7, 112, 115-16, 122, 155, 165, 172, 175
    on Dartmoor 87, 88
    at Dorking, Surrey 83
    at Hatfield Forest, Essex 85, *86*
    at Langford Warren, Norfolk 83
    at Mildenhall, Suffolk 83, *105*, 107
    at Minchinhampton Common, Gloucestershire 84-5
    at Rushton, Northamptonshire 83-4, 88, 166-7
    at Rylstone, Yorkshire 83
    at Thetford, Norfolk 82-3, 88, 107
warrens 9, 12-18, 30-1, 48-53, 55-9, 62, 65-6, 68-9, 73, 76-7, 80, 83, 85-7, 89-91, 93-7, 98-100, 103, 105, 107-14, 116-18, 120-6, 128-9, 133-5, 137-8, 140, 150, 152-3, 160-5, 167-70, 172-3, 175, 177
    and designed landscapes 169-73, *174*, 175
    and earlier features 62-4, *65*, 70, 93
    and parks 14-15, 25, 28, 52-3, 71, 89, 103, 118
    as expressions of status 28, 66, 86, 88, 160, 163-4, 168-9
    'breaking' of 15-16, 28, 163-4
    cultivation within 21, 26, 71, 96, 107-8, 122
    decline/destruction of 27, 71, 88, 91, 93, 97, 108, 115, 121, 123, 125, 175
    disputes over 91, 107, 161-4
    ecology of 26
    enclosure of 14, 20-2, 26, 65-70, 91, 96, 107, 113-14, 125-6, 160-1
        with banks 69, 70
        with fences 68, 70
        with walls 68-70, 113-14
        with wire 22, 69-70
    enclosures within 34, 70-1, *72*, 75-6, 88, 96, 99, 107-8, 115, 119, 122
    escape from 20-1, 26, 65-6, 89, 91, 97, 115, 161
    facilities in 24
    grazing of 24, 71-2
    leases of 21, 23-5, 32, 52-3, 57, 77-8, 95, 103, 105, 107
    locations of 13-14, 47, 89-126
    maintenance of 24
    origin of term 17
    ownership of 66, 103, 126
    sizes of 26, 53, 67, 89, 91, 96, 99, 103, 109, 118, 122, 125-6
    stocking levels in 21, 24-6, 57, 68, 95, 99, 107
    subdivisions of 20, 26, 70-2, 77, 107-8
    symbolic significance of 28, 155-75, 177-8
waste *see* marginal land
watercourses 70, 97, 99, 113-14, 145
Wessex 17, 34, 89, 90-1, 93, 125-6
Wheeler, M. 135
Wigber Low, Derbyshire 63, *65*
Winterbourne Stoke, Wiltshire 62, 73
Wolds 111, 125-6
    Lincolnshire 17-18, 25, 77, 95-6, 97
    Yorkshire 17, 18, 77, 89, 95-7, 99, 149
woodland 15, 94, 156
Wood Hall, Carperby, Yorkshire 19, 69, *70*, 77, *78*
wood-pasture 25, 94, 156

Y Foel, Powys 39, 44, *45*, 49, 62, 121-2, *123*, 140
Ystradfellte, Powys 51, 59, 71, 77, 118-20, *121*